The Causes and Prevention of War

Second Edition

Seyom Brown
Brandeis University

St. Martin's Press
New York

For Jeremiah, Matthew, Benjamin, Nell, Eliot, Steven, and Lisa

Executive editor: Don Reisman
Manager, publishing services: Emily Berleth
Publishing services associate: Kalea Chapman
Project management: Publication Services, Inc.
Art director: Sheree Goodman
Cover art: Tom Kowal

For information, write:
St. Martin's Press, Inc.
175 Fifth Avenue
New York, NY 10010

ISBN: 0-312-04906-4

Published and distributed outside North America by
THE MACMILLAN PRESS, LTD
Houndmills, Basingstoke, Hampshire RG21 2XS and London Companies and
representatives throughout the world

ISBN 0-333-61850-5

A catalog record for this book is available from the British Library

Preface

On the verge of the completion of this project, and learning that a dramatic breakthrough for peace in the Middle East was materializing, I experienced a range of reactions. I was seized by a rekindling of the hope, so often dashed, that the energies and talents of the peoples of the region might at last be freed from their preoccupation with war and revenge and devoted instead to the elaboration of peace and justice prophesied as their destiny. At the same time, the author's ego in me wondered (with anxiety) whether what I had been writing about the causes and prevention of war would be supported or contradicted by the events now unfolding.

In probing for the sources and implications of the Israeli-Palestinian rapprochement of September 1993, I find that in considerable part they are products of the even more momentous changes in the world at large associated with the end of the Cold War—changes that prompted the decision to do a second edition of the book.

The first edition, written when the rivalry between the United States and the Soviet Union dominated world politics, reflected the preoccupation of analysts and statespersons with the nuclear balance of terror between the superpowers. A U.S.–Soviet strategic war could have jeopardized the survival of the human species, and I gave its prevention the highest priority in my work, concentrating on bilateral measures of conflict moderation, arms control, and deterrence. I discussed normative and structural reforms of the international system but for the most part considered them unrealistic means of reducing the role of war in the context of the U.S.–Soviet rivalry.

Then came the world-transforming events of 1989 to 1991: the collapse of the Soviet sphere of control, the demise of the U.S.–Soviet rivalry, the Gulf War. The fate of humanity no longer hinged precariously on the stability of the U.S.–Soviet nuclear balance. Don Reisman of St. Martin's Press and I began to talk of a new edition reflecting the changed parameters of conflict and cooperation in international relations. We met at the end of March 1991 in Vancouver at the International Studies Association (ISA) convention to firm up plans. It was just three weeks after Desert Storm had routed Saddam Hussein's troops from

Kuwait. George Bush's "new world order" had already proven illusory, as Saddam, ever defiant, initiated his protracted campaign of undermining the cease-fire accords. Secessionist movements with the potential for violence were erupting in the Balkans among and within the republics of a disintegrating Yugoslavia. A similar fate seemed in store for many of the nations of Eurasia with the falling apart of the Soviet empire. Reisman and I agreed that world peace was hardly about to break out and that serious work on the causes and prevention of war would continue to be in demand—a judgment no less warranted in the fall of 1993.

At the ISA convention I was a panelist in the roundtable discussion titled "What Do We Know about Peace?" organized by Matthew Melko of Wright State University. The other panelists were Kenneth Boulding of the University of Colorado, Jack S. Levy of Rutgers University, Manus Midlarsky and John A. Vasquez also of Rutgers, Laure Paquette of Queens University, and Michael Wallace of the University of British Columbia. This turned out to be a defining moment in my scholarly odyssey, for it was at the Vancouver roundtable, while exchanging ideas with my distinguished colleagues on the systemic causes of war and peace, that I was struck by the realization that my own work had concentrated too much on the structural factors and not enough on the emotional and cognitive states of mind of key decision makers. I thereupon resolved (and it was reflected in the thrust of my comments during the session) to remedy this imbalance in my future research and writing.

The present edition of *The Causes and Prevention of War* reflects my enlarged interest in the psychological variables and the mind-sets of particular decision makers—notably in the chapters "Why Humans Fight" and "The Role of Diplomacy." I also give greater weight to the ideational, especially moral, norms that predispose nations and their leaders toward violent or nonviolent means of dealing with conflict— thus the added chapter "The Culture of War." These emphases are prominent in a new concluding chapter on the elements of a comprehensive and flexible strategy for the prevention and control of war in the post– Cold War era.

Another feature of the post–Cold War edition is the greater attention given to ethnic and nationality conflicts. I am deeply indebted to my Brandeis University colleague, Steven L. Burg, for insights on the causes of and methods of dealing with these precipitants of civil and interstate violence.

Others who read drafts of the manuscript and provided me with valuable comments include Martin O. Heisler, University of Maryland at College Park; David Hendrickson, Colorado College; Jeffrey Kimball, Miami University; Steven L. Lamy, University of Southern California; Carolyn Landau, Marist College; John A. Vasquez, now at Vanderbilt University.

In addition to Don Reisman, whose encouragement and commitment to this project had much to do with its fruition, I would like to thank Kalea Chapman at St. Martin's Press and Al Davis, Veronica Scrol, and Joseph Vittitow at Publication Services for their superb guidance and technical assistance during the editing process.

Finally, I am specially proud of the index — constructed by my two youngest sons, Matthew and Jeremiah, with general oversight and occasional kibitzing from their father. The boys also ran a newspaper clipping service over the years (for remuneration, of course) to help me keep up to date on many of the situations analyzed in the book.

S. B.

Contents

Introduction: Scope and Focus

This book is about the causes, prevention, and control of violence between countries, involving intentional physical destruction of people and material assets—that terrible human activity called *war*.

Psychological violence (efforts to manipulate an opponent's will through language, sometimes abusive, sometimes seductive, and through the proffering and withholding of various carrots and sticks) will be dealt with, but only to the extent that it is conducive to, involved in, or meant to prevent physically destructive warfare. I justify this distinction on the premise that the threshold separating assaults on the mind from assaults on the flesh is one of the most profound demarcations in human life, and that once this threshold has been crossed in a real conflict (as distinguished from body-contact sports, such as football), the prospects of avoiding terrible and irreversible brutality are drastically reduced.

The subject matter here is *international war*—that is violence between organized political entities claiming to be sovereign nations. The book is primarily about war between *nation-states,* or "countries," but it also covers secessionist wars by political subdivisions of a country and wars of "national self-determination" instigated by geographically concentrated national or religious communities who believe themselves to be illegitimately subordinated by a larger state. Internal revolutions and "civil wars" among rival domestic groups for control of the the state apparatus are not the subject, except insofar as they may induce the intervention of external powers or otherwise affect interstate alignments and balances of power in ways that significantly affect the prospects of international war or peace. However, civil and other domestic violence, including interpersonal violence, will be examined for the insights such examination can contribute to the analysis of war between nations.

The analysis of war, so defined—physically destructive war between nations—has been a major preoccupation of international relations scholars. But knowledge relevant to the causes, prevention, and control of such war can also be gleaned from the disciplines of political science, economics, sociology, anthropology, psychology, biology, and physics as well as the transdisciplinary fields of history and philosophy. None of these fields has a monopoly on scholarly questions and answers about war and peace.

Similarly, with respect to the practical politics of war prevention and control, no segment of the political spectrum has a monopoly on the search for effective policy initiatives. I have worked with officials in the Department of Defense who have been as determined to live up to the Pentagon motto, "Peace is our profession," as colleagues in the Peace Studies Program at Brandeis University or participants in the Avoiding Nuclear War Project at Harvard have been to devise realistic measures for peace consistent with the hard facts of geopolitics.

My net for seeking insights is therefore cast widely across fields of knowledge, professions, and ideological orientations. The approach is inclusive and eclectic, but it is neither a survey of views nor neutral with respect to the merits of the views analyzed.

My larger, more ambitious objective is to develop a comprehensive strategy for the prevention and control of war that can help to reduce the role of violence in world politics. More modestly, I hope to help enhance analysts' and practitioners' awareness of the menu of policies available to governments and political movements for preventing, controlling, and terminating particular wars.

THE RANGE OF DIAGNOSES AND PRESCRIPTIONS

The chart on page 3 displays the range of frequently offered causes of war outbreak and escalation and the range of frequently offered remedies. It represents types of analyses and prescriptions applicable both to the problem of war in general and to specific cases—historical, contemporary, or anticipated—of war or war prevention. It thus previews the more detailed discussion of topics in the body of the book.

The chart shows that each of the the explanations commonly given for the prominence of war in the international system or for the occurrence and escalation of a particular war tends to lead to a cluster of remedies specific to the causes believed to be dominant. For example, theories that find the causes of war primarily in the distribution of military power usually produce policy prescriptions emphasizing diplomacy, deterrence, or arms control, whereas theories that locate the sources of war in prevailing attitudes about when the use of force is legitimate often give rise to calls for broad changes in what is taught in the schools

PRESCRIPTIONS FOR PREVENTING AND CONTROLLING WAR

CAUSES OF WAR	Selection and training of decision makers	Society-wide education	New social and economic policies	Reform of domestic political system	Restructuring of international system	Diplomacy, including deterrence and arms control
Structural factors:						
The international system						
distribution of military power					◉	◉
distribution of economic power			◉		◉	◉
institutions					◉	◉
Domestic systems			•	◉	•	
Prevailing culture of war and peace		◉	•	•	•	◉
Decision makers (their psychological characteristics)	◉	•	•	•	•	•

-    •   *Prescription often associated with the category of cause*
- ◉   *Prescription most often strongly recommended to deal with the category of cause*

3

and media. Systemic diagnoses are closely associated with systemic remedies, just as analyses that focus on the psychological idiosyncrasies of certain leaders or peoples tend to search for means of minimizing their influence or providing them with therapy.

The chart also reflects the fact that levels of analysis and prescription are often merged or skipped. This is entirely appropriate both for policy making and for scholarly analysis. If the larger system is deemed to be in a violence-prone configuration (for example, an unstable balance of military power), it may be more imperative than ever that extraordinarily skillful diplomats are at the helm and that decision processes are micromanaged so as to reduce the likelihood of emotional or cognitive mistakes. Conversely, if ignorant or emotionally unstable individuals happen to be at the national switches that could ignite a general conflagration, there is all the more reason to have in place international mechanisms for quarantining, controlling, and terminating such wars as may break out.

ORGANIZATION OF THE BOOK

The search for "causes" is the principal preoccupation of Part I. Chapter 1 focuses on the violent behavior of individuals. Chapter 2 explores the sources of collective violence. Chapter 3 reviews the justifications national leaders typically give for deciding that war is an appropriate way for dealing with the country's situation. Chapter 4 analyzes elements in the basic structure of the relationships among and within nations that are conducive to war. Chapter 5 deals specifically with the distribution of military power and the strategies for using it. Chapter 6 explores the culture of violence prevailing at various times and places that can affect the likelihood of war and the way it is fought. And Chapter 7 examines how the skill or ineptitude of particular governments and leaders can determine whether conflicts are handled peacefully or violently.

The search for effective methods of preventing and controlling war is the preoccupation of Part II. Chapter 8 analyzes proposals for purging war from human society by fundamentally transforming the structure and norms of the world polity. Chapter 9 assays less radical efforts to reduce the prominence of war and control the escalation of international conflicts. The more specialized problems of arms limitation and control are the focus of Chapter 10. The Conclusion draws on these various prescriptions in arguing for a multifaceted and flexible approach to war prevention and control for the post–Cold War era.

PART I

The Causes of War

You are interested, I know, in the prevention of war,
not in our theories . . .
Yet I would like to dwell a little
on this destructive instinct.

— *Sigmund Freud*

Wars kill people.
That is what makes them different
from all other forms of human enterprise.

— *General Colin L. Powell*

The Semai are not great warriors . . . .
Many did not realize that soldiers kill people.
When I suggested to one Semai . . .
that killing was a soldier's job,
he laughed at my ignorance and explained,
"No, we just tend weeds and cut grass."

— *Anthropologist Robert Knox Dentan*

CHAPTER 1

Why Humans Fight: Explaining the Violent Behavior of Individuals

The extent to which virtually any human being, because of the inherent physiology and characteristic mental processes of the species, is predisposed to act violently or refrain from violence in various situations will surely affect the actions of nations toward one another. This proposition might be too obvious to state were it not for the view frequently propounded by international relations scholars of the so-called realist school (with some notable exceptions) that little, if anything, about international war and peace can be learned from the fields of biology or psychology.

Common sense and detailed research alike point to the crucial role of the *emotional dispositions and cognitive mind-sets of particular individuals* in national decisions

- To regard another country's actions as hostile or benign
- To fight or negotiate
- On strategy and tactics during a war
- To stop fighting
- On terms of peace

The answers to the underlying questions—What's at stake? How do we get or defend it? Is war the best available means? Will the contemplated result of war be worth the expected costs and risks?—are always profoundly affected by what is going on in the heads *and* glands of the involved decision makers, whether these be only a restricted elite at the very top echelons of the interacting governments or also include parliaments and broad segments of the population. Knowledge about the sources of these crucial ideas and impulses is therefore essential to an adequate understanding of the causes and prevention of war.

7

BIOLOGICAL DETERMINISM

The theory that violence is natural to human beings has been advanced by some biologists in the fields of ethology and sociobiology, most prominently by Konrad Lorenz and Edward O. Wilson. The empirical scientific observations by these biologists have been mostly of nonhuman species, and the inferences they make from their studies of insect and lower-animal behavior to human behavior are highly conjectural (indeed they admit to this).

In his book *On Aggression,* Konrad Lorenz speculates that the human animal contains a store of aggressive energy that seeks release and can be rather easily triggered in situations of rivalry and perceived threat. In this respect, the human being would be like many other species in the animal kingdom whose survival has been aided by such instincts. By a process of natural selection (the most aggressive would be most likely to survive, to mate, and to pass on their aggressive traits to their offspring), the evolutionary process may well have favored the development of human beings with high intelligence and a propensity to fight.[1]

This hypothesis of the survival of the most aggressive is echoed in Edward O. Wilson's contention that human beings are disposed to react with "unreasoning hatred" to perceived threats to their safety or possessions. There is a "profound human tendency to learn violence," says Wilson. "Our brains appear to be programmed ... to partition people into friends and aliens. . . . We tend to fear deeply the actions of strangers and to solve conflict by aggression." He speculates that these "learning rules are most likely to have evolved during the past hundreds of thousands of years . . . and thus, to have conferred a biological advantage on those who conformed to them with the greatest fidelity."[2]

The theory of the natural selection of the most aggressive beings refers mainly to the males among the vertebrate animals. Male proclivities to violence are noted especially among mammals, though there are exceptions: female hamsters, for example, are larger and better fighters than males, and among wolves, various feline species, and even some primates (such as gibbons) there appears to be a rough equality in inclination and capability for fighting. But among most primates, Homo sapiens included, the males within any group tend to be larger, more muscular, and more inclined to physical aggression than the females.[3]

The differences in aggressiveness between primate males and females do appear generally to have been biologically functional, in the sense of contributing to the survival of the group or tribe in most mammalian species prior to premodern humans. The need of the fetus or infant to gain its sustenance directly from the female's body tended to turn the female into a more stationary, domestic creature and cast the male into the role of gatherer, hunter, and protector of the vulnerable mothers and offspring. The mates most attractive to the females, therefore, were males with the physiological attributes for effective hunting and combat against intruders: physical strength, swiftness, and keenly responsive instincts for when and how to attack and defend. The intra-tribal combat games among most primate males were often pre-mating rituals, with the winners getting the most desirable of the available females. The most desirable females tended to be those whose bodies were fittest for productive copulation and for bearing and nurturing the young. (Females needed to be capable of combat, too, for those times when their male protectors were away on the hunt; indeed, the female in most species, particularly when her babies are threatened, but also when fighting a rival for a male partner, can be especially ferocious.)

Only a superficial inference from this particular dynamic in the natural selection process, however, would lead to the conclusion that evolved contemporary man is genetically predisposed toward violence and contemporary woman is still most attracted to such an aggressive male.

Survival from generation to generation also required males and females who were loyal and caring for one another and their young and—to the extent that group survival was a requisite of individual survival—who were emotionally capable of cooperating and sharing with others. Even various insect and animal species lower on the evolutionary scale appear to have instincts that are functionally equivalent to these "altruistic" traits.[4] Moreover, as group welfare and survival came to require agriculture, trans-seasonal storage, irrigation projects, and the rudiments of industry along with more elaborate defense capabilities and strategies, those with the kind of intelligence required for such planning and organization came to be more admired and rewarded with privileges and consequently also to be more attractive as mates. Then, too, because peace might in some communities be more conducive to the group's well-being than frequent and destructive wars, the arts of diplomacy and bargaining could well be the attributes making for the "survival of the fittest."

Given these caveats, most biological determinists (even those who postulate the parallel evolution of cooperative traits along with egoistic traits) maintain that the typical human being is by nature *not strongly inhibited* from killing other humans and that human violence can be quite easily provoked.

PSYCHOANALYTIC INSIGHTS

Sigmund Freud, the founder of the psychoanalytic movement, was centrally concerned in his theory and in his clinical practice with the extreme forms of human aggression—violence directed against others in homicide and against the self in suicide. He devised therapies for helping individuals to cope with and in some cases overcome their violent propensities, but he was not optimistic, as revealed in his dialogue on the subject with the great physicist Albert Einstein, that significant ameliorants were available for reducing the level of violence between countries.

The Death Instinct

Einstein wrote to Freud in 1932 for help in understanding what seemed to him to be an irrational refusal of humans to dispense with the international war system and national military establishments. The physicist could find only one explanation for such stubborn adherence to these presumably obsolete human institutions: the human "lust for hatred and destruction" which at times of international conflict often emerges as a "collective psychosis."[5] Freud's reply[6] drew on his theoretical work on how the pleasure principle, mediated through the death instinct (suicidal impulses to eliminate all pain) and Eros (life-affirming impulses), leads to interpersonal and intergroup aggression; accordingly, for "civilization" to prevail, this instinct-driven dynamic had to be repressed. We see this necessity for repression, Freud explained, in the imposition of discipline by parents over children, by institutions over individuals, and by the state over society. From this he deduced, and Einstein agreed, that a world government was needed to impose the necessary discipline on the otherwise dangerously anarchic international system. But whereas Einstein became a supporter of the United World Federalists and other groups working toward the establishment of world government, Freud doubted that humans have the requisite capacity to overcome their irrational attachments to national and religious groups. The father of psychoanalysis, therefore, remained deeply pessimistic about the prospects for fundamentally reducing the role of war in world politics. Today, however, the psychoanalytic branch of psychiatry is divided on this question.

Narcissism

A variant on Freud's focus on the pathological manifestations of the pleasure principle is the concept of narcissism. Also appearing in Freud's work, this concept has been accorded a central explanatory role by some of his disciples.[7] Named after the Greek mythological character Narcissus, who fell in love with his own reflection in a pool of water, the narcissistic personality is obsessed with his or her self-worth because of deep underlying feelings of worthlessness. The narcissist seeks solace from self-doubt in evidence that others are unworthy or evil. Worthiness, often measured in strength, material success, or victory in contests and conflict, is translated by the narcissist into an intense desire to see others as weak, failures, and losers—even in active efforts to put others down and, at the extreme, to destroy them. In its most pathological form, narcissism appears as sadism.[8]

In the world of statecraft the quintessential narcissist of modern times was Adolf Hitler, followed closely by Benito Mussolini, Joseph Stalin, and, perhaps, Saddam Hussein. These are all too easy to identify. But confirming the psychoanalytical insight that we all harbor narcissistic tendencies, albeit in varying degrees, we take no little pleasure in being able to point to *them* as narcissistic monsters.

The need to enhance one's own self-worth by knocking others down is indulged in the great participatory *and* spectator sport of war. Psychiatrists confirm that combat veterans report never having felt as "high" as when engaged in the act of "wasting" the enemy—even when the targets were villages or cities containing noncombatants. It is often their later, intense feelings of guilt that bring such combat veterans into psychotherapy, but during warfare these guilt feelings are suppressed by the psychological device of dehumanizing the enemy, often with racially denigrating code names—japs, krauts, gooks, and the like. A parallel dynamic operates on the home front, where the supportive populace gains vicarious enjoyment not only from news reports of the country's combat victories, but also through plays, films, comic strips, and other popular art forms that portray the enemy as venal and subhuman. Although this process of "enmification" is most pronounced during wartime, it is also very much a part of *pre*war buildups of patriotic fervor required to mobilize national energies for impending combat.[9] As such, narcissism, when fused into nationalism, can at times be employed for national self-defense, but it is also susceptible of exploitation by demagogues who would lead their peoples into acts of self-righteous aggression. Another consequence of the projection of evil onto the opponent is the opposition this engenders against efforts to limit and terminate wars, particularly when the controls, cease-fires, and peace negotiations would require one's own side to compromise its original war aims.

Alienation

Some of Freud's disciples dispute the emphasis given in orthodox psychoanalytic theory to presumably innate human propensities for violence and give more weight to societal factors as determinants of whether aggression is mainly defensive or malign. Erich Fromm, one of the most influential of these neo-Freudians, maintains that dangerously malign forms of aggression (expressing sadistic and masochistic motivations) have their source in the socio-psychological condition of alienation.

In *The Anatomy of Human Destructiveness,* Fromm portrays the alienated individuals and groups as profoundly separated, in a psychological sense, from their fellow human beings and as irrationally driven to avenge their terrible loneliness and feelings of impotence through godlike acts of destruction. The alienated are ready candidates for recruitment into violent communal and nationalist organizations, where individuals can compensate their lack of human connectedness by "losing themselves" in a group bound together by its hatred of the outsiders.[10]

Fromm's work provides a bridge to the efforts of social psychologists, sociologists, and anthropologists to discover which social conditions are most likely to provoke the intense negative emotions that drive humans to acts of violence and which social conditions are most conducive to more rational and peaceable means of dealing with conflict.

THE FRUSTRATION-AGGRESSION HYPOTHESIS

The key to most human violence is found by many social psychologists to be frustration—that is, substantial interference with or blocking of goal-directed activity. Especially when the frustrated person expects to have achieved the objective were it not for the interference, the result is often intense anger, expressed in attempts to hurt or destroy the object or person perceived to be the cause of the frustration.[11]

In its sophisticated versions the hypothesis does not state that all frustration leads to aggression, for obviously humans, especially adults, have a wide variety of adaptations to frustration, some of them constructive and creative. Even when a frustrating situation produces aggressive *feelings* toward those believed to be the cause of one's discontent, people living in civil society are generally dissuaded from acting violently toward the targets of their animosity because of the social and legal consequences they would suffer unless they repress their anger or deflect it in socially acceptable ways.

What the hypothesis does state is that when violent and destructive behavior occurs it is usually in response to a negative stimulus outside the person—a stimulus that is experienced as frustration of activity directed toward the satisfaction of a strongly desired objective. (The objective does not necessarily have to be a goal still to be attained; it can be the peace and security of the status quo, the safety of one's family and possessions, and the maintenance of one's standard of living, one's way of life; frustration in such cases may take the form of threats to these valued conditions.) Obviously, not all angry violence is directly triggered by frustration so defined. Some people actively seek violent encounters as a way of testing or proving their virility; some revel in it; some may have an insatiable appetite to dominate others and thus provoke violent reactions on the part of those whom they try to push around; and there are severely disturbed individuals who exhibit a chronic state of belligerence. The social psychologists who have developed and elaborated the frustration-aggression hypothesis do not deny these other sources of violence. Their contribution is to focus attention on the immediate situational variables that can provoke or reinforce existing interpersonal or international proclivities for violent action, and by this they also encourage the search for practical ameliorants or alternatives to violence that can be applied or negotiated in specific situations.

RATIONAL AND PRACTICAL VIOLENCE

The biological, psychoanalytical, and frustration-aggression explanations discussed above all postulate an upwelling of emotion, whatever its deeper source in the person's physiology or experience, that is the immediate driving pressure producing acts of violence. Presumably the intensified emotional energy (usually accompanied by measurable changes in body chemistry) takes over in such situations, overwhelming rational calculations of costs and benefits that could result from the violence. The actor loses control to inner primordial or subconscious forces, and attacks.

Yet many of the conventional and legally codified explanations for violence, for both legitimate and condemned acts, assume that the actor retains essential mental control of his faculties up to and throughout the behavior in question. Indeed, one of the standard indictments in murder trials is that the act of violence was premeditated, and one of the standard defenses is that of justifiable homicide.[12] The prosecution and defense alike are claiming that the defendant knew precisely what he or she was doing at the time.

Defense attorneys in murder trials sometimes try to get their clients acquitted on grounds of insanity. But the legal criteria for insanity are stringent and require expert psychiatric testimony to establish that the defendant was totally out of control and mentally incapable of distinguishing right from wrong at crucial phases in the homicidal sequence.[13] More frequently, acquittals are obtained on "reasonable man" grounds: the defendant's actions under the circumstances (being subjected to intense provocation, needing self-protection or to protect others, experiencing chaos and confusion, what have you) were understandable, in that most ordinary persons finding themselves in similar situations could well have acted as the defendant did. (As will be shown in Chapter 3, such "reasonable man" defenses are analogous to many justifications nations typically offer for going to war.)

The conventional and legal definitions of and societal responses to murder reflect the fact of life that in many human circumstances violence is an option, sometimes an attractive option. Violence is one of the means available, frequently regarded as legitimate, for bringing pressure against another human being or group to get one's way when opposed, or to prevent being inflicted with pain or humiliation. And it is a fact, however distressing, that it can and often does succeed.

When There Is No Alternative: The Violence of "Last Resort"

Most communities, as do most social philosophers, grant that violence can be legitimate when it is necessary for self-defense—that is, when one's own survival or protection against extreme violence requires the violent disabling of an attacker. Allowable self-defense ordinarily extends at least to the protection of one's immediate family. Organized societies are expected to provide community resources, including police forces, to help protect people against violent attacks. Law enforcement agencies are provisioned with superior weapons and with generally wide writs of authority to use violence sufficient to overwhelm individuals or groups engaging in illegal activity. But the police are not always close enough to offer timely protection, and when they are not, violent acts of self-defense may well be rational.

Calculated, deliberate acts of violence or threats of violence also are resorted to for purposes other than defending against physical attacks upon persons. Premeditated violence often is used as a last resort to protect property against vandals, thieves, and trespassers when nonviolent prohibitions are disregarded. In most communities, recourse to such violence in the defense of property is normally supposed to be undertaken by the community's police force, but again, when timely protection by the community's law enforcers is unavailable, self-help, even including the use of deadly force, is widely regarded as permissible.

Although acts of violence for reasons of necessary self-defense and protection of property are generally tolerated, they are nonetheless usually subject to after-the-fact review by community institutions to determine whether they really were necessary under the precise circumstances. Such judgments are often highly controversial. Is it justifiable, for example, to shoot someone who has threatened harm to your family when that person enters your immediate residential neighborhood on an obvious mission to carry out that threat, or must the would-be attacker have entered your home? Does a store owner have the right to use force to apprehend or stop a thief caught in the act of robbery? Under what circumstances is shooting to kill and not merely shooting to disable permissible? It is not my intention here to resolve such practical and philosophical issues, but only to observe that there are categories of violence, whether engaged in by organized society on behalf of citizens or by individuals on their own behalf, that some societies consider both rational and morally justified.

Given the enormous destruction war brings to each side, the claim of having no alternative is usually part of the justification for using or threatening to use military force (see Chapter 3) and is associated with the presumed need to protect a vital national interest.

The claim that only violent means are available and that in the circumstances they are both rational and morally justified is often made by leaders of revolutionary movements—*and* by governments attempting to repress the revolutionaries: "When a long train of abuses and usurpations . . . evinces a design to reduce [a people] under absolute despotism, it is their right, it is their duty, to throw off such government" (American Declaration of Independence).[14] "The proletarians have nothing to lose but their chains . . . . Workingmen of the world, unite!" (Marx and Engels).[15] "Only the violent overthrow of the bourgeoisie, the confiscation of its property, the destruction of the whole of the bourgeois state apparatus . . . can ensure the real subordination of the whole class of exploiters" (Lenin).[16] "The great organism of violence . . . has surged upwards in reaction to the settler's violence . . . . [This] violence is a cleansing force. It frees the native from his inferiority complex and from his despair and inaction; it makes him fearless and restores his self-respect" (Fanon).[17]

The prevention of the violence of last resort is especially difficult once the antagonists begin to mobilize themselves for physical combat. Appeals for reasonableness in such situations are likely to fall on deaf ears, not so much because emotions have taken over as because a calculated decision has been made that violence is the only feasible alternative to an intolerable sacrifice of one's basic values.

When Sticks Seem More Efficient Than Carrots

Between individuals, groups, or states, violence is at times resorted to with conscious calculation even though other means of protecting or asserting one's interests are available. Those who initiate the violence calculate—whether on the basis of intuitive assessment or computer-assisted "gaming" of costs and benefits—that they will be better off if they employ (or convincingly threaten) force than if they do not.

Much bullying between children is the product of the simpler variety of such cost-benefit assessments. Two groups of children converge on an unreserved athletic field, both wanting to use it. An argument ensues, but neither will give way. The members of one group, clearly older and stronger, start pushing and shoving their rival claimants, who then concede the field rather than accept the challenge to a fight they are sure to lose. (Czechoslovakia's contrite surrender to Hitler's bullying in 1938 comes to mind.) The older and stronger group has other options—inviting the younger children to play with them, suggesting a time limit on the use of the field by each group, flipping a coin, and so on—but a quick calculation of the balance of power convinces them that they can easily scare off the younger group and have the field entirely to themselves, as they planned.

The history of American frontier settlements in areas not yet under established civil authority is replete with such violent encounters,[18] the plot for many a wild West movie or TV drama:[19] Neighboring ranchers are grazing their herds in the same grassland, and the area is becoming overgrazed. The owners of Circle X ranch erect a fence around roughly half of the grazing area and put "No Trespassing" signs along the fence. The owners of the Bar Y ranch are outraged at this unilateral act and, since their herd is 50 percent larger than the Circle X herd, demand that the fence be moved back closer to the Circle X corral. When their demand is refused, the Bar Y ranchers chop down parts of the fence to allow their cattle again to wander the whole grassland. The Circle X ranchers drive the cattle back and repair the fence, while warning the Bar Y ranchers that any of their cattle found again within Circle X territory will be shot on sight. The possible next steps in this escalating conflict need not be drawn here. The point of the illustration is only the calculated rationality of the steps taken by each side up the conflict-escalation ladder.

In many situations of this sort, alternative moves of a less provocative nature are available but are not taken. Why? If generally established procedures for mediating or arbitrating conflicts are lacking, if there are no enforceable rules prohibiting unilateral preemptive behavior, and if a sense of community among those sharing a particular resource is absent, aggressive moves can be highly tempting. We need not postulate an instinctive predisposition to violence to explain the violence or violence-provoking behavior. The only necessary premises are a modicum of acquisitiveness, a scarcity of some valued amenity, and the absence of strong internal and external inhibitions against violence; given these conditions, the violence is an unsurprising resultant of rational calculations on both sides.

Typically such conflicts can be prosecuted (and sometimes resolved) with either "carrots" or "sticks," or with some combination of positive bargaining and coercive threat. When the sticks available to one or the other of the adversaries appear to be considerably more efficacious than the available carrots, the inclinations to resort to force are highest, and this condition is most likely when the adversaries possess few resources with which they can bargain for positive-payoff exchanges. This is one of the reasons why the calculated resort to violence (or threats of violence) between individuals or groups even of essentially equal power is generally more prevalent between children than between adults, between relatively poor people than between the comfortably affluent, and between the politically disenfranchised than between those with easy access to the central institutions of society.[20]

It is precisely with respect to the phenomenon of violence as negative bargaining that deterrence—the dissuasion of an action through the threat of imposing costs on the potential aggressor in excess of his or her anticipated gains, even though not necessarily prevailing over the aggressor—may appear to be the most efficacious means of controlling violence. In basically anarchic situations (unsupervised playgrounds, unpoliced neighborhoods with high crime rates, countries pervaded by civil conflict, the international system) the deterrence of violent behavior often requires that the individuals or groups trying to protect themselves display a credible ability and will to inflict unacceptable damage on their would-be attackers.

SOME EVIDENCE FROM ANTHROPOLOGY

The existence of even a few societies in which violence (actual or threatened) is virtually absent would call into question the theory of strong innate predispositions to violence in the human species. Anthropologists have discovered remarkably little violence, either against other tribes or as an instrument of internal social control, in as many as ten known tribal societies: the Zuni Indians of the American Southwest, the Kung Bushmen of the Kalahari Desert in southern Africa, the Arapesh of New Guinea, the Semai of Malaysia, the Copper Eskimo of Canada, the Adaman Islanders (Indian Ocean), the Tristan Islanders (South Pacific), the Todas of India, the Siriono of Bolivia, and the Yahgan of Chile.[21]

These societies are not without conflict. They are peaceful to the extent that they rely on nonviolent methods of conflict resolution—intertribal negotiations and intratribal mediation by tribal elders or religious leaders. But, significantly, even the most peaceful of these societies also employ various forms of social conditioning to constrain and deflect the tendencies to resort to violence. Tribal cosmology, rituals, and legends reinforce the nonviolent norms of the society. And social ostracism is typically inflicted on individuals who violate these norms. Thus, none of the societies studied by anthropologists would seem to operate on the premise that its members would automatically refrain from violence, that there is a strong instinct for peace, as it were, operating without community inducements to discourage violence and without instruction in the virtues and arts of nonviolent conflict resolution.

VIOLENCE AS LEARNED BEHAVIOR

The anthropological evidence of significant variations in the way conflict is handled in different cultures is consistent with studies by social psychologists demonstrating that humans can be taught to be more or less violent or peaceful. Explicitly or implicitly, groups (from families to gangs to nations) convey to their members what kind of conflictual or cooperative behavior is admired or disparaged, and such group norms can work to reinforce, channel, or deflect aggressive desires to dominate others or to strike out at those believed to be responsible for one's deprivations and frustrations.

A series of research projects by Albert Bandura and other social psychologists comparing the family environment of adolescent boys exhibiting antisocial aggression with the family environment of nonaggressive adolescent boys discovered a crucial difference: The aggressive boys had parents who (even though themselves not particularly antisocial) encouraged their sons in combative aggressiveness in conflicts outside the family. By contrast, the more pacific boys had parents who discouraged physical belligerency as a method of dealing with interpersonal conflict.[22]

Such direct teaching of how to deal with interpersonal and intergroup conflict also takes place outside the family commands or instructions from authorities that may be accompanied by punishments and rewards to reinforce the verbal or symbolic messages.[23] It is just as often indirect, through myths and legends defining heroism and courage as the willingness to risk one's life in physical combat against the enemies of one's group, through ideologies and propaganda engendering hatred toward members of enemy groups and dehumanizing them, and through religious and ethical concepts and mores that justify killing under certain circumstances.

One laboratory for observing how and to what extent individuals can be taught to act violently is the basic training administered to raw recruits into the military service. Much of the training is designed to remove the inhibitions ordinary civilian youth are thought to have against killing other human beings. A typical basic training drill requires that the neophyte charge a stuffed dummy of "the enemy" and plunge a bayonet into its body (including the face), all the while screaming, "Kill! Kill! Kill!" Armies are not content to dehumanize the enemy, however; universally, their training routines reflect an elemental understanding that fear for one's own life or some residue of reluctance to maim and kill others may interfere with effective performance in actual combat. Accordingly, the basic training rituals also are designed to inculcate absolute and immediate obedience to superiors in the chain of command. The automaton-like marching and saluting, the crisp "Yes, *sir!*" responses, and the requirement that one do exactly as one is ordered, without question, enthusiastically, even when the action is ridiculous or degrading, are meant to program the soldier into a totally reliable cog in the military machine. But a military unit's effectiveness in combat requires more than automaton-like discipline. Initiative, the ability to make smart decisions in situations not anticipated in commands already received, and loyalty to and care for one's buddies — all of these very *human* traits — are also inculcated and nurtured in the training regime of the neophyte soldier. Moreover, the individual soldier is taught and is expected to adhere to various rules of war concerning the impermissibility of attacking noncombatants, the treatment of prisoners, and the like (see Chapter 6), and this can set up considerable tension and psychological disturbance within individual soldiers who are ordered by their superiors to engage in the prohibited acts. Yet the basic approach in military training the world over to the inevitable contradictions encountered in turning human beings into efficient fighting machines is to inculcate reliance on the hierarchical authority structure of the military establishment.

Paradoxically, if being a man is to be an autonomous individual capable of deciding when and how to do what is necessary and right and to have the capacity to control one's behavior accordingly, much of basic military training is structured precisely to *emasculate* the individual soldier. The Marine Corps' traditional recruiting slogan should perhaps be changed to "Give us a few good men, and we'll make them less than that!"[24]

There can be variations from country to country in the susceptibility of young soldiers to basic training in military violence. But some research studies suggest a universal malleability, despite the cultural variances, by indoctrination in the arts of brutality.

Evidence of the ease by which ordinary individuals can be trained to act violently, given the appropriate social environment, is provided in the famous experiment conducted by psychologist Stanley Milgram with subjects selected from a broad cross-section of Americans. The subjects were told that they would be helping to administer an experiment in learning and would serve as teachers for the experiment. The "teachers" were separated by a wall from the person they were told was the subject of the experiment, the "learner." They were instructed to administer electric shocks to the "learner" when the "learner" made mistakes in a simple verbal test. The shocks were increased in voltage each time the learner made a mistake. The "learner," contrary to what the "teachers" were led to believe by the experimenter, was not actually wired to receive the shocks, but pretended to suffer increasing pain to the point where, near the end of the experiment, he was screaming and banging on the wall. The experimenter would urge on "teachers" who appeared reluctant to administer shocks beyond a certain intensity, saying authoritatively that they must continue. Although virtually all of the "teachers" were unmistakably disturbed at having to administer the high-voltage shocks, 65 percent did continue even up through the final level, ominously labeled *XXX*. Analysis of the reactions (and some follow-on controlled experiments) indicated that the crucial determinant of the willingness of the subjects to administer what they believed were violent shocks to an innocent person was the apparent scientific authoritativeness of the experiment and the chief experimental psychologist.[25]

The learning of violent methods of dealing with conflict is also indirect: through assimilating the norms and ethical precepts of the society in which one lives. In traditional society these views of expected behavior were transmitted through myths, legends, literature, and religious instruction. In contemporary society, the media for such normative messages are often films and television programs.

Given the pervasiveness of violence on television and in the movies (especially in the United States, but increasingly also in other countries), there are grounds for the concerns of many parents, educators, and psychologists that the populace is being acculturated to regard violence — and presumably, therefore, also war — as normal. A study conducted under the auspices of the Harvard Medical School's Center for Psychological Studies in the Nuclear Age found that in watching the most popular adventure cartoon shows on American television,

> children learn that the world is a dangerous place in which they
> . . . have to be ready to defend themselves against the arbitrary
> attacks of an evil, foreign enemy who lurks behind every corner.

... They learn that the world is one in which only violence is
effective in settling differences....

Heroes and enemies never get together to negotiate. They only
meet to fight. As a result, children are socialized to believe in
peace through a notion of strength that is synonymous with hatred
and violence.[26]

Are these messages translated into excessive violence in the home,
street, and school? Is what is learned carried over into the psyches of
adults who are charged with the responsibility for making crucial life-
and-death decisions for the nation and the world? Psychologists disagree
in their assessment of the behavioral impact of television violence on
children and are even farther apart when it comes to assessing the impact of media violence on adults. At one extreme is the psychoanalyst
Bruno Bettelheim, who contends that the contemporary media offerings
to children are no more violent in their plots than traditional fairy tales
and, like the fairy tales, are a useful catharsis for children in working
out their otherwise repressed fears about violent tendencies, even those
within themselves.[27] Most studies by social psychologists, however, do
show a significant correlation between frequent watching of television
violence and acting violently, even while there continues to be substantial professional controversy over the causal dynamics.[28]

More research is required in order to determine more precisely under
what conditions (social and within the individual) violent media stories
and images are most conducive to violent behavior. Even if a heavy determinative influence is established, it will remain difficult to legislate
effective legal controls on the exposure of children and other susceptible individuals to negatively stimulating material without infringing on
various important civil liberties.

MISPERCEPTION AND OTHER
COGNITIVE FAILURES

Despite the evidence from biology and psychology that most humans are quite capable of acting violently toward other humans, especially when they are involved in intense conflict over some seemingly
indivisible object, those political leaders and bureaucrats who rise to
the top of their country's foreign policy decision-making apparatus are
usually highly self-controlled individuals. Such officials have learned to

keep their violent impulses in check and to use violence (or its threat) instrumentally in pursuit of their personal or group's important interests. Yet even these leaders, whose use of military power is almost always deliberate and calculated, can make terrible mistakes, taking their countries into enormously destructive and expensive wars when available nonviolent options would have been at least as effective in gaining their objectives and would have involved substantially less human and material sacrifice.

Such crucial mistakes, leading to otherwise avoidable violence, are often the product of one or both of two basic types of cognitive failure: (1) the *failure to obtain crucial information* on the intentions and capabilities of the adversary and of other parties that could help either side, and (2) the *failure to predict correctly the effects of the actions* of the relevant parties upon one another, a failure sometimes directly traceable to misinformation but possibly also the product of the concepts and theories by which one processes information. The first type of cognitive failure is often referred to as *misperception*. The second is often called *miscalculation*.

These failures frequently play a large role in interpersonal and intergroup violence, in which there are relatively small sets of capabilities and intentions to assess; no wonder there is such an awful record of misperception and miscalculation leading to avoidable international war, given the vast number of material and human variables that need to be analyzed by the relevant decision makers in order to assess the interactive effects of their contemplated actions correctly. Some of the classic cases of avoidable war, however, have not been mere products of cognitive failure traceable to the complexity of the information or the unavailability of good analysis. As often as not, disaster has resulted from a stubborn rejection, bordering on the pathological, to use the relevant information and analysis at hand.

A prototypical scenario of homicide committed during a robbery illustrates how misperception and miscalculation can take over in crises and transform them from dangerous confrontations to calamities: A man wearing a ski mask enters a convenience store late at night, points a handgun at the manager, who is behind the counter, and demands all the money in the cash register. The store manager, saying "You're not going to get away with this," starts to reach under the counter to activate an alarm. The robber shoots the manager, fatally wounding him. What began as a minor robbery is changed into an irredeemable horror involving the loss of an innocent life and bringing great pain and suffering to many people.

The robber, as we learn later at his murder trial, *misperceived* the store manager's move to activate the alarm as an effort to reach under the counter for a weapon, probably a gun, and shot the manager in panic. The store manager *miscalculated,* however, in failing to anticipate that the robber could rationally mistake the purpose of his move to reach under the counter as a grab for a gun. A rational robber in such a situation probably would have fled, calculating that the risks of completing the job had suddenly escalated way out of proportion to the possible gains. But the robber, under stress, imagined only an inevitable lethal confrontation, calculating that unless he shot first he might be killed or seriously wounded and not able to escape. The store manager was thus also at fault in acting without sufficient information about the mental condition of the masked robber. To be sure, if the robber were a cool professional, he would have recalculated his risks and run. As it turned out, it was a fatal error on the part of the store owner to have done anything other than promptly emptying the cash register and *later* reporting the robbery. Why did he make such an error? Was it simple stupidity? Or was it perhaps the product of a subconscious desire to compensate self-doubts about his manliness?

The kinds of misperception and miscalculation that can turn confrontations between nations into war are strongly analogous in their dynamics to such scenarios of accidental escalation of ordinary crimes into criminal homicide. And international relations scholars, arms control analysts, and policy makers—fearful of the rapidity and scope of escalation possible with modern weapons—have begun to pay increasing attention to the problem. Historical and contemporary crises are being studied to better understand the effects of misperception and miscalculation on policy and the sources of such mistakes.[29]

Some terrible but avoidable events in recent world history are revealed to have been at least partly attributable to these psychological processes: World War I, substantially a result of Kaiser Wilhelm's overestimation of the British desire to remain neutral in the summer of 1914 and his assumption that the war would be short; Hitler's aggressive rampages across Europe at the outset of World War II, encouraged by the misperception on the part of Neville Chamberlain and Edouard Daladier in the Munich Conference of 1938 that his aims were essentially limited to absorption of the Sudetenland; the United States–China war of 1950–1952, brought on by General MacArthur's grossly mistaken conviction that the Chinese were bluffing when they warned that a drive by U.S. forces toward the Manchurian border would compel them to intervene in the Korean War; the escalation of the civil war in South Vietnam into a full-blown United States–Vietnamese war lasting nearly a decade, a result of the assumption in U.S. policy-making circles that Ho Chi Minh would be frightened by the prospect of fighting against the world's most powerful country; General Galtieri's assumption in 1982 that an Argentine invasion of the Falkland Islands would have the blessings of the Reagan administration and that therefore the British would not intervene; and the Gulf War of 1990–1991, a consequence of Saddam Hussein's belief, encouraged by the Bush administration's policy of building him up as a counterweight to Iran's diplomacy, that he had virtually carte blanche to bully Kuwait and his other neighbors.

Studies of these cognitive failures have discovered that the crucial misperceptions and miscalculations often persisted in the face of evidence available to the responsible decision makers that strongly contradicted their assumptions. This record of blotting out cognitive dissonance has been explained by some analysts on the basis of psychological principles featured in the psychiatric literature on the defense mechanisms individuals resort to to protect their egos from the recognition that the assumptions on which they have been operating may be disastrously wrong. Richard N. Lebow's book *Between Peace and War: The Nature of International Crisis* devotes a central, fifty-page analytical chapter to "Cognitive Closure and Crisis Politics," in which concepts such as repression, chronic anxiety, and dissociative reactions are applied to the behavior of European heads of state and policy elites during the month between the assassination of the Archduke Ferdinand in Sarajevo and the outbreak of World War I.[30] And in his book *Avoiding War: Problems of Crisis Management* Alexander George, one of the most respected national security analysts, himself coauthor of a classic psychological study of President Woodrow Wilson, includes an essay by a psychiatrist on how national decision makers in international crises, particularly when they are under stress and fatigued, will variously misperceive information and miscalculate consequences according to whether they have a "compulsive personality," "narcissistic personality," or "paranoid personality."[31]

My discussion in this chapter has been based on the the premise that an understanding of human biology and psychology is a necessary part of the understanding of the violent behavior of nations, but the insights we gain from the fields of biology and psychology are an insufficient basis for understanding the highly organized and usually premeditated international violence we call war. To understand the causes of war and how it can be prevented and controlled, we must grapple as well with a wider array of factors, encompassing the material conditions, social structures, and cultural and moral norms that influence the behavior of nations.

NOTES

1. Konrad Lorenz, *On Aggression* (New York: Harcourt Brace & World, 1966). Instinctivist hypotheses are also advanced by Irenaus Eibl-Eibesfeldt, *The Biology of Peace and War* (New York: Viking, 1979).
2. Edward O. Wilson, *On Human Nature* (Cambridge: Harvard University Press, 1978), p. 119.
3. John Paul Scott, *Aggression* (Chicago: University of Chicago Press, 1975), pp. 68–88. See also Anthony Storr, *Human Aggression* (New York: Atheneum, 1968), pp. 59–71.
4. A work in the tradition of biological determinism that gives major attention to the counterviolent tendencies in various species is Irenaus Eibl-Eibesfeldt, *Love and Hate: The Natural History of Behavior Patterns* (New York: Holt, Rinehart & Winston, 1972). It should also be noted that Lorenz and Wilson themselves, in parts of their work that have occasioned less public controversy, have discovered variations among species and even within species in the counterviolent traits of bonding and altruism. See, for example, Wilson, *On Human Nature,* chap. 8.
5. Letter of Albert Einstein to Sigmund Freud, July 1932 (Geneva: League of Nations, International Institute of Intellectual Cooperation, 1933); reprinted in William Ebenstein, *Great Political Thinkers: Plato to the Present* (New York: Rinchart, 1951), pp. 802–804.
6. Sigmund Freud, letter to Albert Einstein, September 1932, included in the above League of Nations publication, reprinted in Ebenstein, pp. 804–810. Freud's theories on the sources of human violence, which he summarized for Einstein, are found in Freud's *Beyond the Pleasure Principle* (New York: Liveright, 1950); *Civilization and Its Discontents* (New York: Norton, 1962); and *An Outline of Psychoanalysis* (New York: Norton, 1959).
7. Otto Kornberg, *Borderline Conditions and Pathological Narcissism* (New York: Jason Aronson, 1975).
8. On the widespread phenomenon of narcissistic projection, see Andrew Bard Schmookler, *Out of Weakness: Healing the Wounds That Drive Us to War* (New York: Bantam Books, 1988); see also Schmookler's *The Parable of the Tribes: The Problem of Power in Social Evolution* (Berkeley: University of California Press, 1984).
9. Robert W. Rieber and Robert J. Kelly, "Substance and Shadow: Images of the Enemy," in Robert W. Rieber, ed., *The Psychology of War and Peace: The Image of the Enemy* (New York: Plenum Press, 1991), pp. 3–39.

10. Erich Fromm, *The Anatomy of Human Destructiveness* (New York: Holt, Rinehart & Winston, 1973); and *Escape from Freedom* (New York: Holt, Rinehart & Winston, 1941).

11. The original version of the frustration-aggression hypothesis is in John Dollard, Leonard W. Doob, Neal E. Miller, et al., *Frustration and Aggression* (New Haven: Yale University Press, 1939). Subsequent refinements are well reflected in Leonard Berkowitz, *Aggression: A Social Psychological Analysis* (New York: McGraw-Hill, 1962).

12. Wayne R. LaFave and Austin W. Scott, Jr., *Criminal Law,* 2d ed. (St. Paul: West Publishing, 1986), pp. 642–646.

13. LaFave and Scott, *Criminal Law,* pp. 302–331.

14. Carl L. Becker, *The Declaration of Independence: A Study in the History of Political Ideas* (New York: Harcourt, Brace, 1922).

15. Karl Marx and Friedrich Engels, *The Communist Manifesto* (New York: Appleton-Century-Crofts, 1955).

16. V. I. Lenin, "Theses on the Fundamental Tasks of the Second Congress of the Communist International," (July 4, 1920) in *Selected Works,* vol. 10 (New York: International Publishers, 1935), pp. 162–179.

17. Frantz Fanon, *The Wretched of the Earth,* trans. Constance Farrington (New York: Grove Press, 1963), p. 73.

18. See Eugene Hollon, *Frontier Violence: Another Look* (New York: Oxford University Press, 1974).

19. For an analysis of typical movie scenarios of violence on the Western frontier, see Will Wright, *Six Guns and Society: A Structural Study of the Western* (Berkeley: University of California Press, 1975).

20. For data on how a scarcity of resources for exchange correlates with violence, see Robert Bensing and Oliver Schroeder, *Homicide in an Urban Community* (Springfield, Ill: Charles C. Thomas, 1960). For an exposition of the logic of this relationship, see H. L. Nieburg, *Political Violence: The Behavioral Process* (New York: St. Martin's, 1965).

21. James M. Wallace, "Is War a Cultural Universal? Anthropological Perspectives on the Causes of Warfare in Human Societies," in Jongsuk Chay, ed., *Culture and International Relations* (New York: Preager, 1990), pp. 21–33; David Fabbro, "Peaceful Societies," in Richard Falk and Samuel S. Kim, eds., *The War System: An Interdisciplinary Approach* (Boulder: Westview Press, 1980), pp. 180–201; and Alexander Lesser, "War and the State," in Morton Fried, Marvin Hawk, and Robert F. Murphy, eds., *War: The Anthropology of Armed Conflict and Aggression* (Garden City, NY: Natural History Press, 1967), p. 95.

22. Study of adolescent aggressiveness by Albert Bandura and Richard Walters, described by Myriam Miedzian in *Boys Will Be Boys: Breaking the Link Between Masculinity and Violence* (New York: Doubleday, 1991), p. 62.

23. Albert Bandura, *Aggression: A Social Learning Analysis* (Englewood Cliffs; N.J.: Prentice Hall, 1973). On the philosophy and techniques of stimulus-

response behavior modification see B. F. Skinner, *Beyond Freedom and Dignity* (New York: Knopf, 1971).

24. The film *Full Metal Jacket* directed by Stanley Kubrick, 1987, vividly portrays the training of recruits in a U.S. Marine Corps boot camp.

25. Stanley Milgram, *Obedience to Authority* (New York: Harper & Row, 1974).

26. Petra Hesse and John E. Mack, "The World Is a Dangerous Place: Images of the Enemy on Children's Television," in Rieber, *The Psychology of War and Peace*, pp. 131–153, quotation from pp.147–148.

27. Bruno Bettelheim, *The Uses of Enchantment: The Meaning of Fairy Tales* (New York: Vintage, 1989). See also his "The Importance of Play," *The Atlantic*, March 1987, pp. 35–46.

28. Hesse and Mack, "The World Is a Dangerous Place," pp. 145-146.

29. Insightful analysis of the crucial effects of official misperceptions and miscalculations on the conduct of international crises is provided in Robert Jervis, *Perception and Misperception in International Politics* (Princeton: Princeton University Press, 1976); Richard Ned Lebow, *Between Peace and War: The Nature of International Crisis* (Baltimore: Johns Hopkins University Press, 1981); Ole R. Holsti, "Crisis Decision Making," in Philip E. Tetlock, Jo L. Husbands, Robert Jervis, Paul C. Stern, and Charles Tilly, eds., *Behavior, Society, and Nuclear War*, vol.1, ed. (New York: Oxford University Press, 1989), pp. 8–84; John Stoessinger, *Why Nations Go to War* (New York: St. Martin's, 1993); and the essays by Alexander George himself in Alexander George, *Avoiding War: Problems of Crisis Management* (Boulder: Westview, 1991).

30. Lebow, *Between Peace and War*, pp. 101–147.

31. Jerrold M. Post, "The Impact of Crisis-Induced Stress on Policy Makers," in George, *Avoiding War*, pp. 471–494.

CHAPTER 2

Why Communities Fight: Understanding Collective Violence

Knowledge about why individuals fight does not tell us enough about why and how entire communities go to war. A fighting response by an individual to a particular situation emanates from the brain — the organism's command center. This neurological dictator of the body not only processes information and renders decisions almost instantly but, through the body's central nervous system, can order the rest of the body to act and have these orders readily obeyed (within the limits of the body's physiological capabilities). By contrast, no large human group is such an integrated organism, subject to total behavioral direction from a single center of command and control. Members of communities, unlike the "members" of a human body, usually must be *convinced* (sometimes coercively) to participate in a violent action and to perform the roles assigned to them.

Not only wars between countries but also civil or revolutionary wars and major protests and strikes that provoke violent repression by governments often involve the activation of large organizations, with elaborate administrative structures. Sociologist Charles Tilly, one of the leading scholarly authorities on collective violence, finds that

> The groups engaged in collective action with any regularity
> usually consist of populations perceiving and pursuing a common
> set of interests. And collective action on any considerable scale
> requires coordination, communication and solidarity extending
> beyond the moment of action itself.[1]

The mobilization of these organizations to fight requires advance planning and provision directed toward an impending battle with a definable enemy. This preparation presupposes that the recourse to force has been seriously considered during a period of intensifying tension, usually featuring a series of demands and counterdemands between adversaries.

Moreover, although some interpersonal violence may grow out of extended periods of hostility and may be systematically premeditated and planned out in advance (for example, a murder committed in order to collect insurance benefits), much interpersonal violence, probably the large majority of instances, occurs in acts of uncontrolled suddenly-burgeoning emotion. By contrast, most violent conflicts between human communities, although sometimes triggered by unanticipated provocations, assassinations, or surprise attacks, are not primarily unthinking acts of passion. The collective resort to force is usually rational in the sense of being the product of conscious motivation and a calculated decision on the part of at least the community leaders to involve their warriors in battle.

This is not to exclude from consideration those situations in which large segments of a community engage in expressive, unorganized violence, such as the periodic religious riots in India or the destructive rampage by inner-city African Americans of Los Angeles in May 1992 in response to the acquittal of policemen on trial for beating an African American they had arrested. Even though such explosions of community anger tend to be short-lived and spasmodic, they sometimes galvanize protracted campaigns of violence between the police forces of a jurisdiction and paramilitary units representing the opposition or between rival organized gangs. The initially spontaneous violence then becomes *war,* and it partakes of all the characteristics of collective action identified by Tilly.

Throughout history organized violent encounters between communities—tribes, towns, feudal principalities, religious orders, cities, economic classes, states, empires—have arisen out of a range of material conditions and ideational motivations. Various schools of social science typically focus on certain of these conditions and motivations as the most important sources of intercommunity violence. This chapter will summarize those social science insights that are applicable to the general phenomenon of collective violence, of which war between countries, the subject of the subsequent chapters, is a special category.

CONFLICT OVER COVETED RESOURCES

Economists and other social scientists who seek the sources of human behavior in material conditions tend to attribute much of the world's collective violence to conflicts over highly valued resources, especially in zero-sum situations, where one group's getting what it wants diminishes another group's ability to satisfy its wants. The situations of this sort most conducive to violence involve severe scarcities of the resources that the basic subsistence of a community requires, but rivalries over luxuries and simple greed can also breed intense, violence-prone conflict.

The relationship between scarcity and intercommunity violence is supported by anthropological studies of relatively peaceful simple societies. Most of these peaceful societies have provided for their subsistence by hunting and gathering rather than by breeding animals and planting crops.[2] The peaceful hunter-gatherer communities typically have flourished and coexisted in regions where game and vegetation were abundant and access to a particular locale was therefore not a matter of survival. If one tribe encountered another already exploiting the resources of a given site, there could be a confrontation, but each tribe had the option of moving on to another site. Not all preagricultural communities have been peaceful, however. Desert areas with scarce water and vegetation have characteristically produced nomadic tribes having fierce fighting traditions. Yet Ashley Montagu appears to be essentially correct in his generalization that "at the level of the non–politically organized gatherer-hunter stage of human development the coefficient of aggressiveness is relatively low."[3]

On the other hand, where there are not enough of the valued goods in a fertile area to satisfy those to whom the area is physically accessible, a test of will and strength among rivals for its control can be expected, and the winners will attempt to secure exclusive ownership of the area. This dynamic is closely related to the development of agricultural and industrial societies, in which property rights are established and enforced among members of the victor community and the frontiers are defended against covetous outsiders.[4]

Some communities, through the development of technologies allowing them to operate large-scale agricultural and industrial economies and to overpower weaker neighbors militarily, will be inclined to expand their frontiers forcibly over vast regions, sometimes striving to encompass entire continents. The huge ancient riverine empires of Eurasia—notably Mesopotamia, Egypt, Persia, India, and China (all of them established by the sword)—originated primarily out of the desire to gain control over fertile irrigation basins. The period of modern overseas colonization, involving wars to subdue indigenous empires (such as the Spanish exploits in Mexico and Peru), was characterized by the quest for precious metals, furs, and spices. From the fifteenth century on, many of the great wars of the world were between rival European colonial powers attempting to gain exclusive control over the resources of major parts of Africa, South and Southeast Asia, the Middle East, and the Americas.[5] Some economic historians (especially those with a Marxist orientation) give weight to the drive by industrialized communities to obtain additional markets for their goods—presumably an urgent need of countries experiencing the contradictions of advanced monopoly capitalism—as a cause of the nineteenth and twentieth-century wars among the imperialist powers.[6]

Economists of different schools of thought offer widely varying interpretations of the conditions under which the competition for resources (and markets) promotes intense social conflict—or, conversely, cooperation—in modern society.

The classical and neoclassical free market theorists from Adam Smith (in the eighteenth century) to Milton Friedman (in the twentieth) trace much of the world's large-scale collective violence to political distortions of natural market mechanisms of supply and demand. Left to its natural dynamics, the free market is supposed to induce specialization of labor and production of particular goods and services by those who can produce them most efficiently, and therefore also create a high degree of commercial interdependence, which in turn leads to intra- and intercommunity cooperation and cultivation of the arts of conflict resolution. The principal culprits, from the point of view of the free market devotees, are the promoters of national or parochial self-sufficiency, the quest for which generates beggar-thy-neighbor protectionism, imperialistic expansionism, and war. Within countries the most intense political conflicts, sometimes leading to revolutionary violence or civil war, are seen by the champions of market capitalism to inhere in statist societies where those in control of the government determine the economic winners and losers; in such societies, who controls the government can easily become a fighting issue.

Marxism and some varieties of democratic socialism, on the other hand, attribute much of the world's civil and transnational violence to uneven and allegedly inequitable allocation of goods effectuated by the capitalist market. Those already in control of society's most productive resources, it is claimed, will attempt to preserve and expand their control by underpricing or buying out their competition; the free market, therefore, leads inexorably to monopoly capitalism, in which those who have cornered the market in certain product lines also become the major source of jobs for large segments of the population. The monopolists, in order to maximize their profit margins, attempt to reduce factor costs by keeping wages low, scrimping on health and safety standards, and substituting automation for human labor, setting the scene for intense, sometimes violent, labor-management conflicts.

The Marxists (still influential in many parts of the world despite their falling out of favor in the former Soviet sphere) have the starkest view of this capitalist dynamic, which they view as merely one phase of the elemental and historically determined course of social progress. Human inventiveness inevitably alters the forces of production within a society, and these forces, according to Marx and his followers, outgrow and come into conflict with the established relations of production, or the ownership of property, capital, and other property relationships. The maturing of these contradictions ushers in an epoch of social revolution in which the "immense superstructure" of society (the relations of production and the institutions and laws that reflect and reinforce them) is overturned and a new system of ownership and control consistent with the new productive forces is instituted. Such social revolutions, in the Marxist analysis, almost always involve violent conflict between the social classes that have benefited from the old order and the emerging classes, whose time has come to run the society.[7]

Many non-Marxist political sociologists, although rejecting the absolutist economic determinism and class-conflict theories of Marx, locate the sources of collective violence mainly in social and economic conditions that produce angry resentment on the part of the economically disadvantaged sectors of the population. This is a sociological version of the frustration-aggression hypothesis prominent in psychological literature, with the frustrated group the analog of the frustrated individual. The relationship between economic deprivation and the kind of anger that is mobilizable into collective violence has been evident in most anti-government revolutions in the Third World since the 1960s. A major comparative study of these uprisings identifies "population and urbanization exceeding economic opportunities" as a principal source of mass mobilization in virtually every case.[8] The social scientists reporting on these studies are careful to refute the popular notion of a direct causal relationship between poverty and collective violence, however.

Starving populations lack the energy and resources to organize themselves for violent uprisings. Usually a period of improving conditions, involving the development of literacy, intergroup communication and, in general, rising (but unsatisfied) expectations are preconditions for the mobilization of activist discontent.

The function of rising expectations is captured by the *relative deprivation* theory of rebellion. According to this theory, groups are susceptible of being mobilized for militant revolutionary action when they perceive that the established regime is unjustly depriving them of amenities enjoyed by other groups.[9] Significantly, the objective condition of having less than other groups is not the crucial determinant of intense resentment. Rather, the group must *believe* itself to be unjustly deprived (or to be threatened with such deprivation), whether or not this belief conforms to the reality of presumably objective observers. This formulation is consistent with the phenomenon of collective violence by groups that are still relatively well off in tangible assets or social status against upwardly mobile groups. The violence against immigrant communities in Western Europe in the early 1990s is a case in point. Note also that perception of *injustice* in the social distribution of amenities is an important element in the generation of the violence-prone anger. Thus, groups wedded to the ideology of a market economy may take their lumps without intense reaction when their lesser share of society's amenities results from the interplay of market forces, but groups adhering to egalitarian doctrines of social justice may become violently antagonistic to the system and those running it when the prevailing distribution of amenities appears to be grossly to their disadvantage.

ETHNIC HOSTILITY: DEFENDING AND SPREADING WAYS OF LIFE

Anthropological and archaeological studies of the earliest human communities reveal that the transition from hunting and gathering to agriculture is characteristically accompanied by the elaboration of idea-cultures—ways of life that communities feel the need to fight to defend no less than their material possessions. Stable husbanding of the land requires community-wide language and norms for resolving interpersonal conflict, facilitating barter and trade, determining shares of work and output, and maintaining organizational hierarchies. Although such social functions are the requisites of community life everywhere, the ways of performing them evolve differently from place to place. Each society develops its practices and sets of myths, symbols, and rational justifications, which usually are held to be superior to those of other societies.

The defense of the community against outsiders, perhaps originally motivated simply to protect assets and exploit scarce resources productively, becomes inseparable from the defense of the community's way of life. And just as material reasons for self-sufficiency can turn communities toward economic imperialism, so the ideational justifications for autonomy can turn them into presumptuous civilizers of other peoples.

Whatever the original reasons for one community's political annexation or absorption of another, the dominant community almost inevitably attempts to subordinate the culture of the annexed community to make it conform to the norms of the dominant community. The subordinated culture—even where there are no legal or political impediments to equalization of the material status of the absorbed population—then becomes a breeding ground for the cultivation of ethnic secessionist or irredentist movements. A precondition for the transmutation of the grievances of ethnic groups into secessionist movements is the geographic concentration of their populations in particular regions within countries dominated by other ethnic groups. Ethnic enclaves of this sort are often the product of the forced territorial incorporation of an area in war or the redrawing of state boundaries in a diplomatic settlement to terminate or avoid war; such legacies become part of the cultural identity of the ethnic community and are particularly conducive to the community's militant mobilization in times of crisis.

Chauvinistic ethnic enclaves can also develop in immigrant communities. Sometimes this segregation is largely self-willed, for the purpose of preserving a way of life that the community values; more often than not it is also forced upon the immigrant community by the hostility and chauvinism of other groups in the area. Sometimes ethnic alienation and hostility combined with poverty and economic class divisions can contribute to their involuntary or coerced segregation long after their initial arrival within a jurisdiction—the ghettos of African Americans and other minority groups in the United States being a prime example.

Since the last quarter of the eighteenth century, the rallying cries of the French and American revolutions have provided inspiration to many such aggrieved ethnic communities, who have sought to give additional legitimacy to their demands for political autonomy by marching under the banner of national self-determination. The idea common to these otherwise two very different revolutions was that governments are legitimate only to the extent that they have the consent of the governed. Most of the anticolonial revolutions of the 1950s and 1960s, which in barely two decades tripled the number of recognized nation-states from 50 to over 150, were activated by a hybrid of concepts from the American Declaration of Independence and the French Declaration of the Rights of Man, sometimes fused with the doctrines of Marx, Lenin, and Mao Zedong.

The appeal of national self-determination has also been exploited by established nation-states to sow disorder and disintegration in the domains of their rivals, and the doctrine has been invoked by imperialistic aggressors and their opponents alike as justification for intervening in other countries. France under Napoleon Bonaparte went on a rampage of imperial expansion ostensibly to help subordinated nationality groups throughout Europe obtain their independence. World War I was precipitated by imperialistic exploitations of ethnic rivalries in the Balkans. Ironically, Hitler used the national self-determination concepts embedded in the Covenant of the League of Nations to justify his *Anschluss* of Austria and invasion of Czechoslovakia. The Cold War superpowers engaged in competitive interventions throughout the Third World under the mantles of their respective versions of self-determination (the Soviet Union to assist "wars of national liberation" and the United States to support "freedom fighters").

In the post–Cold War period, the retraction of active sponsorship by the superpowers of the political claims of client ethnic groups has paradoxically created a more permissive environment for the escalation of ethnic conflicts. The virtual epidemic of ethnic violence in Africa in the early 1990s was thus one of the unintended consequences of reduced competition between the superpowers for influence in the Third World. Another consequence of the end of the Cold War has been the flareup of ethnic conflict in the former Soviet Union and the countries of eastern and central Europe previously in the Soviet sphere of control. The reformist ideologies of *glasnost* and political pluralism stimulated separatist agitations for full national independence in both the national republics of the USSR and ethnically homogeneous enclaves within Russia and other states in the Commonwealth of Independent States. But the leaders of post-Soviet Russia, having accepted the sovereign independence of the fifteen former republics of the Soviet Union, have not been willing to extend the right of secession to the provinces of the

Russian federation itself, many of which contain substantial minorities of ethnic Russians. The situation in many regions of the Russian federation is accordingly highly volatile and violence prone.

The transmutation of ethnic or way-of-life consciousness into large-scale collective violence is rarely a dynamic that simply arises spontaneously out of intergroup antagonisms between communities that are in contact in daily life. To be sure, way-of-life antagonisms are potentially combustible raw materials, but their activation into sustained communal warfare is most often the work of political demagogues in the business of mobilizing fanatic support for themselves.

The sudden transformation of ethnic communalism into large-scale and sustained collective violence in the Balkans in the early 1990s was very much the work of sophisticated political leaders deliberately cultivating historically rooted resentments on the part of the non-Serbian populations in Croatia, Slovenia, and Bosnia-Herzegovina against the Serb-dominated federal state of Yugoslavia. Exploiting interprovincial economic rivalries and the political fractiousness occurring in the Yugoslavian Communist party during the decade following the death of strongman Josip Broz Tito, provincial party bosses one after another cynically demanded greater power for their regimes. Opposition leaders injected the explosive demand for "national self-determination" into the cauldrons of ethnic conflict stirred up by the Communists to enhance their bargaining power in the federal government and party organizations. These demands were converted by newly elected opposition governments into declarations of secession and full independence in the spring of 1991, having been given additional legitimacy by Western applause for the self-determination movements then spreading across most of Sovietized Eurasia.[10]

But where national self-determination is presumed to legitimize the right to statehood (and recourse to whatever means it takes to achieve it), particularly in regions with overlapping concentrations of different ethnic groups, chain reactions of violence can destroy large populations. In such regions the questions of who is the nation and who is the self that is supposed to determine the makeup of the state are what is up for grabs.

The Balkan region in the early 1990s once again provides a bloody case in point. The absolute determination on the part of Croatia, Slovenia, and Bosnia-Herzegovina, member provinces of the Yugoslav federation, to be fully independent sovereign states (as expressed in formal declarations of independence by each of them in the summer and fall of

1991) produced an equally absolute determination on the part of the defenders of the federation, led not only by the government of Serbia but by the Serbs within the secessionist provinces, to resist Yugoslavia's disintegration. The result was a multitiered civil war pitting the forces of the federal government, in alliance with militias of local Serb populations, against each of the seceding provinces. First came war in Slovenia between the federal government and the Slovenian militia. Then came war in Croatia between a newly created Croatian army and irregular national troops on the one side and irregular Serbian forces on the other. In Bosnia, Serbian irregular forces (militarily supported by Belgrade) asserted their own "self-determined" right to union with Serbia, and fighting took place between them and the armed forces of both the Croat and Muslim ethnic communities as well as between Croat and Muslim forces.

Other such self-determination conflicts, some already violent, some with a high potential for violence, are very much a part of the contemporary world scene.[11] A sampling of the most combustible conflicts includes the following:

- The conflict between the Palestinians and the government of Israel (not fully resolved by the accords of 1993) over the degree of political autonomy to be exercised by the Palestinian population of the Israeli-occupied West Bank and Gaza Strip
- The dispute between the two former Soviet republics Armenia and Azerbaijan over the demand of the largely Christian province Nagorno-Karabakh to join Armenia or, at a minimum, to be granted independence from predominantly Muslim Azerbaijan
- The assertion of independence from Moldova by the peoples of the Deniester region, mainly Russians and Ukrainians, who fear that the ethnic Romanian majority of Moldova will seek to merge the former Soviet state with Romania
- The demand of the Kurdish peoples for an independent Kurdistan, which pits them against the governments in whose jurisdictions they are located (especially Iraq, Iran, and Turkey) and is exploited by these neighbor countries in order to weaken each other
- Autonomy movements against the federal government of India on the part of peoples in ethnically homogeneous areas, such as the Muslims of Kashmir, the Sikhs of the Punjab, and the United Liberation Front of Assam

- The separatist movement of the Hindu Tamils in Buddhist Sinhalese–dominated Sri Lanka
- Christian East Timor's secessionist rebellion against the Indonesian government, largely controlled by Javanese Muslims
- The uprising of the Tibetans against the Chinese government
- The Basque and Catalonian demands for autonomy from Spain
- The violence between Catholics and Protestants of Northern Ireland (Ulster), stoked by the clandestine Irish Republican Army's terrorist campaign on behalf of Ulster's separation from Britain and union with the mostly Catholic Republic of Ireland

All of these are appropriately regarded as conflicts between ways of life, not because the struggle for material amenities is absent but because regardless of the material grievances that may have contributed to the outbreak of the militancy or may be sustaining it, the principal self-definition by the community is ethnocultural or religious and what mobilizes the community for extreme campaigns of violence is the conviction that their entire way of life is at stake.[12]

POWER RIVALRIES

Periods of intense disputes between communities focus the attention of those involved on the prevailing distribution of *coercive power*. Realists will come to the fore, claiming that the ability of the community to obtain or protect what it values will be determined by its ability to force opponents to adhere to its will or to fight off opponents' efforts to make it adhere to their will. Presumably, the side having more coercive power can usually get its way, regardless of the substance of the issue in dispute. Coercive power is thus more than simply a means to achieve victory or avoid defeat in a particular conflict; because it is seen as a crucial instrument for performing well in a wide range of disputes with other enemies as well, its acquisition and enhancement become ends in themselves.

This recognition that the community has to rely on coercive power to preserve or further its values may prompt it to go to war not only to affect the intercommunity balance of tangible coercive resources but also to affect perceptions of its psychological capacities for engaging in violent conflict. Such raw power motivations are central to a broad spectrum of conflicts, from full-scale revolutions seeking to take over and transform a country's governing system to turf wars among rival urban gangs.

Violence by and against Established Political Regimes

Given that national governments characteristically claim the right to possess military and police forces more powerful than those of their constituents—as put by the German sociologist Max Weber, "A state is a human community that (successfully) claims the monopoly of the legitimate use of physical force within a given territory"[13]—*who runs the state* may itself become a fighting issue. But not only the state's superiority in coercive power makes the control of the state a matter of such high stakes. The relative well-being of a society's contending groups can be crucially affected by the state's constitutional provisions that determine who can attain high political office and how laws are to be made and implemented; these determinants of political regime will in turn vitally affect the substance of the rights and amenities enjoyed by or denied various economic classes and ethnic groups.[14]

It is not unusual for a regime to become established through a violent revolution against an old order seen to favor a particular class or ethnic group. The new regime may feel compelled to institute a "reign of terror," as did the successful French revolutionaries in 1789, to consolidate its power against those in society who were loyal to the previous rulers. Moreover, the new regime, in its procedures for selecting its officials and for making and implementing laws, will also inevitably create opponents who regard the new constitution and laws as instruments of the ruling class.

Not only in weak states bordering on anarchy but also in presumably stable and well-established nation-states political violence by and against national and local governments is a recurring phenomenon. Many regimes rely heavily on force to maintain themselves in power and to ensure that general community rules are obeyed within their jurisdictions: in performing self-protective and law-enforcement functions, governments are normally expected to apprehend, disarm, or even destroy the perpetrators of illegal violence. In democracies as well as autocracies, as pointed out by Charles Tilly in a study for the Presidential Commission on the Causes and Prevention of Violence, "the extent, location, and timing of collective violence depend heavily on the way the authorities and their agents handle the challenges offered them."[15]

No governing regime will admit that it maintains itself in power primarily by controlling the instruments of coercion. Even autocracies and totalitarian dictatorships claim that their power is based on popularity with the general citizenry and that they use force only against criminal elements and subversive minorities, especially those aided by the state's foreign enemies that want to overthrow the legitimate order.

To be sure, governments have their justifications, credible at least to themselves and their loyal supporters, for resorting to force inside their own countries. Leading the list is the need to suppress illegal violence. Next is the need to counteract even nonviolent acts of subversion that could prevent the government from performing its essential functions or that could weaken the country's ability to resist its foreign enemies. Finally, as in the Chinese government's violent repression of the student democracy demonstration in Tiananmen Square in June 1989, there is the residual justification of the need to uphold the law when crowds do not obey official orders to disperse, when lawbreakers resist arrest, and so on. Usually the governments claim to have exhausted their nonviolent options.

A good deal of antigovernment domestic violence in contemporary society, however, cannot be attributed only to lawless and unruly elements. Sometimes it is a function of government nonreaction or negative reaction to legal and nonviolent pressures. When groups that consider themselves unjustly deprived find their peacefully asserted demands for rectification repeatedly ignored or rebuffed, and especially when their defeats are processed through a political system they believe is stacked against them, their willingness to resort to violent pressure grows. The more undemocratic a political system is, the more it is prone to engender such violent inclinations in aggrieved groups, who in turn are likely to stimulate repressive policies by the fearful government. Democratic systems also may develop this precipitating condition, since the full, legitimate working of the democratic process, based on a one person–one vote electoral system, can severely offend minorities. Even groups constituting numerical majorities in democratic systems sometimes conclude that the normal political system works against them when more affluent minorities appear able to control government policy through expensive media advertising and other means of "buying" votes in decision-making bodies and electoral contests.

Gang Warfare and Intergroup Violence amid Domestic Anarchy

The distinguishing characteristic of this kind of intergroup violence is that the warring groups operate in a largely anarchic arena: no overarching norms for determining who is right and wrong and no legitimate and effective superordinate institutions or processes for resolving the territorial claims, allocating the material goods, or redefining the societal roles over which the conflict has developed. The rival groups are essentially on their own in a world resembling the state of nature (postulated by Thomas Hobbes) where might makes right.

In such locales, gangs, groups of vigilantes, and other unofficial paramilitary units become substitutes for government offering protection in exchange for money and loyalty. Units of territorial jurisdiction ("turf") are established and maintained through violent encounters among rival gangs.

CONSUMMATORY AND CATHARTIC VIOLENCE

Communities, like individuals, can come to rely on paroxysms of violence for satisfying or giving release to emotional needs. Sometimes there is the motive of revenge for past harms and humiliations suffered by the community, and the targets of the violence are those considered to be directly or indirectly responsible. But sometimes the violence is almost only cathartic, and those who are its victims just happen to be convenient targets.

Participating in such acts of collective violence can engender a sense of power among members of a community otherwise depressed by feelings of impotence. The particular campaigns of violence need not have any rational objective and need not produce an obvious win over opponents in order to provide the existential experience sought by the community. The French sociologist, Emile Durkheim, writing at the end of the nineteenth century, traced the availability of ordinary citizens for participation in irrational campaigns of violence to the disintegration of the moral foundations of community brought on by industrialization and its extreme specialization of labor; Durkheim found the resulting alienation of persons from one another and from the community as a whole to be a major source of both suicide and susceptibility to mobilization by violently militant groups.[16] The revolutionary leader and professional psychoanalyst Frantz Fanon similarly located the roots of twentieth century anticolonial violence in the profound disintegration of the foundations of native society resulting from the policies of the colonial powers. He regarded the violence of the national liberation movements as being in many respects emotionally consummatory rather than rationally instrumental but as positive nonetheless: "a cleansing force" that "frees the native from his inferiority complex and from his despair and inaction; it makes him fearless and restores his self-respect."[17]

TERRORISM

All of the categories of collective violence so far considered can involve terrorism, in the sense that acts of violence or threats of violence are directed against individuals who are not themselves in direct opposition to those acting violently. Official police and armed forces engage in terrorism when they attack noncombatants. Insurgent or revolutionary groups become terrorists when they attack or threaten to attack unarmed government officials or supporters of the government. And communal antagonists are terrorists when they violently disrupt the civic life in their rivals' places of commerce, culture, or religion. A form of terrorism that has received considerable media attention in recent years involves the taking of civilian hostages who have nothing to do directly with the terrorists' grievances and threatening to do them harm unless the enemies of the hostage takers accede to their demands.

Some degree of terrorism in one form or another has always been an element of acts of political violence. Today, however, terrorism may be increasing because of the widespread vulnerability to terrorist attack of those able to influence government policies. Representatives and ordinary constituents of governments travel a lot, using highly exposed transportation systems, and so invite hijackings, airport bombings, and the like. When those threatened are constituents of advanced democratic systems, fears of citizens and governments that they may not be able to conduct their normal everyday activities can be exploited by the terrorists to force democratically elected officials at least to pay attention to their demands.[18]

TOWARD A MULTI-CAUSAL ANALYSIS
OF COMMUNITY VIOLENCE

The search by social scientists and theorists for that crucial independent variable or set of factors that determine whether communities in conflict resort to violence has not succeeded. Overarching grand explanations, such as the absence or presence of a superordinate system of governance or a social consensus against the use of force, border on being tautologies—not explanations but merely restatements, using other words, of the condition we are trying to understand.

An alternative approach, which I find appropriate for diagnosing the causes of human violence at all levels—interpersonal, intergroup, and interstate—starts with the expectation that most cases of violent behavior are resultants of the complex interaction of numerous psychological pressures and social forces, which vary from case to case. The various theories sampled in this and the previous chapter are useful for directing our attention to possible specific sources and precipitants of violence, which may indeed be the most crucial factors in a particular case. And in any analysis, at least initially, the widest range of plausible diagnostic suppositions ought to be applied to the case at hand for the purpose of discovering which factors are in fact at work and how they interact with one another.

Generating virtually every case of large-scale violence (especially those large enough to be considered wars) is a mix of influences: physiological and psychological, inherited and contemporaneously conditioned, rational and irrational, material and ideational, political/institutional and cultural. A thoroughgoing analysis of any major episode of collective violence will reveal all of these to be at work. This does not mean that in particular conflicts some subset of these factors will not be of dominant influence, and certainly it is the function of good analysis to be able to weight the most important factors. However, their relative influence cannot be derived from any general theory but must be ascertained for each situation by detailed empirical investigation. Such fidelity to the facts of each case—which will often manifest a degree of complexity not conducive to elegant theorizing—is especially important when the purpose of the diagnosis is the prevention and control of violence. Just as the physician or psychiatrist, no matter how skilled, should examine each patient individually before prescribing a cure, so the formulators and executors of plans for preventing the violent escalation of conflict are best advised to proceed under the assumption that the devil (or angel) resides in the details.

The eclectic diagnostician, however, is primed to be on the lookout for characteristic conditions in the patient usually associated with pathological symptoms. Similarly, social scientists are appropriately on the lookout for those societal conditions that comparative analysis shows often predispose communities to act violently. These *characteristic predispositions* can be grouped into four interrelated categories:

Predisposition Category A: Intense grievances. The pervasiveness in a community of intense feelings of being unjustly treated by those in a position to affect their well-being is usually a precondition for the mobilization of the community for collective acts of violence. (The role played by such grievances, or justifications, in the decisions of nations to go to war is analyzed in Chapter 3.)

Predisposition Category B: Structural determinants. The intensity and durability of violence-inducing grievances are usually functions of structural relationships in the society that pit class against class, ethnic group against ethnic group, community against community, or nation-state against nation-state. These structural determinants may include the basic constitutional and governance system, the economic system, and the demographic distribution. (The influence of such structural factors on the disposition of countries to resort to military force is analyzed in Chapter 4.)

Predisposition Category C: The distribution of coercive power. Underlying grievances and structural conditions that can predispose a community to deal with its predicaments violently will not usually translate into systematic and sustained campaigns of violence unless the community is able to calculate, on the basis of an assessment of the fighting capabilities and will to fight of the potential belligerents, that a violent engagement with its adversaries would leave the community in a better situation than would be achieved if it refrained from fighting. (The characteristic role of balances of military power in affecting the inclination of countries to go to war is discussed in Chapter 5.)

Predisposition Category D: Attitudes toward the use of force. Finally, even given the presence of the other predispositions to use force, the likelihood of its actual employment will depend on the community's dominant normative culture concerning the circumstances under which violence is justified. A community in which there is a tradition of resolving disputes with outsiders by nonviolent means and for whom force is legitimate only as a last resort to ensure the community's very survival will react very differently to the same objective circumstances than a community with a pugnacious tradition. (The way such different cultures of violence affect patterns of war and peace in the interstate system is the subject of Chapter 6.)

Even where all these predispositions for collective violence are present, however, the resort to force and the escalation of violence are not inevitable. The material may be combustible, but someone still has to light the fire and fan the flames. There are almost always some strategies available to those determined to avoid or control the destruction and bloodshed. (The crucial role of leaders and decision makers in propelling their countries into avoidable wars and escalation is analyzed in Chapter 7.)

Efforts to prevent and control war through countering the violence-inducing predispositions of national communities and decision makers are analyzed and evaluated in Part II (Chapters 8 through 11).

NOTES

1. Charles Tilly, quoted in James B. Rule, *Theories of Civil Violence* (Berkeley: University of California Press, 1988), pp. 174–175.

2. David Fabbro, "Peaceful Societies," in Richard A. Falk and Samuel S. Kim, eds., *The War System: An Interdisciplinary Approach* (Boulder: Westview Press, 1980), pp. 180–203. See also Elizabeth M. Thomas, *The Harmless Peoples* (New York: Knopf, 1959).

3. Ashley Montagu, *The Nature of Human Aggression* (New York: Oxford University Press, 1976), p. 268.

4. Douglas C. North, *Structure and Change in Economic History* (New York: W.W. Norton, 1981), pp. 72–112.

5. Paul Kennedy, *The Rise and Fall of the Great Powers: Economic Change and Military Conflict from 1500 to 2000* (New York: Random House, 1987).

6. A prototypical Marxist argument on the causes of imperialist wars is V. I. Lenin, *Imperialism: The Highest Stage of Capitalism* (New York: International Publishers, 1939). Originally published in 1917.

7. Karl Marx, *Selected Writings,* edited by David McLelland (Oxford: Oxford University Press, 1977).

8. Jack A. Goldstone, Ted Robert Gurr, and Farrokh Moshiri, eds., *Revolutions of the Late Twentieth Century* (Boulder: Westview Press, 1991).

9. The most prominent scholarly proponent of relative deprivation as an explanation for collective violence is Ted Robert Gurr; see his *Why Men Rebel* (Princeton: Princeton University Press, 1970). Precursors to Gurr's work are Ivo Feierabend and Rosalind Feierabend, "Aggressive Behavior Within Polities, 1948–1962: A Cross-National Study," *Journal of Conflict Resolution*, 10 (1966), 249–271; and James Chowning Davies, "Toward a Theory of Revolution," *American Sociological Review*, 27 (1962), pp. 5–19.

10. Steven L. Burg, "Nationalism and Democratization in Yugoslavia," *The Washington Quarterly*, Fall 1991, pp. 5–19.

11. Useful brief synopses of most of these contemporary self-determination conflicts are provided by Morton H. Halperin, David J. Scheffler, and Patricia L. Small, *Self-Determination in the New World Order* (Washington: Carnegie Endowment for International Peace, 1992), pp.123–160.

12. Ted Robert Gurr in his "Minorities at Risk" project found that in 1990 more than 17 percent of the world's population belonged to at least 233 "politically assertive communal groups." Nearly half of these groups have engaged in organized violence of one form or another since the end of World War II, and since 1950 the incidences of violent protest or rebellion have quadrupled. Ted Robert Gurr, *Minorities at Risk: A Global View of Ethnopolitical Conflict* (Washington, D.C.: United States Institute of Peace Press, 1993). In this work, Gurr moves away from the emphasis on "relative deprivation" that characterized his earlier work (see note 9, above) and toward a multifactored analysis of the causes of ethnic violence similar to my analysis.

13. Max Weber, *From Max Weber: Essays in Sociology*, trans. and ed. Hans Gerth and C. Wright Mills (New York: Oxford University Press, 1946), p.78.

14. Milton J. Esman, "Political and Psychological Factors in Ethnic Conflict" in Joseph V. Montville, ed., *Conflict and Peacemaking in Multiethnic Societies* (New York: Lexington Books, 1991), pp. 53–64.

15. Charles Tilly, "Collective Violence in European Perspective," in High Davis Graham and Ted Robert Gurr, eds., *Violence in America: Historical and Comparative Perspectives* (New York: Signet, 1969), pp. 39–40.

16. Emile Durkheim, *The Division of Labor in Society* (Glencoe, Ill.: Free Press, 1964).

17. Frantz Fanon, *The Wretched of the Earth*, trans. Constance Farrington (New York: Grove Press, 1963), p. 73.

18. See Paul Wilkinson, *Terrorism and the Liberal State* (New York: New York University Press, 1986); and Michael Stohl, ed., *The Politics of Terrorism* (New York: Marcel Dekker, 1983).

CHAPTER 3

Why Nations Fight:
Their Standard Justifications

The leaders of the world's mammoth and highly institutionalized human collectivities we call nation-states, or countries, particularly need to engender support from large groups of people and diverse organizations when taking their nations into war. When fought by modern nation-states, war risks involvement of the whole population, not only as provisioners of the massive war machines but also as targets of attack. Consequently, the interests that propel most economically developed countries into war almost invariably are presented by the advocates of war as vital interests of the whole nation and not merely the special interests of a segment of society. Conversely, opponents of going to war usually insist that the pro-war party has not demonstrated that vital national interests really are at stake. If a particular war risks confrontation with an enemy armed with nuclear weapons or other weapons of mass destruction, the burden on the pro-war groups is all the heavier to show both that the alternative to war is the sacrifice of vital national interests and that the war can be fought to a successful conclusion without subjecting the country to massive destruction or terrible economic dislocation.

The more elaborate and institutionally mediated the decision-making structures of the polity, the more important, and also the more difficult, it is to obtain the needed support. In other words, modern democracies usually find it harder to go to war than do traditional autocracies. Ironically, but understandably, democracies involved in wars also find it more difficult to terminate them.

WAR AS A CONSIDERED AND DELIBERATE POLICY CHOICE

Nations typically "go" to war, in the sense of *choosing* to fight. This may involve starting a war by physically attacking the adversary or responding to an attack by active defense or retaliation. Even though they are capable of crucial misperception and stress-induced emotional instability, those who choose war over other courses of action invariably believe they are deciding rationally and attempt to justify their choice to those whose support is needed to prosecute the war. The country's lawyers, defending the decision in the courts of domestic and world opinion, always plead justifiable homicide, as it were. However, virtually every decision to go to war is also believed to be unwarranted by some elements of the nation, even when the enemy has struck the first blow. Sometimes objections are proffered by a small and politically ineffectual minority; at other times the antiwar party is strong enough to reverse the momentum toward war or to compel the government to enter war-termination negotiations rapidly.

Thus few if any wars are inevitable. They are for the most part willed acts, products of conscious calculation (possibly distorted by unconscious emotions and other sources of cognitive failure) that convince the responsible decision makers and relevant support groups on each side that this is the time and place to commit their countries to lethal combat.

REASONS OF STATE: THE STANDARD JUSTIFICATIONS FOR GOING TO WAR

Officially, countries go to war for reasons of state: to secure or advance important national interests. Even though war is a "normal" feature of international relations, in the sense of being one of the options traditionally available to states engaged in conflict, in most societies in the contemporary world it is seen as an extreme action that should not be undertaken without substantial practical and moral justification.

What are the presumably vital interests that governments or pro-war groups are likely to invoke to justify going to war?

Some are physical, tangible interests, such as territory and economic assets that supposedly need to be defended or acquired for the nation to sustain itself in an acceptable material or economic condition.

Some are ideational interests, such as a religion, an ethno-linguistic culture, or a political system, without which life itself presumably would have drastically diminished value.

Other interests that may be deemed worth a war are derived, by strategic reasoning or psychologically, from the basic material and ideational interests of the nation-state. Foreign military interventions on behalf of allies and friends are often justified by such strategic or psychological extensions of basic national interests.

When modern countries enter into major wars, especially wars likely to require protracted fighting beyond their home territory as part of an international coalition, all or most of these kinds of national interests nearly always are asserted to be in jeopardy. Those pointing to the dire consequences of not fighting may or may not actually believe their own arguments. But even where the arguments reflect sincere beliefs, the prevailing negative assessments of the nonwar alternatives may be mistaken or the costs to the nation of fighting miscalculated out of simple ignorance. On the other hand, the prevailing assessments of consequences for the national interests that draw countries into particular wars may, in historical retrospect, turn out to be basically correct.

Material Interest Justifications

The territorial integrity of a country is, by definition and a priori, a vital national interest. No part of the country's territory can be violated (intruded upon without permission, invaded, physically struck) without the country's treating the action as an attack on the whole. It does not matter that the violated part is of little strategic or economic value or that no one lives there; the fact that it is organically a part of the nation normally is sufficient to evoke demands for a violent response.

Still, though violations of a country's territorial integrity are universally regarded as acts of war, aggressors can sometimes get away with such violations without having to engage their victims in combat. This can occur when the violated country knows it will be beaten badly if it puts up a fight. For example, Hitler invaded Czechoslovakia's Sudetenland in 1938 without firing a shot because despite the good training and fortifications of the Czech military, President Benes knew that his country could not stand up to Hitler's *Wehrmacht* unless Czechoslovakia's Western friends were willing to come to its assistance—which, as they had made clear in the appeasement of the dictator at Munich, they were not willing to do.[1]

It is also true that, although countries claim a vital interest in protecting their citizens and material interests from harm even when these are located outside the national territorial jurisdiction, attacks on extraterritorial deployments do not necessarily provoke a violent response. Whether or not an attack against one's nationals or extraterritorial assets is defined as an act of war in a case depends on many considerations, not the least of which are estimates of one's ability to retaliate or defend against subsequent attacks without great cost or risk—in contrast to the claim that no cost is too great to pay to defend the nation's territorial integrity. Another consideration is how central the extraterritorial assets are to other important interests. Are they a dispensable luxury? Are they of high political value as symbols of one's international power, like the Falkland Islands, which the British fought to retrieve from an Argentine invasion in 1982? Are they essential components of global military capability, like the U.S. Sixth Fleet that the Navy periodically deploys in the Persian Gulf to signal resolve? Or are they important but marginal assets, like the military communications facility at Kagnew, Ethiopia, that the United States did not value sufficiently to justify any kind of military action to prevent the change of regime that took Ethiopia into the Soviet camp in the 1970s?

Countries have traditionally regarded their ships at sea (navies or major commercial vessels owned by their nationals) as if they were organic extensions of the nation. But again, the translation of this sentiment into a definition of an attack on the ships as an act of war is likelier for the maritime powers than for countries with relatively small navies. When Kuwait wanted to convey to Iran in 1987 that Iran was asking for war in attempting to prevent Kuwait's merchant ships from sailing freely in the Persian Gulf to Iraq and other countries, Kuwait felt the need to have its ships fly the flag of one or another of the great naval powers—either the Soviet Union or the United States—to deter Iran from harassing Kuwaiti ships. (The United States, by putting its flag on a Kuwaiti ship, was saying: "This will now be treated as if it were a U.S. ship. Any attack against this ship is therefore an attack against the United States.")

The norms regarding aircraft are a bit fuzzier, in large part because of the ease with which aircraft can violate sovereign airspace and also because of the rights governments claim—and exercise rather often—of shooting at trespassing planes. The norms for satellites, though not yet fully elaborated in international treaties, can be deduced from the proposition, iterated in numerous United Nations resolutions, that all of outer space is an international realm, like the high seas: thus another country's direct attack on a nation's orbiting spacecraft would be regarded as an act of war.

Apart from territorial integrity, the national interest of highest priority for most countries is the maintenance of military capabilities, their own and those of reliable allies, sufficient to deter attacks on their territory and other interests and to defend these successfully when attackers are not deterred. Countries, therefore, resort to war and claim to be justified in doing so to avoid a disadvantageous balance of military capability when they perceive war to be the most feasible way of maintaining the balance they believe they need. The Japanese government's decision to bomb Pearl Harbor in December 1941 was evidently motivated in large part by the hope of avoiding a confrontation with the United States later when the U.S. Pacific Fleet would be much more powerful.[2] The question of whether the Soviet deployment of nuclear ballistic missiles to Cuba in 1962 would change the balance of military power once the missiles became operational was a central issue in the Kennedy administration's deliberations over using military force to get them out. Under the premise that they appeared to change the global balance of power, Kennedy administration officials decided that the Soviet missiles had to be removed—by force, if other means failed.[3] Similarly, Israel justified its 1981 air raid on Iraq's fledgling nuclear plant at Osirik by the need to prevent Iraq from gaining a nuclear weapons capability that would have drastically altered the regional military balance.

An additional national interest often thought worth a war to advance or sustain is the basic economic well-being of the country. During the centuries of great-power imperial expansion, this motive was as important as any other in initiating major wars, many of which started in remote overseas areas as empire builders got in each other's ways. The United States–Japan war of 1941–1945 had its sources in Japan's burst of imperialist effort in Asia to establish what the Japanese called their coprosperity sphere. The Japanese conclusion in the fall of 1941 that war was inevitable, leading to their decision to strike first, was prompted by the U.S. government's decision, in reaction to Japan's invasion of Indochina, to freeze Japanese economic assets held by American financial institutions while embargoing the shipment of oil to Japan.[4]

In the post–World War II period, with the breakup and delegitimization of colonial empires, economic aggrandizement has become a less obvious motive for war, but countries still claim the right to go to war defensively to prevent others from hobbling their economies. U.S. Secretary of State Henry Kissinger, for example, would not rule out war against the oil-producing countries of the Middle East if their restrictions of supplies or pricing policies threatened a "strangulation of the industrialized world."[5] And a major rationale for the Bush administration's war to reverse Iraq's takeover of Kuwait in 1990 was to prevent Saddam Hussein from controlling a large portion of the world's oil.

Ideational Justifications

In addition to fighting to obtain material sustenance for themselves and their loved ones and to satisfy desires that are rooted in biology (such as for sexual pleasure or power over rivals), humans can become violent toward one another over competing views of the universe, god and morality, and abstract claims of rights and duties. The century of religious wars preceding the Peace of Westphalia (1648), featuring intercommunal slaughter of genocidal dimensions between Muslims and Christians and between Protestants and Catholics, was one of the bloodiest eras in history. In subsequent centuries, secular religions, such as nationalism or Marxism, have also pitted peoples against peoples in highly destructive wars. Some of these have started as civil wars for control of the governing apparatus of a particular state, but frequently the partisans of the contending causes would form alliances across state lines, and the war would become international or transnational.

Protecting the national way of life.   Nearly as sacrosanct as a country's territorial integrity and often closely bound up with it is the national government's insistence (often backed up by its citizenry) on its sovereign authority over the country's system of public order and justice. Every nation-state (or would-be nation-state) claims the right to make its own rules for what behavior is to be encouraged or prohibited among its people; the corollary is that other countries must respect its jurisdiction over what happens within its borders.

Thus, an active policy by one country to subvert another's way of life through material and organizational aid to groups that reject the legitimacy of the existing domestic regime, especially groups attempting to disrupt the society's activities by general strikes or terrorism, can provoke open warfare against the sponsor of the subversion. Austria's stated reason for going to war against Serbia in the summer of 1914 and thus starting World War I was not only to retaliate for the assassination of the Archduke Francis Ferdinand by a Serbian terrorist but to prevent Serbia from further organizing nationalist-separatist revolutionary movements among the Serbs and other Slavic peoples within Austria-Hungary.[6]

The claim of national sovereignty is a two-sided sword in the international system. Though it cuts at foreign sponsors of subnational separatism and can be used to justify making war against them, the claim also cuts at a state that forcibly denies self-determination to the nationalities within its jurisdiction, and it can be used to justify making war against such a repressive state. If all nations are to be sovereign, no government has the right to lord it over my nation: my nation will wage war, if need be, to establish its autonomy. Further, if my war for national independence is a just war, surely other countries have a right to intervene on my behalf to help ensure my success.[7] Such logic, invoked many times to justify foreign intervention in civil conflicts, was Napoleon Bonaparte's justification for his imperialistic wars to help "nations" in other countries obtain their "liberty" in the late eighteenth and early nineteenth centuries. In recent times, preventing Pakistan from putting down the Bangladesh independence movement was India's justification for going to war against Pakistan in 1971. Arab nations attempted to justify their protracted warfare against Israel by claiming the goal of statehood for the Palestinians.

"Making the world safe for. . . ." The willingness to fight to the death to protect a way of life often emanates from a conviction that one's own way is the best for all human beings—that it is more in accord with human nature, or the will of God, or some self-evident universal standards of justice. And when other people with the same conviction ask for help in securing such a way of life in their areas, there is a great temptation to come to their aid and even to do violent battle on their behalf.

Transnational religious conflicts are one variant of this phenomenon. Governments are not nearly so inclined to intervene in foreign religious wars as they were during the sixteenth century and the first half of the seventeenth century, but religious differences sometimes still feed intense hostility among the peoples of countries in dispute over other issues and often become part of the mix of motives that bring these countries to blows. Examples are conflicts between the mostly Muslim

Turks and the mostly Orthodox Greeks in Cyprus; between the mostly Hindu Indians and the Muslim Pakistanis over Kashmir; between the Jewish Israelis and the Muslim Arabs over the size and shape of the state of Israel; between the fundamentalist Shiite Muslims in Iran and Iraq and the more secular Sunni Muslims in control of the Iraqi government; and in the Balkans between the Roman Catholic Croatians, the Greek Orthodox Serbians, and the Muslim Bosnians.

Universal secular ideologies have been more typical justifications of the modern industrialized great powers for going to war beyond their borders. Napoleon Bonaparte led France in a military rampage across Europe ostensibly to extend the "rights of man" to all people. President Woodrow Wilson, provoked by Germany's submarine attacks on U.S. shipping in 1917, asked Congress to declare war on Germany in order to "make the world safe for democracy."

In the period of the Cold War the rival secular ideologies threatened to plunge most of the world into a Third World War, just as the religious conflicts of the late feudal period engulfed the major countries in bloody interstate conflicts. From the late 1940s through the late 1960s, the antagonism between those who professed adherence to some variant of Marxist state-run socialism often brought them into intense confrontation—domestically and internationally—with those who professed adherence to a free capitalist political economy. For the countries in which these ideologically defined conflicts broke out, the rival partisans mobilized themselves to fight against enslavement by their totally venal enemies. For the external protagonists and interveners on both sides, the objective of not allowing the other side to expand its sphere of influence was worth a war. The Korean War (1950 to 1953) and the Vietnam War (1945 to 1973) were justified in both camps by the need to keep the other from forcing its way of life on the world. Each side was led by a military superpower (the United States and the Soviet Union) to whom fell the role of organizing a worldwide coalition of states and political movements to countervail against the presumed power of the rival coalition. Being a contest between good and evil, it was regarded as credible that any member of the coalition, although its own territory or vital material interests was not initially subject to attack, would nonetheless come to the defense of its coalition partners. Even pledges by the superpowers to enter into strategic nuclear war against one another on behalf of lesser members of their coalitions were accorded widespread credibility, although not without considerable dissent from some strategists and opinion leaders, who argued that the threat of employing strategic nuclear forces was justified only as a means of deterring a direct military attack against one's own country.

To recognize the central role of ideology in the Cold War does not mean that all confrontations between the coalitions during that era were motivated entirely, or even predominantly, by ideological as opposed to material or geostrategic considerations. It means that whatever the hard interest calculations involved in a particular crisis or war, the justifications offered by the responsible decision makers to gain public support for military hostilities tended to emphasize the ideational or "way of life" interests presumably at stake. Moreover, once invoked as an appropriate *causus belli,* the ideological stakes would become an essential part of the motivation henceforth for waging the good fight and not backing down.

The formulation of and debate over the Truman Doctrine reveals the central (and problematical) role of ideology in globalizing the brink-of-war mode of diplomacy that characterized the Cold War. In order to gain congressional and popular support for an emergency economic and military aid package for Greece and Turkey in 1947 (both countries were thought to be targets in the Soviet Union's grand strategy of gaining direct access to the Mediterranean), President Truman defined the Soviet-American rivalry as a global struggle between freedom and communist totalitarianism. This definition of the situation made it highly likely thereafter that the United States would go to war anywhere in the world where it seemed that American military force was a feasible means of preventing communists from dominating a country. George Kennan, then head of the Policy Planning Staff of the State Department, argued in vain to get Truman to tone down his rhetoric, fearing that it would give nations around the world a blank check on American assistance, one they could cash by simply defining their internal opponents as communists. Kennan also worried that the doctrine's failure to make distinctions between geopolitically significant threats and lesser provocations would give rise to indiscriminate public pressures for military intervention where vital interests of the United States were not in jeopardy.[8]

Kennan's apprehensions about allowing ideology to influence the definition of U.S. interests strongly were borne out, as successive administrations—in order to contain communism—involved U.S. forces in combat, or came very close to doing so, even when vital national security or economic interests were not clearly threatened.

Ideologically driven military moves show up in the Eisenhower administration's brink-of-war policies against China in the Formosa Straits in 1954 and 1958, in its covert military operation against the Arbenz regime in Guatemala in 1954, in its close decision of 1954 not to become militarily involved in Indochina on the side of the French, and in its deployment of marines to Lebanon in 1958.[9]

Examples of ideological determinism at work during the Kennedy-Johnson years include the abortive Bay of Pigs invasion of Cuba by CIA-organized Cuban exiles in 1961, President Johnson's dispatch of Marines to the Dominican Republic in 1965, and, most prominently and disastrously, the U.S. military intervention in Vietnam.[10]

U.S. policy seemed to be turning away from an ideological anticommunist definition of vital interests during the Nixon and Ford administrations under the tutelage of Henry Kissinger's realpolitik, in which the containment of Soviet power, not necessarily communism, was the principal objective. Obviously, considerations of the global balance of power and not ideology dictated the rapprochement with the People's Republic of China. And the first two years of Jimmy Carter's presidency included an attempt to move even further beyond these Cold War preoccupations.[11]

With the election of Ronald Reagan in 1980, however, the good-versus-bad definition of America's worldwide struggle with the Soviet Union was revived. The president of the United States championed a renewed global crusade for freedom against Marxist-Leninists generally, charging the Kremlin leaders with being liars, cheats, atheists, and the focus of evil in the world. Under this restored self-righteousness, the United States invaded Grenada to prevent a Marxist dictatorship from consolidating its power on the island, openly aided the insurrectionary *contra* movement against the Marxist regime in Nicaragua, and prepared a range of contingency plans, not excluding the direct employment of U.S. military forces, to counteract an alleged Soviet grand design to establish a satellite empire in Central America.[12]

The Soviet Union's use of force beyond its borders also was affected in part by its ideological definition of the world struggle. The Marxist-Leninist theory of universal class conflict between the communists and the capitalists, fused during the Cold War with traditional Russian fears of a hostile outside world, prompted the Kremlin to employ tanks and troops to put down changes of regime in Hungary in 1956 and Czechoslovakia in 1968 that the Soviets feared would have brought into power elements insufficiently loyal to the interests of the Marxist camp, as defined by the Communist Party of the Soviet Union. Clearly, the geostrategic consideration of a reliable security belt in Eastern Europe was the dominant element in the Kremlin's decisions to intervene militarily to structure the internal political situation of its Warsaw Pact allies, but the strategic rationale was reinforced and given legitimacy by the transnational Marxist ideology. And on the southern flank of the Soviet Union, it was primarily the fear of losing control over a strategically significant border region, not an ideologically stimulated desire to communize another nation, that led the Soviets to invade Afghanistan in 1979; here too, however, the Kremlin tried to justify its intervention on grounds of protecting the "progressive" and secular Marxist-Leninist modernizers in Kabul against the "reactionary" forces of Islamic fundamentalism.[13]

Ideological motives, in addition to the Kremlin's perceptions during the Cold War of the country's military and economic self-interests, were among the determining reasons for the Soviet Union's occasionally generous transfer of economic and military resources to Marxists in the Third World. From their vantage point in the most powerful Marxist country, the leaders of the Soviet Communist Party felt compelled to give the historical dialectic a push from time to time. A case in point was the Soviet Union's relation with Fidel Castro's Cuba, whose sugar the Soviets purchased beyond their needs and whose economy they bankrolled until 1992, when Boris Yeltsin informed Havana that it would have to make it on its own. To be sure, during the period of United States–Soviet global rivalry, Cuba did provide the Soviets with forward military and communications facilities in the American hemisphere, but these were not essential to the security of the Soviet Union. Moreover, providing military protection to Cuba turned out to be extraordinarily expensive and at times, as in the Cuban missile crisis, risky to the Soviet Union itself. Premier Nikita Khrushchev's deployment of missiles in Cuba in 1962 was dictated by Soviet intercontinental strategic deficiencies, but these were rectified by the late 1960s. The Kremlin's continued support for Castro was motivated to some extent by the obligation felt in Moscow to help other Marxist regimes secure themselves against the principal capitalist enemy. Soviet support for Marxist Nicaragua in the 1980s was an even clearer case of ideology potentially putting the Soviets in harm's way. The considerable expense of playing big brother to the Sandinistas and the resulting risk of direct confrontation with the United States surely was not a geopolitical necessity, given the fact that the Soviets already had a military outpost in Cuba, unless the ideological factor—the fraternal obligations among Marxist-Leninists—were a heavy consideration. Similar mixed motives were behind the Soviet and Cuban support of Marxists in Africa.

Derived Interests

Many of the interests for which countries fight or have said they are prepared to fight do not appear to have the characteristics of either highly valued material assets or sacrosanct ways of life. Among the numerous cases in point are Germany's support for Austria's invasion of Serbia in 1914, the Soviet Union's threat to launch missiles at Britain, France, and Israel in 1956 if they did not pull their forces out of Egypt, the Kennedy administration's 1961 threat to use force to maintain access to West Berlin, the American involvement in the Vietnam War from 1963 to 1973, Britain's military action against Argentina in 1982 to regain possession of the Falkland Islands, and the United States–led military action against Iraq in 1991 to drive Saddam Hussein's forces out of Kuwait.

Geopolitical concepts.   Decisions about whether a country can afford to lose a particular place on the globe to potential enemies or, conversely, whether it can afford to pass up an opportunity to gain access to or control of a place from which it has been excluded are affected profoundly by the geopolitical theories its decision makers carry around in their heads. These are notions—sometimes arrived at through systematic analysis, sometimes only intuitively developed—about the significance of a country's geographic situation for its ability to fight wars successfully.

Countries with long coastlines usually formulate very different defense and security requirements from those of landlocked countries. Countries separated from their neighbors by rugged mountain ranges are less likely to be intensely and continually watchful of political developments across their borders than countries that share the same open plain.

Geopolitical theories include an amalgam of assumptions about the current and future lineup of the country's probable allies and adversaries around the globe, assumptions derived from assessments of their material and ideational interests.

The geopolitical views prominent in the United States and the Soviet Union during and immediately after World War II—and taught in their respective military academies—contributed significantly to the onset and perpetuation of the Cold War. The views on both sides were strongly influenced by the classical Anglo-American geopolitical theories developed at the turn of the century by Sir Halford Mackinder and Captain Alfred Thayer Mahan and refined in the 1940s by Nicolas J. Spykman. This theoretical legacy provided the intellectual muscle for the military and alliance-building policies by which the United States after 1947 confronted Soviet expansionary moves, and essentially the same geopolitical worldview, reinforced by Marxist-Leninist theories of global class conflict, infused Kremlin grand strategies until the latter 1980s, when Mikhail Gorbachev demanded new thinking from his advisers about Soviet national interests.

The classical geopolitical theories postulated a natural, or geographically determined, rivalry for great-power dominance of the vast rimland of the Eurasian landmass. This was because the great powers that were largely dependent upon the sea for their military protection and economic well-being, the "insular" powers, needed secure dominions on the rimland, or at least spheres of influence, for naval bases, servicing facilities for their commercial fleets, lines of communication, and raw materials; at the same time, the power or powers who dominated the central expanse of Eurasia, the heartland, considered it imperative to have secure access to this same rimland and freedom of movement through it to ensure commerce with the rest of the world. A position of dominance by the insular powers would accordingly be viewed by the central heartland power as threatening encirclement. In the event of war, control of the rimland would be absolutely crucial to both sides. For the insular powers, the rimland was seen as a staging ground for attacks into the heartland; for the heartland powers, in addition to providing a necessary buffering area against such attacks, the rimland provided a staging ground for disrupting strategic lines of communication and navigation between the insular powers and their allies.

The understandable and geopolitically rational efforts of the United States and its allies on the one hand and of the Soviet Union and its allies on the other to cultivate rimland clients were regarded by each side as hostile and part of the rival's grand design to achieve global dominance. The Soviets, looking at the world from a different geographic vantage point but through very similar geopolitical lenses, labeled the rimland activities of the United States and its allies capitalist encirclement, and the rimland countermoves by the Kremlin, particularly its drive to obtain bases and servicing facilities for the Red Navy, were branded by the West as Soviet imperialism. With good reason President Jimmy Carter's National Security Adviser, Zbigniew Brzezinski, called the region "the arc of crisis" and military planners on both sides saw it as a likely tinderbox for the ignition of World War III.

The fact that the Middle East contains about 30 percent of the world's petroleum has strongly added to the classical geopolitical focus on the rimland since World War II and was one of the compelling reasons why the United States was able to mobilize a coalition in 1991 to throw Iraq's occupying army out of Kuwait. Although the Soviet Union was no longer a primary rival of the United States for influence in the Persian Gulf, Saddam Hussein's takeover of the oil-rich sheikdom put him in control of 20 percent of the world's oil reserves and created fears that, bloated with success and a newly acquired reputation as the Gulf's military *hegemon*, he would use Kuwait as a stepping stone to domination of the other oil-producing countries in the Middle East.

Credibility, prestige, and national honor.   Once a nation publicly articulates the material interests and social values it considers important at home and in the world, striking postures simultaneously to reassure friends and warn adversaries that it will fight for them militarily if necessary, it creates the additional vital interest of making these promises and threats believed. The value calculations that produced the initial national commitment can change to the extent that a reassessment would indicate that a particular interest is no longer worth fighting for; but the original, now objectively obsolete commitment may still be adhered to, even if war results, because of the perceived need of the country to sustain a reputation for honoring its commitments. Similarly, circumstances may tempt an adversary to challenge vaguely formulated or very general commitments, only to be confronted with more belligerence than is warranted on a relatively minor issue.

The fashionable catchall term for the considerations that enter into such thinking and actions is *credibility* — maintaining the credibility of a nation's commitments or, more grandly, maintaining its own credibility.

The United States fought the first big war of the post–World War II period, the Korean War of 1950–1953, precisely because of a concern for the credibility of its new security commitments to the NATO countries and Japan rather than because of a military-strategic judgment that possession of South Korea as well as North Korea by a Soviet ally would adversely change the balance of power in Asia. Indeed, the Joint Chiefs of Staff in 1947 had considered the Korean peninsula to be of minor strategic importance in another war and had advised against deployments and commitments that could lock the United States into defending South Korea. But President Truman and his top national security advisers, having publicly drawn the line in the North Atlantic Treaty and other international undertakings against further communist expansion (after the Soviet takeover of Czechoslovakia in 1948), suddenly saw the credibility of all such U.S. commitments to be at stake once the North Korean communists invaded South Korea. For this reason, and no other, the United States went to war again in Asia, albeit under the United Nations' flag, after just five years of peace. The American "police action" resulted in the deaths of over 34,000 American soldiers. More than 800,000 South Koreans, at least 500,000 North Koreans, and perhaps as many as 2,000,000 Chinese also died in the war.

When President Dwight D. Eisenhower prepared the American public for a possible U.S. military intervention in Vietnam to save the French from defeat in 1954 by comparing Indochina to the first of a row of dominoes, he was concerned not with the strategic value of Indochina itself, but rather with how a failure to help the French in their hour of peril might embolden enemies of the United States and demoralize its friends.

Once again it was primarily credibility, accorded the heightened emotional definition of national honor, that first prompted the direct entry of the United States into the Vietnam War in 1965 during the administration of Lyndon Johnson and then prevented the Nixon administration from finally terminating U.S. participation in the war until 1973—on what turned out to be humiliating terms—after 50,000 young American men had lost their lives in the futile effort to prevent communist control. "The commitment of 500,000 Americans [troops deployed to Vietnam] has settled the issue of the importance of Vietnam," explained Henry Kissinger. "For what is involved is confidence in American promises. However fashionable it is to ridicule the terms 'credibility' or 'prestige,' they are not empty phrases; other nations can gear their actions to ours only if they can count on our steadiness."[14] For President Nixon, the worst fate to be avoided in Vietnam was humiliation. His most aggressive moves, including the 1970 invasion of Cambodia, which enlarged the war, were rationalized by this anxiety. "If and when the chips are down," said Nixon,

> the world's most powerful nation, the United States of America, acts like a pitiful, helpless giant, the forces of totalitarianism and anarchy will threaten free nations and free institutions throughout the world. It is not our power but our will and character that is being tested.[15]

A similar invocation of national character and resolve, this time in the guise of an opportunity to revive lost glory, was operative in Prime Minister Margaret Thatcher's dispatch of the British Royal Navy to take back the Falkland Islands from Argentina in response to Argentina's April 1982 military occupation of the British-controlled islands off the South American coast.

A felt need to demonstrate an unsqueamish willingness to use force to defend the national honor can drive national leaders to relatively easy-win power plays against largely defenseless opponents. Such a compulsion appears to have been present in President Reagan's successful but probably unnecessary marine invasion of the tiny Caribbean island of Grenada in 1983. His stated justifications were, first, to prevent American medical students from being taken hostage by the island's new Marxist regime and, second, to depose a regime that, with Cuban and Soviet aid, was planning to subvert its neighbor governments. The timing was especially welcome in the White House, coming in the wake of the terrorist car-bombing attack on a U.S. Marine barracks in Lebanon, for which the United States had been unable to find an effective reprisal. Grenada gave the administration's frustrated constituents the catharsis they had been denied in Lebanon.

At any moment in history some nations somewhere in the world will be bloodying one another for one or more of these reasons of state. Does this fact of international life confirm the views of the instinctivist theorists, such as Konrad Lorenz and Sigmund Freud, that the human organism is naturally predisposed to behave violently? Or does it suggest rather that the *structure and norms of human society,* which humans have themselves created, are responsible for the frequency of war in the world? Do we live in war systems of our own making? If so, to what extent are such systems subject to reform?

NOTES

1. For a vivid description of Czechoslovakia's decision not to fight Hitler's invading armies, see Leonard Mosley, *On Borrowed Time: How World War II Began* (New York: Random House, 1969), pp. 75–88.

2. See Scott D. Sagan, "The Origins of the Pacific War," in Robert I. Rotberg and Theodore K. Rabb, eds., *The Origin and Prevention of Major Wars* (New York: Cambridge University Press, 1989), pp. 323–352.

3. Robert Kennedy, *The Thirteen Days* (New York: Norton,1969).

4. Sagan, "The Origins of the Pacific War."

5. Interview with Secretary of State Henry Kissinger, *Business Week,* January 13, 1975.

6. Austria's reasons for war were contained in her government's notorious forty-eight-hour ultimatum to Serbia on July 23, 1914, in which the Austrian government asserted that the Serbs had the "duty of putting an end to the intrigues which form a perpetual menace to the Monarchy." Among the intrigues that Vienna demanded the Serbs stop immediately were anti-Austrian publications, anti-Austrian instruction in the Serbian public schools, and allowing the existence of anti-Austrian societies. See Laurence Lafore, *The Long Fuse: An Interpretation of the Origins of World War I* (New York: J.P. Lippincott, 1971), pp. 225–226; and John G. Stoessinger, *Why Nations Go to War* (New York: St. Martin's, 1985), Chapter 1.

7. Michael Walzer, *Just and Unjust Wars: A Moral Argument with Historical Illustrations* (New York: Basic Books, 1977).

8. George F. Kennan, *Memoirs: 1925–1950* (Boston: Little, Brown, 1967), pp. 314–315, 319–320.

9. Seyom Brown, *The Faces of Power: Constancy and Change in United States Foreign Policy from Truman to Reagan* (New York: Columbia University Press, 1983), pp. 65–145.

10. *Ibid.*, pp. 149–307.

11. *Ibid.*, pp. 321–561.

12. *Ibid.*, pp. 567–628.

13. Raymond L. Garthoff, "Detente and Afghanistan," in Erik P. Hoffmann and Frederick J. Fleron, Jr., eds., *The Conduct of Soviet Foreign Policy* (New York: Aldine de Gruyter, 1980), pp. 756–761.

14. Henry Kissinger, "The Vietnam Negotiations," *Foreign Affairs* (January 1969), 47(2): 218–219.

15. Richard Nixon, radio-television address to the nation, April 30, 1970; full text in *Department of State Bulletin*, No. 1612 (May 18, 1970), 62: 620.

CHAPTER 4

Why Nations Fight: Basic Structural Determinants

The previous chapter reviewed the standard reasons statespersons and publics give for going to war. These reasons are usually offered in connection with a particular war and are prompted by the need to create domestic and international support for the nation's actions. Such public justifications characteristically recount the enemy's immediate war-provoking acts and portray the need to fight as dictated by vital national interests. Sometimes leaders and publics will work themselves into a war fever when vital national interests are not really at stake. But more often than not, in cases of major war the immediate war-provoking situation is a symptom of very real, long-term conflicts of interest between the belligerents that are deeply imbedded in the larger structure of their relationship.

Frequently the intense conflicts of national interest that lead to war are rooted in economic rivalries or hegemonic-dependence relationships that at least one side finds intolerable. Moreover, such rivalries and grievances are prosecuted through a virtually anarchic interstate system that—lacking authoritative processes of conflict resolution and relying heavily on the distribution of military power to determine who gets what, when, and how—often is itself one of the determinants of war. These kinds of basic structural sources of serious international conflict ought to be part of the search for the causes of particular wars as well as for the causes of the continuing prominence of war in world society.

THE NATION-STATE SYSTEM
AS A CAUSE OF WAR

Much academic writing in the field of international relations, particularly the school of thought that calls itself realist, either contends or implies that the nation-state system is essentially a war system. The dominant view is capsulized by Kenneth Waltz: "With many sovereign states, with no system of law enforceable among them, with each state judging its grievances and ambitions according to its own reason or desire—conflict, sometimes leading to war, is bound to occur."[1]

The "realist" analysis gives determinative weight to the assumption (seemingly borne out by history) that in the nation-state system individual countries cannot depend on the community of states to enforce interstate agreements or even to protect their most basic right: sovereignty itself. Enforcement of international agreements and the defense of a nation's vital interests, including national survival, ultimately depend on a country's own ability, sometimes in conjunction with allies, to impose enough costs on aggressors to outweigh any gains they might hope to achieve.

Accordingly, countries normally maintain large arsenals and permanent military establishments to enable them to hold their own in conflicts that may turn violent. Even countries with populations of basically peaceful dispositions are compelled, by the system, to threaten the use of force—the *ultima ratio* of international politics—to avoid being pushed around and humiliated by opponents more disposed to employ military power. For many governments this translates into a requirement to maintain credible war-fighting capabilities and, on occasion, to use them in shooting wars.

In contrast to domestic society, where the outbreak of intergroup violence often places the whole system in jeopardy, wars and threats of war have traditionally been regarded as normal attributes of the world of nation-states. As Hans Morgenthau, the intellectual godfather of contemporary "realism," put it, "All history shows that nations active in international politics are continually preparing for, actively involved in, or recovering from organized violence in the form of war."[2]

The view that the principal cause of international war is the anarchic nation-state system itself has precedents in a long line of prominent thinkers, including not only the ancestors of modern "realism," such as Niccolò Machiavelli and Thomas Hobbes but also proponents of world government such as Emeric Crucé, William Penn, John Bellers, the

Abbé de Saint-Pierre, Bertrand Russel, Albert Einstein, Robert Maynard Hutchins, and Richard Falk.[3] Agreeing with the diagnosis but not the prescription, the "realists" see no politically feasible way of transforming the system of sovereign nation-states into a durable world state. Any controls on violence in the international system will have to be accomplished *within* its basic anarchic structure, through attention to the distribution of power, especially military balances, and crisis-management diplomacy. The "realists" and world-order idealists are as one, however, in their basic prognosis that war will continue to be a normal feature of international life as long as the world polity retains its essentially anarchic structure.

The international system does seem to be prone to violence. Yet many countries do not go to war against each other when their important interests clash. Some regions of the globe have lower frequencies of war than others. Some periods in history have fewer wars than others. Some wars are fought in highly constrained ways—localized and limited in their destructive intensity. Some even stop before either side has won. What explains these variations?

Much of the scholarship and theorizing about war, taking the nation-state system as a given, attempts to pinpoint the conditions under which international conflicts are most likely to result in war. Some of this work also concerns itself with the the conduct of wars—the hows and whys of their escalation, control, and termination. Five factors have received the most attention: the international distribution of power; the internal structure of states; the balance of military power; the normative culture; and the quality of diplomacy. The first two of these—the basic structural determinants of war—are the subject of this chapter.

THE INTERNATIONAL DISTRIBUTION OF POWER

The term *power* is subject to a wide range of definitions. As used here, it refers to *the ability to mobilize human and nonhuman resources,* where *mobilize* means organize to accomplish some definable purpose, and *resources* is a general term that covers natural as well as artificial phenomena, information and ideas as well as tangible things. This leaves open the question of what the ingredients of such ability might be in a particular relationship. There is elementary wisdom in the recognition by many analysts that a key to the location and prevalence of war or peace in the international system is the distribution of power, so defined, among countries.

The components of any such distributions of power will vary with the issues over which a set of countries are in conflict, with the particular set of countries involved in the conflict, and with the kinds of coercive capabilities available to these countries. The tendency of countries to resort to military intimidation as opposed to economic coercion, for example, will be different in a conflict about jurisdiction over an ethnic group from what it will be in a conflict over currency devaluations. The kinds of power the countries in conflict have at their disposal and are willing to bring to bear on the situation will also affect whether the conflict is prosecuted and resolved with or without violence.

Thus, if the overall balance of power between countries in an intense altercation favors one side when nonmilitary resources are counted but relatively even when military forces are compared, the economically weaker side may be tempted to provoke a war over the issue. Such a dynamic played a large role in propelling the United States and Japan into war in 1941. On the other hand, when both sides are able substantially to affect the well-being of the other in the economic sphere but the military balance is lopsided, war may well be avoided. A case in point is the series of altercations during the 1970s about oil pricing and supply issues between the Arab oil producers on one side and the United States and its NATO allies on the other side. Public hints by the Western governments that they would consider military action were very much a part of the bargaining and probably helped keep the economic disputes from escalating to actual military confrontation.

Generally, countries engaged in a rich range of transactions across a number of issue areas can invoke many bargaining counters—promises and threats to provide or withhold items of value to each other—without restoring to military coercion. The converse also holds: when a conflict arises between countries not normally engaged in nonviolent bargaining across a range of issues, there will be a tendency to jump quickly to the military level to influence each other.

The Distribution of Power as a War-Provoking Issue

Not only does the distribution of power affect the willingness of countries to go to war over particular issues, but the distribution of power itself, particularly the power that comes from control of foreign areas with economic resources and geographic features crucial to military performance, can be the issue over which wars are fought.

As indicated in Chapter 3, the geopolitical consideration of preventing an adverse change in a country's power vis-à-vis its adversaries is one of the standard reasons of state for which countries feel justified in fighting. Kaiser Wilhelm's decision at the end of the nineteenth century to turn Germany into a global naval and seagoing commercial power stimulated France and Britain to collude against Germany and to draw Russia into their entente. The determination of France and England to counter the Kaiser's challenge to their imperial dominance even if this meant going to war against Germany had much to do with the escalation of the 1914 Balkans crisis into World War I.

Another cause of war related to distribution of power is an impending defection from an established alliance which could affect the regional or global balance of power to the detriment of the other members of the alliance. This was the main reason the Soviets invaded reform-minded Czechoslovakia in 1968 and why the United States was prepared to use all means necessary during the Cold War to prevent a pro-Communist government from coming to power in Iran (when such a threat loomed in 1953, the CIA engineered a coup to bring the pro–United States shah back into power, but the United States had contingency plans on the books to go much further if the Marxists gained a position of dominance in Teheran).

Hegemonic War

Throughout history, large-scale wars have been fought between rival imperial states or between established imperial states and those seeking to dislodge them from their hegemonic position. Such hegemonic war can arise out of any of four basic situations:

- Expansionary imperial states get in each other's ways, as in the conflicts between the Netherlands and Spain in the sixteenth century and between France and England during the eighteenth and nineteenth centuries.
- States considering themselves to be disadvantaged by the existing distribution of power try to revise the distribution by force (this can take the form of a number of states concerting with one another, as did Germany, Japan, and Italy prior to World War II, to attack those advantaged by the status quo).[4]

- A state at the top of the heap (globally or regionally), fearing that an impending change in the distribution of power would negate its hegemony, initiates (or provokes) war while still in possession of superior capabilities (as in Russia's 1904–1905 war against Japan) in order to hobble its potential rivals.
- States configured in a rather even distribution of power strike, individually or in combination, at one of their number to prevent that state from realizing its hegemonic pretensions (a recurrent feature of European interstate politics during the eighteenth century, often referred to as the classical balance of power.)[5]

Some theorists have sought deeper explanations, locating the basic causes of such hegemonic wars in underlying broad and long-term shifts in the global distribution of economic and industrial power produced by differential rates of economic modernization.[6] These shifts bring about incongruities between existing international domains of *political* control (empires, spheres of influence, hegemon-led coalitions) and the emergent socioeconomic realities. Efforts to bring the political domain into congruence with the socioeconomic realities can rarely be accommodated peacefully by the dominant imperial powers, and as the incongruence becomes more severe, either the old imperialists or their challengers are likely to attempt to settle the hegemonic issue by war.[7]

The Polarization Factor

Decisions by antagonists to conduct their conflict by war are strongly affected by their respective calculations of the fighting power that can be mobilized on each side (see Chapter 5), and these calculations, in turn, are affected by the prevailing pattern of alliances and the extent to which alliance members and other prospective parties to the action are bound to one another and for what reasons. Thus, if most of an international system is polarized into only two camps and if the bonding between countries in each camp is known to be tight across a range of issues, almost any war within the system has the strong potential for becoming a systemwide war. In such a tightly polarized system, however, war-inducing miscalculations of the military balance of power due to false assumptions about which countries will fight on each side are less likely, and therefore war should be less likely, than in more loosely structured international systems.

Abstracted from other complicating factors, the effects of various degrees and types of polarization on the war-proneness of an international system and on the geographic extent of the violence if war does break out are represented in the following chart.

POLARITY AND THE LIKELIHOOD OF WAR AND ITS GEOGRAPHIC EXPANSION[8]

Higher roman numerals indicate greater likelihood of war; higher arabic numerals indicate greater likelihood that war will involve most states in the system.

	Tight	Loose
Unipolarity	I (1) [in theory only]	IV (1)
Bipolarity	I (5)	III (4)
Multipolarity	II (2) [in theory only]	IV (3)
Polyarchy (no dominant coalition pattern)		V (1)

This model, admittedly simplifying reality, highlights the effects of two variables on the chances and shape of war in any regional international system or in the world system as whole.

The first variable is the number of dominant power centers, or poles of attraction, in the system being analyzed: One power center is called *unipolar;* two power centers are called *bipolar;* a few, say three to ten, are referred to as *multipolar;* and many, more than ten, perhaps even hundreds, are termed *polyarchic.*

The second variable is the degree of coalescence of major actors around the dominant power centers (the relevant actors include states, nongovernmental organizations, political movements, corporations and trade associations, ethnic and religious groups, and so forth). In a refined model the degree of coalescence could be plotted on a continuum, but for present purposes it is sufficient to establish the two categories *tight* and *loose.*

Summarizing the likelihood of war and its geographic expansion for the various international configurations, the chart represents the following six hypotheses:

1. *Tightly organized unipolar systems are (in theory only) the least prone to intrasystem war and best equipped to terminate local violence.* In practice, especially in the contemporary world, such systems are inherently unstable and vulnerable to violent assertions of autonomy by the subordinated nations. Tightly controlled unipolar systems have existed in ancient history in the form of autocratic empires such as Egypt, Sumeria, Persia, the early Chou dynasty in China, and Rome during the reign of Julius Caesar. But the only modern example (if viewed as a self-contained regional system) was the Soviet Union and its sphere of control in Eastern Europe. As demonstrated by the fate of the relatively short-lived Soviet empire (a mere 45 years, as compared with the centuries-long durations of the ancient empires), rigidly hierarchical multinational empires are inconsistent with the dispersal throughout the realm of the requisites of modernity: literacy, organizational/political skills, technological competence, commercial capital, and entrepreneurship. The local, national enclaves of human energy that are the correlates of modernity can only be subordinated into the multinational empire by force or the temporary exigencies of security vis-à-vis a hostile empire. Take away the latter "legitimate" excuse for empire, as happened with the demise of the Cold War, and the diverse peoples of the realm are likely to resist, with violence if necessary, dictation from a single polar center. In other words, the internally peaceful multinational empire has become a fiction.

2. *Loosely organized unipolar systems are no less prone to war than loose multipolar systems but are substantially better at avoiding a system-wide spread of violence.* The lack of tight identification between the hegemonic power and others in the system—a function of the system's pluralistic structure and norms—is responsible for both the prevalence of war and its susceptibility to localization. Because the system's single hegemon does not need to preempt or restrain a rival great power's exploitation of a local conflict, lesser states may be tempted to engage in local aggression under the assumption that the hegemon will not want to assume the costs of intervention. If this assumption is indeed borne out, the local war can take its course without infecting the entire system. If on the other hand (as in the 1990–1991 Gulf War) the hegemon, for reasons of world order or because some of its interests are involved, does intervene, its overwhelming power and the lack of a rival hegemon will likely allow it to accomplish its purposes

swiftly in the particular conflict without high risk of provoking a larger conflagration.

3. *The most dangerous international systems tend to be those characterized by either loose bipolarity or loose multipolarity.* They are dangerous in two respects: the likelihood of war and the likelihood that war anywhere in the system will engulf the whole system. War is likelier because the ambiguity of mutual security commitments in the loose coalitions leads to miscalculation and bluffing. These characteristics also provide temptations for the system's dominant powers to intervene in local conflicts and the need for weaker powers to invoke coalition ties, however loose, to deter their adversaries from bullying them. If these dangers are indeed inherent in bipolar systems, it can be asked, what explains the "long peace" between the United States and the Soviet Union during the four decades of Cold War bipolarity?

4. *War is highly unlikely in tight bipolar systems, but once started it is most difficult to isolate.* War is unlikely because as a system becomes more tightly polarized into two opposing camps members of each camp have little opportunity for unilaterally engaging in war-provoking action against others in the system; any such action usually must be authorized by the whole coalition or at least the coalition's leader. War is also discouraged because an attack on any member of the rival coalition would be an attack on the whole coalition, and therefore the attacker could not hope to control his risks by attacking a weak opponent under the assumption that the victim's allies would not want to become involved. The temptation to nibble at or "salami slice" the rival coalition that characterizes loosely polarized configurations is minimized in tightly polarized systems.

The risky side of tight bipolarity is that it operates as an all-or-nothing deterrence system. If despite the built-in inhibitions against war a conflict between members of each camp should escalate to open hostilities, the war—unless terminated at once—would very likely expand into a systemwide war with few or any sanctuaries.

5. *Tight multipolar systems (in theory only) would have few interstate wars, and these could be easily quarantined.* Divided into a number of regional (or subregional) subsystems, each a highly integrated and self-contained security community, a tightly multipolar global (or regional) system should be able to keep conflict contained within each of its separate parts, with little likelihood that members of these internally self-policing security communities would be tempted to intervene in one another's affairs. But although it is a *theoretical* possibility, the tight multipolar system is no more plausible as an actual pattern of international relations than the tight unipolar system.

The idea of self-contained subsystems is inconsistent with the growing interdependence of nations across all traditional regional lines and with the increasing economic and strategic importance to all major countries of common areas (the oceans, the biospheric environment, and outer space) where countries can get in one another's ways. Why should new regional subsystems, any more than the regional empires of the past, be expected to be content with what they have and refrain from balance-of-power games against each other?

Even the *formation* of such self-contained regional subsystems appears entirely theoretical, for there no longer are universally acceptable definitions of which peoples constitute what regions. Are not some countries in the Middle East, for example, part of Africa, southwestern Asia, or southeastern Europe? Even the European Community, especially with Eastern Europe no longer imprisoned in the Soviet empire, has no settled view of its proper membership. Who is to decide disputes over such regional definitions, and by what criteria? In most continents there is profound jealousy and suspicion that would-be regional hegemons, such as Brazil or Japan, would lord it over other members of a self-contained regional community.

6. *The polyarchic configuration is more war-prone than others but more likely than any of the others to keep wars localized.* Pervaded by crosscutting loyalties and associations—based on nationality, domicile, ethnicity, religion, economic role, social class, occupation, and ideology—many of them traversing state boundaries, some of them intercontinental in reach, polyarchic systems are not conducive to firm multinational alliances. Mutual security pacts lack credibility. Every nation needs to be prepared to fend for itself. War is therefore less likely to be deterred than in the polarized systems. On the other hand, as exhibited in the rapprochement between Israel and her neighbors in 1993, the growth of cross-cutting associations can inhibit the scope of hostility that must be generated to fight large wars. In general, however, the prognosis for polyarchy is for more war than in any of the polar systems, but no system-wide war.[9]

DOMESTIC STRUCTURE

There is considerable ideological and scholarly disagreement over how much influence the domestic structure of a country has in inclining it toward a basically warlike or peaceable mode of international behavior.

Marxists see war in the modern era as an external expression of the contradictions of capitalism within nonsocialist states. Neoclassical economists are wont to find the sources of war in imperialist/mercantilist conflicts produced by statist distortions of the free market. Some political sociologists attribute the international pugnacity of certain countries to the political insecurity of traditional elites who turn to war as a means of enhancing their otherwise declining influence in the high councils of power. Many liberal democrats hold that states structured on democratic principles of representation and accountability are basically pacific whereas autocracies are usually the instigators of war.

What does the historical record show? First of all, and generally speaking, the domestic structure of a country does significantly affect its crucial decisions on war and peace. The stage and kind of economic development of a country and the related structure of relationships between governing elites and the society's socioeconomic classes and communal groups have a lot to do with when and how the country is inclined to use military force in its relations with other countries.

These connections between internal structure can be demonstrated through a comparison of (*a*) the European state system during the period of the classical balance of power, and (*b*) the period of rising nationalism, comprising the French Revolution, the Napoleonic wars, and the post–Napoleonic concert of Europe.

Diplomacy and War among Aristocratic Monarchies: The Classical Balance of Power

Usually dated from the Peace of Westphalia (1648), ending the wars of religion, and prevailing until about 1775, this pattern of statecraft was characterized by a flexible system of shifting alliances among the half-dozen or so major dynasties of Europe. The classical diplomatic minuet of combinations and recombinations directed toward ensuring that no one of the states would become the hegemon was inseparable from the fact that during this period the principal states of Europe were aristocratic monarchies (the only exception being the 1653–1660 republican interregnum in England under the Cromwells).

The states of the day were not yet true *nation*-states. The economic and social ties between peoples within each country were still flimsy. The state was little more than an administrative overlay on the still relatively distinct enclaves of homogeneous ethnic, linguistic, or religious populations. Monarchs often would recruit their top ministers, including diplomats and generals, from other countries. Indeed, it was not unusual for the monarch himself to speak a different language or practice a different religion than the majority of his subjects. The monarchs of the time would arrange marriages, successions to kingship, and treasury deals with one another, redraw the boundary lines demarcating their states of Europe, trade colonial possessions, form reform alliances and counteralliances, and even go to war, without bothering to determine whether the populations within their jurisdictions liked it or not.

Wars were frequent and fought by professional mercenary armies, hired soldiers who as often as not had no prior connection with the land and peoples they were paid to defend. The citizenry at large were not asked to fight or even to do much to support the wars going on around them. Accordingly, the aristocratic monarchies were wont to order their generals into war for any of a wide range of state and personal interests, from vital to trivial: one war might be fought to prevent a major shift in the interstate balance of power; another might be fought over the right to fish in a disputed area; still another might be fought to salvage the reputation of a general who was outmaneuvered by a rival general in the preceding war. Because the ruling elite did not have to justify their actions to anyone but themselves, wars could be started quickly and stopped quickly before serious and irretrievable costs were incurred.

The role of war in the period of the classical balance was also influenced by the ways military forces were recruited, organized, and provisioned. Although some soldiers fought for the glory of it, most were simply in the business of renting out their bodies; if they were not fed and clothed well, if the work was too hard, or if there was too much risk of their getting killed, they would desert. Consequently the generals of the time were constrained to avoid frequent or sustained battle. In a sustained battle not only one's soldiers but also their supply trains, ammunition, and weapons would be lost, and all of this was very expensive to replace. Moreover, without the revenue to finance costly wars (the nobility being generally exempt from taxation), most monarchies were very constrained to limit their war aims and to fight highly controlled and brief wars. Like chess, war was a game of maneuver, and the brilliant general not only knew how to win without getting into a big engagement but also knew when to concede defeat, sometimes even prior to any major exchange of gunfire. Clever statespersons played on these incentives in order to establish bargaining advantages over enemies by convincing their enemies that their resolve and staying power had not reached their limits.

The central imperative of diplomacy in this period—to maintain as much flexibility as possible in the choice of alliance partners—was highly interactive with the incentives to fight limited wars. In order to preserve the option of forming alliances tomorrow with today's enemies, statespersons would refrain from pushing their advantages to the point of destroying or humiliating a defeated country. Fortunately, because of the material and personnel constraints on warfare, there were few temptations to exceed this rule of prudence.

Underneath the military statecraft of limited war for limited means, new forces were at work eroding the socioeconomic foundations of the aristocratic/monarchical order that had sustained it.

The Rise of the Nation in Arms

As eighteenth-century technological and economic developments in Europe made the sectors of societies dependent upon one another for the enjoyment of the amenities of modern life, states were transformed into integrated nations. Functions of government within the evolving nation-states that had previously been centralized in the monarchy—the controls on public order and commerce, the collection of taxes and tolls to construct and maintain commonly used roads and waterways, and the raising of armed forces to enforce the rules of civic order within the country and to protect it against hostile outsiders—now needed to be adapted to the new nation-forming forces.

More and more, the power of a country vis-à-vis other countries was dependent upon the ability of its rulers to gain cooperation from many sectors of the country in building modern fleets and armies, constructing and maintaining nationwide roads and transportation systems, and fostering industries that could engage in profitable international trade. This put the merchant and commercial classes in an especially strong bargaining position (particularly when it came to the mobilization of the country's resources for large projects, such as the expansion of the navy), since it was they who really controlled the country's industry and finances. The hereditary dynasties and aristocracies were compelled to co-opt these new elites into the regime, inviting them into the chambers where policy was made. Thus were born the institutions of the nation—councils of state and parliaments—to which the monarchy was accountable. Interstate diplomatic maneuverings and power plays were accordingly constrained by this need of the governing elites to persuade broader and broader segments of society that particular alliances, foreign adventures, and wars were indeed in the nation's interests.

In order to generate sufficient support for their policies, monarchs, aristocrats, and prime ministers increasingly had to identify with the people of their countries rather than stand aloof from them. They had to speak the peoples' languages and champion their causes. They had to embrace the ideology of nationalism, the idea of the nation-state as an organic whole.

But the equation of state and nation and the spread of the ideology of nationalism were at odds with some of the basic requirements of balance-of-power statecraft. Foreign adventures, especially wars, now being more difficult to initiate because they required widespread national support, would be much more difficult to keep limited in their intensity. National fear, anger, and pride had to be whipped up in order to go to war; the reasons of state for which war was required had to be reasons of nation—the nation's survival, its honor, its glory; the enemy had to be made to be venal and therefore deserving to be severely punished, hobbled if not destroyed.

Developments in weapons technology and military logistics reinforced the sociopolitical and economic factors making for highly destructive wars. New weapons, military transportation systems, and navies required provisioning from an industrial base that in turn required a virtual mobilization of the entire nation. The munitions factories, transportation networks, and indeed the entire industrial infrastructure of belligerent countries became crucial (and thus legitimate) military targets.

No longer could a country depend on hired mercenaries to fight its wars. Loyal citizens would have to be recruited to fight and to provide the generalship. This dependence on citizen armies further reinforced the requirement that wars and military alliances be entered into only for vital national purposes.

In short, wars were harder to start than in the previous century, but once they were started, there would be hell to pay.

Democracy and War

The analysis of the impact of domestic structures can be narrowed to the question of what difference it makes for war or peace whether or not a country is a representative democracy. The philosopher Immanuel Kant argued in his famous 1795 pamphlet *Perpetual Peace* that it made all the difference: governments based on the consent of the governed, which he called republican, would be unlikely to initiate war, since ordinary citizens do not want to disrupt their lives to fight or to pay the costs of fighting and repairing the devastation that war leaves behind.[10]

Contemporary social scientists attempting to test the Kantian proposition by statistical studies on the incidence of war have found no significant correlation between democracy and noninvolvement in war or between the lack of democracy and initiation of war.[11] The data do suggest, however, that pluralistic democracies are unlikely to fight one another. Depending on the way political systems are categorized, and excluding cases such as the U.S. Civil War and anticolonial wars, there are very few if any instances of war *between* democracies.[12]

Analyses of the data have also found an apparent correspondence between the political structure of countries and the objectives (other than direct self-defense) for which they use military force beyond their borders. A government with unlimited executive authority presiding over a domestic system with very little political competition seems to be the most likely to undertake military operations to enlarge its country's territory or dominion over foreign resources. And governments of open and competitive pluralistically organized polities seem to be the most likely to involve themselves in wars over the legitimacy of particular forms of government or the right of particular elite groups to govern—so-called wars of liberation.[13] There are, of course, some important deviations from this apparent pattern. Britain acquired some of its colonial possessions when it was the most democratic of the European countries. And the democratic United States in its fling at empire obtained Cuba and the Philippines by going to war against Spain. Wars waged ostensibly on behalf of the self-determination of peoples have been launched by autocrats: Napoleon Bonaparte, Adolph Hitler, and the rulers of the Kremlin.[14]

Despite these refinements and complications and the inability of the statisticians to extrapolate a coherent pattern from the quantitative data, Kant's hypothesis of the comparative reluctance of democracies to become involved in war is sustained by case studies of major twentieth-century conflicts (see Chapter 7). It is another matter, however, to establish that this reluctance has contributed to reducing the incidence of war in the international system. Indeed, it can be argued that the structural inhibitions democracies experience in mobilizing their societies for war have been partly responsible for some of the most glaring failures in modern times to deter aggression by the world's less inhibited dictatorships.

NOTES

1. Kenneth Waltz, *Man, the State, and War* (New York: Columbia University Press, 1959), p. 159.

2. Hans J. Morgenthau, *Politics Among Nations: The Struggle for Power and Peace* (New York: Knopf, 1978), p. 42.

3. The content of various proposals for world government are analyzed in Chapter 8.

4. Morgenthau, in *Politics Among Nations,* pp. 42–76, sees major international war as a characteristic consequence of inevitably arising rivalries between "imperialist" and "status quo" powers.

5. Edward V. Gulick, *Europe's Balance of Power* (Ithaca: Cornell University Press, 1955); and Morton A. Kaplan, *System and Process in International Politics* (New York: Wiley, 1962), pp. 49–50.

6. The power-differential explanations for hegemonic-war theorists include, most prominently, those of A. F. K. Organski, *World Politics* (New York: Knopf, 1968); Robert Gilpin, *War and Change in World Politics* (Cambridge, England: Cambridge University Press, 1981); and George Modelski, *Long Cycles in World Politics* (Seattle: University of Washington Press, 1987).

7. A special version of the hegemonic-war theory, found in classic Marxist-Leninist works, forecasts a final desperate war started by the capitalist-run states at a late stage of capitalism's demise in the face of the global success of socialism. Neo-Marxists such as Immanuel Wallerstein, however, see a long-term era of global dominance by the capitalists, who will continue to fight imperialist wars among themselves while continuing their rapacious exploitation of peripheral societies. See Wallerstein, *The Politics of the World Economy* (Cambridge, England: Cambridge University Press, 1984).

8. The polarity model represents relationships similar to those hypothesized by Richard Rosecrance in his *International Relations: Peace and War* (New York: McGraw-Hill, 1973).

9. The war-inhibiting effects of multiple and cross cutting coalitions are analyzed in Karl W. Deutch and J. David Singer, "Multiple Power Systems and International Stability," *World Politics,* 16(3):390–406; and in Seyom Brown, *New Forces in World Politics* (Washington: Brookings Institution, 1974), pp. 109–119.

10. Immanuel Kant, *Perpetual Peace* (New York: Macmillan, 1917).

11. Jack S. Levy, "Domestic Politics and War," in Robert I. Rotberg and Theodore K. Rabb, eds., *The Origin and Prevention of Major Wars* (New

York: Cambridge University Press, 1989), pp.79-99. See also Melvin Small and J. David Singer, "The War-Proneness of Democratic Regimes, 1816–1965," *Jerusalem Journal of International Studies,* 1 (1976), 50–69.

12. Levy, "Domestic Politics and War"; and Michael W. Doyle, "Kant, Liberal Legacies, and Foreign Affairs," *Philosophy and Public Affairs,* 7 (1983), 205–235, 323–353.

13. William K. Domke, *War and the Changing Global System* (New Haven: Yale University Press, 1988), pp. 72–106.

14. Seyom Brown, *International Relations in a Changing Global System: Toward a Theory of the World Polity* (Boulder: Westview, 1992), p. 70.

CHAPTER 5

Military Arsenals and Balances

"Guns Don't Kill People, People Kill People" asserts the automobile bumper sticker of the National Rifle Association. An analogous view of international relations is that national military arsenals are not the cause of war, but rather the symptom of the intense conflicts among countries that cause war.

This partial truth omits consideration of some essential relationships between military forces and war. Armaments are never merely a symptom of an underlying conflict. Their very presence in a conflict situation, along with the specific characteristics of the arsenals of the antagonists, are among the crucial determinants of whether a conflict will express itself in war and, if it does, what kind of war will be fought.[1]

Nor are the size and characteristics of a country's military arsenal directly deducible by objective scientific analysis from the country's international political relations. As shown in Chapter 3, the highly subjective factors of ideology, prestige, credibility, and honor often are parts of a country's definition of its national interests and affect its assessments of the international threats it faces and the characteristics of the military forces needed to counter them. (Most countries also maintain some of their armed forces to deal with domestic conflicts.)

Even when a country's grand strategists can simplify reality sufficiently to give their military experts a set of carefully defined and prioritized national security objectives, the experts, more often than not, strongly disagree among themselves about the kinds of military capabilities needed to attain these objectives.

However, to recognize these complexities does not preclude making some general observations about how the size and other characteristics of military forces around the world can affect the likelihood and shape of war and the prospects for peace.

WHY COUNTRIES ARM

The national armaments countries maintain for possible use against each other result from two basic features of the nation-state system. The first is that every country has some adversaries that it suspects would injure it if they could do so with relatively little risk of being injured in return. The second is that the virtually anarchic structure of the nation-state system compels each country to rely on its owns means of self-defense, sometimes combined with help from allies. Even without considering any of the aggressive motives for using force discussed in previous chapters, no nation could hope to remain an independent state able to preserve public order within its jurisdiction, facilitate peaceful domestic commerce, operate a regime of social justice, and maintain its cultural values if it could not defend itself against destructive attack by external opponents.

Although the levels and kinds of armaments that a country maintains must depend on varied, sometimes changing factors—its unique set of foreign adversary and alliance relationships, its internal security needs and domestic political economy, its style of diplomacy, and its national-security doctrines—no country allows itself to be completely without military force for external defense.

The Uncertainty of How Much Is Enough

Military planners find it difficult to estimate just which of the many possible combinations of their country's allies and adversaries are likely to be directly or indirectly involved in future belligerencies. Some typical uncertainties follow:

- Should Pakistan attempt to match India's manpower or can the Pakistanis lessen their requirements by counting on China's help in pinning down Indian troops on the Sino-Indian border in the event of war?
- Can the Indians count on the Russians to pin down China's troops on the Sino-Soviet border?
- Given the Israeli-Egyptian peace treaty of 1979, can the Israelis, in establishing their military requirements, subtract the Egyptian armed forces from the combined Arab front they would have to counter in a war? Should they add the forces of Libya? Of Algeria?

• If Angola should attack Zaire across its northern border, would the Republic of South Africa attack Angola from the south? Would Mozambique stand idly by?

To such political uncertainties must be added the wide range of technical uncertainties caused by inadequate intelligence about the quantity and quality of even a single opponent's armaments. Military technology is, in fact, so volatile that today's estimates of what would happen if Country X fought Country Y tomorrow can be made obsolete literally overnight. Assume that Country X has a vast superiority over Country Y in battlefield tanks; Country Y's successful test of a precision guidance system for its antitank artillery could portend a neutralization of this superiority in ways that would be too expensive for Country X to counter.

Rapid changes in existing military balances can also be brought about by transfers of military technologies through sales or military assistance agreements among countries. Thus the Israelis are made very jittery by new purchases of sophisticated air defense systems by any of the Arab countries: it has been primarily through air superiority that Israel has compensated for the overwhelming advantage of its neighbors in numbers of troops.

Since a nuclear arsenal can give a country decisive superiority over an opponent lacking such weapons, the possibility that a rival may develop or otherwise acquire its own nuclear weapons engenders special fears and suspicions. It is widely believed that in addition to the five countries now openly deploying them, at least twenty-five other countries could produce nuclear weapons within ten years. Among the twenty-five are many pairs of intensely antagonistic countries: India and Pakistan, Israel and Iran, Egypt and Libya.[2] Some countries, specifically India and Israel, may already have nuclear arsenals and choose not to reveal them for fear of the reactions of other countries. If any one of them were to admit that it has the bomb, its rivals would not be far behind in deploying their own—if not home-produced, then either bought or stolen.

Given the rapidity with which balances of military power can change, military planners for most governments, including basically peaceful countries that maintain arms only for defensive purposes, usually want to hedge against uncertainty by overarming. The worst the hedger fears is to be charged with having asked for more than is really needed. Yet he or she will probably be praised if the result is either military superiority over the enemy or the enemy's reactive military buildup, which the hedger then can point to as justifying the original recommendations! By contrast, the military planner who asks for too little runs the risk of being blamed for endangering the country's security. In sum, the psychological dynamics combined with bureaucratic and technological factors tend to push governments in the direction of too much arming rather than too little.

The Role of Military Doctrine

Decisions countries make about the size and qualitative characteristics of their military arsenals are also affected by the military doctrines that gain favor in their governments. A case in point is the U.S. strategic nuclear arsenal from the 1960s to the 1980s.

Assured destruction and MAD. In the 1960s Pentagon strategists developed a crude formula for determining the minimum strategic capability the United States would have to maintain to deter a strategic attack on the United States by the Soviet Union. This formula defined the minimally necessary arsenal as including strategic forces that, after absorbing the most devastating first strike the Soviets could mount against the United States, could still inflict a retaliatory blow to destroy at least a quarter of the population of the Soviet Union and one-third of its industry. The Soviet Union seems to have had a similar crude basis for determining the minimum strategic capability it would need to deter a U.S. attack, but the Russians have not yet publicly revealed the details of such Soviet planning concepts.

Secretary of Defense Robert McNamara in the mid-1960s turned this minimum criterion for deterrence based on an assured level of retaliatory destruction into a maximum as well: "This much and no more." The rationale for imposing such a limit on the strategic arsenal was that the United States should forget about winning a thermo-nuclear war or even limiting damage to this country if deterrence failed, for there could be no winners and the horrors of survival in the aftermath of nuclear holocaust would be worse than death. Moreover, if both sides would adopt this restrictive criterion for determining their strategic force requirements—if, in other words, the strategic balance was simply one of mutual assured destruction, or MAD—there would be stable mutual deterrence.

During the early and mid-1970s, both superpowers appeared to be ready to adopt MAD as a sufficient criterion for strategic force planning. The Strategic Arms Limitation Talks (SALT), the SALT 1 Treaty and Agreement of 1972, and the follow-on negotiations for SALT II were expressions of movement toward a deterrence-only definition of the role of strategic forces: Most strategic counterforce weapons (those with the function of destroying the opponent's strategic weapons) were to be prohibited. Both sides agreed that it was legitimate for each to maintain levels of forces sufficient to destroy the other's key cities and industries but that anything more was unnecessary for deterrence and therefore either should not be deployed or, if already deployed, should be negotiated away.

Credible deterrence and beyond.   Despite the SALT accords, new weapons developments accompanied by second thoughts of strategists on both sides about the validity of a MAD-only regime for strategic deterrence had generated a brand new arms race by the mid-1970s.

The anticipation of greater accuracy in Soviet intercontinental ballistic missiles (ICBMs), which some U.S. planners estimated could by the middle or late 1980s give the Soviets the ability to destroy perhaps as many as 95 percent of America's ICBMs, was a window of vunerability, as it was called, that stimulated research and development efforts. The vulnerability-reducing options included efforts to make the U.S. ICBMs mobile, to hide them, to put them in deeper and harder silos, to protect them with antiballistic missiles (ABMs), or to program the ICBMs to be launched on warning that an enemy attack was on its way. Anticipation of the increasing vulnerability of the land-based strategic forces also accelerated programs for enhancing the striking power of American strategic weapons carried by submarines and airplanes.

Missile guidance improvements and other developments making for high accuracy in targeting, in conjunction with the maturing of capabilities for launching many warheads on a single missile—multiple independently targeted reentry vehicles, or MIRVs—made it impossible to distinguish counterforce strategic missiles from those threatening cities. The MIRV technology allowed either side to multiply the number of its deployed warheads virtually overnight, perhaps without immediate detection by the opponent. Accordingly, even the deterrence-only posture seemed to require considerable redundancy, perhaps double or even triple the lethal megatonnage demanded for the assured-destruction mission, simply as insurance against technological breakthroughs or surprise deployments by the other superpower. In the absence of such redundancy, the opponent might be tempted to believe that a well-executed first strike could preclude intolerable retaliation.

The rethinking by strategic analysts of the implications of a MAD-only regime centered on two possibilities. The first was the increased temptations for limited-war power plays under the canopy of absolute mutual deterrence of all-out strategic nuclear war. The second was the terrible "what if" problem: What if for some reason—miscalculation, accident, irrationality, for example—a strategic nuclear attack by one superpower against the other should occur? Would the next step inevitably be a preprogrammed massive nuclear retaliation, which certainly would provoke a massive nuclear attack in reply? If so, wasn't MAD truly insane?

The implications of absolute superpower inhibitions against nuclear escalation were potentially shattering to NATO. A central premise of the alliance was that if a Soviet attack on Western Europe could not be contained and thrown back by the NATO forces deployed in Europe, the United States would be willing to employ its strategic arsenal against the Soviet Union to reverse the tide. But under a MAD regime, this NATO strategy would lack credibility, and the Soviets might therefore be more inclined to start a conventional war under the assumption that the risks were controllable.

Furthermore, some American strategists argued that even the credibility of strategic retaliation in response to the enemy's strategic first strike against the U.S. homeland might be questioned if U.S. forces were designed only for assured destruction of the enemy's cities and industries.[3]

In addition, evidence that Soviet strategists and force planners had never really bought the MAD concept anyway and, despite the SALT agreements, were proceeding to deploy a war-fighting (as distinct from war-deterring) strategic arsenal finally compelled even those U.S. policymakers who had initially championed the MAD concept to favor giving U.S. forces greater clout against Soviet military installations and forces.

These reassessments and alterations of the MAD concept were codified in Jimmy Carter's Presidential Directive No. 59 of August 1980. Labeled "The Countervailing Strategy," the revised criteria for determining what kind of strategic arsenal to deploy provided a nonpartisan rationale for the incoming Reagan administration's plans to substantially enhance the U.S. strategic arsenal. As outlined in the January 1981 report to Congress of Carter's secretary of defense, Harold Brown, the countervailing strategy responded to the "unquestioned Soviet attainment of strategic parity," which "put the final nail in the coffin of what we long knew was dead—the notion that we could adequately deter the Soviets solely by threatening massive retaliation against their cities." It also addressed what had been learned of the Soviets' strategic doctrine: their contemplation of a relatively prolonged nuclear war; the "evidence that they regard military forces as the obvious first targets in a nuclear exchange, not general industrial and economic capacity"; and the fact that "certain elements of the Soviet leadership seem to consider Soviet victory in a nuclear war to be at least a theoretical possibility."

Our national military deployments, said Brown, are designed to tell the world that the United States has the capability and will to deter aggression, whatever the level of conflict contemplated.

> To the Soviet Union, our strategy makes clear that no course of aggression by them that led to the use of nuclear weapons, on any scale of attack and at any stage of conflict, could lead to victory, however they might define victory. Besides our nuclear power to devastate the full target system of the USSR, the United States would have the option for more selective, lesser retaliatory attacks. . . .

> Our planning must provide a continuum of options, ranging from the use of small numbers of strategic and/or theater nuclear weapons aimed at narrowly defined targets, to employment of large portions of our nuclear forces against a broad spectrum of targets. . . .

> At any early stage in the conflict, we must convince the enemy that further escalation will not result in achievement of his objectives, that it will not mean "success," but rather additional costs. To do this, we must leave the enemy with sufficient highly valued military, economic, and political resources still surviving but still clearly at risk, so that he has a strong incentive to seek an end to the conflict.[4]

Secretary of Defense Brown's advocacy of limited and flexible strategic options was a sign of the times. He had been one of

McNamara's protégés, flirting with the idea of controlled counterforce in 1961 and 1962, but rejecting damage-limiting strategies and forces as futile in the mid-1960s, and criticizing the Pentagon for departing from the assured-destruction-only criterion during the Nixon and Ford administrations. At his 1977 confirmation hearings, the secretary designate gave every indication of wanting to reinstitute the regime of mutual deterrence through MAD that Secretaries Melvin Laird and James Schlesinger had begun to dismantle. Now here he was, leading the fight from the Pentagon against the force-planning assumptions he had earlier championed.

At the end of the Carter administration, both superpowers were ordering new strategic forces designed to fight a nuclear war effectively— albeit justified on grounds of credible deterrence. Both sides henceforth would be competitively augmenting their forces considerably beyond what they needed to destroy each other's cities. Many laypersons saw this as overkill, while many, but by no means all, national security planners regarded the increased counterforce deployments as strategically essential.[5]

The case for increasing U.S. counterforce capabilities was strongly asserted in 1983 by President Reagan's Commission on Strategic Forces, chaired by Brent Scowcroft. "Deterrence is not, and cannot be, bluff," said the commission's report. "In order for deterrence to be effective we must not merely have weapons, we must be perceived to be able, and prepared, if necessary, to use them effectively against the key elements of Soviet power."[6]

The Scowcroft commission pointed to Soviet deployments of SS-18 and SS-19 ICBMs as reflecting evidence of Soviet plans to attack the main U.S. strategic forces in the event of a nuclear war. Its principal justification of various U.S. strategic force modernization measures, including the controversial MX (the new highly accurate ten-warhead missile), was to avoid "a one-sided strategic condition in which the Soviet Union could effectively destroy the whole range of strategic targets in the United States, but we could not effectively destroy a similar range of targets in the Soviet Union." Such a one-sided condition, argued the commission, would be "extremely unstable . . . and would clearly not serve the cause of peace." It even "could tempt the Soviets, in a crisis, to feel they could successfully threaten or even undertake conventional or limited nuclear aggression in the hope that the United States would lack a fully effective response."[7]

Notably, the Scowcroft Commission frontally rejected the notion that the only purpose of the U.S. strategic arsenal was to deter a Soviet strategic attack on the United States:

> The Soviets must continue to believe what has been NATO's doctrine for three decades: that if we or our allies should be attacked—by massive conventional means or otherwise—the United States has the will and the means to defend with the full range of American power. . . . [E]ffective deterrence requires that early in any Soviet consideration of attack, or threat of attack, with conventional forces or chemical or biological weapons, Soviet leaders must understand that they risk an American nuclear response. . . .

> Similarly, effective deterrence requires that the Soviets be convinced that they could not credibly threaten us or our allies with a limited use of nuclear weapons against military targets, in one country or many. . . .

> In order to deter such Soviet threats *we must be able to put at risk those types of Soviet targets—including hardened ones such as military command bunkers and facilities, missile silos, nuclear weapons and other storage, and the rest* [my emphasis]—which the Soviet leaders have given every indication by their actions they value most.[8]

Internal Pentagon guidance for force planners during the early 1980s went even beyond these criteria for effective and credible deterrence to set forth the requirement that the United States must be able to "prevail" over the Soviet Union in a "protracted" nuclear war.[9] Secretary of Defense Caspar Weinberger publicly denied any intention of operating under a "war-winning" strategy, insisting that the planning objective was only to "acquire the capability to respond appropriately to any potential level of aggression against us," including the "prolonged" nuclear strike strategy he attributed to the Soviets. But he refused to disassociate himself from the concept of "prevailing."[10] If, indeed, both the Soviets and the Americans were modernizing their strategic arsenals with the objective of winning a nuclear war, there would be no foreseeable limit to the ever-spiraling arms race.

Strategic defense of the population—and SDI.   A military doctrine that includes the imperative of protecting the population during a strategic nuclear war substantially changes the design requirements for the strategic arsenal from those needed to provide assured destruction or credible deterrence. When added to the deterrence objectives, this objective calls for vastly augmented strategic capabilities.

In the 1960s Secretary of Defense McNamara dropped this objective, which then went under the name of *damage limitation,* because of its highly uncertain technical feasibility, the great cost of even attempting to achieve such a capability, the relative ease with which an opponent could overcome it, and its inconsistency with arms limitation agreements based on the premise that neither side should need any more nuclear weapons than would provide it with an assured-destruction deterrent. McNamara turned down proposals for a nationwide shield of antiballistic missiles and convinced his Soviet counterparts that it would be to the advantage of both superpowers not to attempt to negate the vulnerability of their societies to the other's strategic weapons, since this could only provoke new and awesomely expensive offensive arms buildups to preserve the levels of assured destruction on which deterrence rested. It was this logic of McNamara's, adopted temporarily by Richard Nixon and Henry Kissinger, that produced the ABM treaty of 1972, curtailing ballistic missile defenses, as well as the accompanying accord putting a ceiling on new offensive strategic forces.

The surprise announcement by President Reagan in March 1983 that the United States was now going to make a determined effort to achieve a population defense produced shock waves in the military planning communities of both the United States and the Soviet Union, for it suggested that the doctrines that guided strategic force design and arms control during previous two decades were being thrown overboard.[11]

Background briefings to the press indicated that the president was particularly intrigued with the possibility of accomplishing this goal through the development of a space-based ABM system that, with lasers or other exotic technologies, could efficiently destroy enemy ICBMs just after launch in their "boost phase" before they let loose their multiple warheads. Dubbed "Star Wars" by journalists, the orbiting interceptor idea was soon revealed to be just one element of a mammoth research and development project for a multilayered shield against ICBMs: the Strategic Defense Initiative (SDI). The overarching concept of the SDI is that the ABM system would attack ICBMs at various stages along their trajectories—including liftoff, inertial flight through space, reentry into the atmosphere, and terminal homing in on their targets. Since enemy ICBMs that were missed at the first stage could be attacked at the second stage, and so on, the assumption was that very few would finally get through to their targets.

Proponents of the SDI argued that the feasibility and desirability of a population-defense ABM system looked very different in the light of new technological developments: new and improved means for sensing and discriminating targets, for directing interceptors to targets, and for destroying targets demanded at least an agnostic view toward whether ABMs would prove to be cost-effective.[12]

Opponents of the SDI argued that all of the projections of technical feasibility were highly conjectural, being based on still largely untested technologies and unsupported assertions about a new ability to overcome what has been the stark nuclear-age reality that aids to offensive penetration are cheaper than defensive screens. They also pointed out that the SDI, in its current concept, was directed only at the threat from ICBMs. Even if a perfect defense were someday designed against ICBMs, the population would still be vulnerable to nuclear attacks delivered by nearby submarines, by aircraft, and by clandestine means. In addition, a large-scale commitment to develop the ABM by either superpower would surely challenge the other side's assured-destruction capability, stimulating a new and enormously expensive round of competition in offensive weapons, which then would pose an even larger threat for the ABM system to counter.[13]

Some proponents of the SDI, under the barrage of criticism from respected strategic experts and weapons technologists, retreated to a more limited rationale for justifying the new ABM effort: that the technologies spawned in the quest for the ambitious, and possibly elusive, goal of population defense meanwhile could be applied to good effect in reducing the ICBM threat to the deterrent forces and other military targets, thereby further reducing any incentive the enemy might have to initiate strategic nuclear war.[14]

The end of the Cold War changed the entire context of the SDI debate, as indicated in Chapter 10.

DO ARMS RACES CAUSE WAR?

Apart from the drain on resources that otherwise might be used for more constructive purposes, are high levels of armaments and arms races necessarily bad? As a means of ensuring that adversaries don't dare attack, perhaps arms buildups are preferable to efforts to augment national power by imperialistic expansion, to attempts to subvert an opponent's government, or to direct military blows to disable an opponent. When there is mutual suspicion of a temptation or an inclination to attack, intensive arming by both sides may be the only way to discourage war—by denying the prospect of easy victory to either.

The historical record shows that wars were most frequent between the major powers of Europe in the era characterized by relatively low levels of armament: that is, when military establishments were organized for fighting limited wars of minimum destruction and short duration during the period of the classical balance of power (from the Treaty of Westphalia, 1648, to the French Revolution, 1789). In modern times, as war has become more destructive, the major powers have been more constrained from going to war than previously because of the prospects of large-scale suffering even for those who may emerge victorious.

Most analysts attribute the "long peace" between the United States and the Soviet Union—their forty-year "cold" war—largely to their nuclear balance of terror.[15] The historian John Mueller argues that the emphasis on nuclear weapons is overdone—that the whole panoply of modern mass-destruction warfare has made the direct use of force anachronistic among the great powers.[16]

Just as competitive arming can sometimes help prevent war, however, it can also contribute to bringing on a war.[17] Even if much depends on the political circumstances surrounding particular military balance, we should not concentrate only on nonmilitary variables and forget that armaments can play a crucial role in precipitating war.

There probably are optimal levels of armament to discourage war between adversaries. If the armament of one or both of the parties is either above or below this optimum, war is more likely than if both countries remain at this optimum, even with the same degree of political hostility. The difficulty, of course, is in knowing just where the optimal armament levels are in an adversarial relationship, as well as in inducing both sides to stabilize their arsenals at those levels. At the center of the difficulty is the problem we have already identified: what is perceived by one country or alliance to be the optimum for deterring its opponents may be perceived by the opponents to be intolerably threatening.

Certain kinds of military balances (or imbalances) are inherently more threatening than others, and some of them may provide more incentives to one or both sides to launch an attack. Frequently what is most provocative is an impending dramatic augmentation in an opponent's force levels that seems to threaten an imbalance.

Gross Imbalances

If there exists between intensely antagonistic countries a large imbalance of military power favoring the country dissatisfied with the prevailing political or economic relationship, the imbalance will tempt the dissatisfied but militarily superior country to escalate conflict to the brink of war and, if this does not induce concessions by the adversary, to launch an attack. Japan's military operations against China in the 1930s were this type of aggression. So were Hitler's attacks on Germany's neighbors before World War II, the North Korean invasion of South Korea in 1950, and India's attack on Pakistan in 1971 to prevent Pakistan's suppression of the Bangladesh independence movement. The military aggressor usually needs a clear prospect of victory in order to attack. A substantial imbalance in military capability usually is a crucial and necessary determinant, though not in itself a sufficient cause, of war. The defending country, on the other hand, does not need a clear prospect of victory to be motivated to fight. All it needs is some likelihood of making the war painful enough to the aggressor country to compel it to modify the expectation that violence can obtain what is desired without great cost; sometimes the victim of attack will fight even without the hope of changing the aggressor's calculations simply because surrender is an intolerable alternative.

Where gross imbalances favor the satisfied power, there usually is peace in the sense of a lack of overt warfare. But if peace is an imposed or imperialistic peace over people who believe their values are being intolerably suppressed and if the suppressed people begin to agitate against being dominated, the imperial power, with overwhelming military force at its disposal, may forcibly intervene to put down the challenges to its dominance. The British military intervention against restless North American colonies in 1776 was of this sort, as were the

French wars against the Vietnamese and Algerian independence movements after World War II. Similarly, it was the overwhelming military power of the Soviet Union in Eastern Europe that allowed the Kremlin to order its tanks and troops into Hungary to shoot down those revolting against Soviet dominance in 1956 and then to inflict the same kind of brutal punishment on the Czechoslovakian reformist movement in 1968. The Soviet invasion of Afghanistan in 1979 was a still more recent instance of the attempt to reinforce dominance by military might. In each case, the superpower acted according to its calculation that the victim was a military pushover and lacked allies that might redress the imbalance of power.

As these typical examples of aggression reveal, the initial calculation by an aggressor that it possesses sufficient military superiority to overpower its opponent may easily turn out to be mistaken. Sometimes, as in an imperial power's wars to hold on to its dominions, the aggressor is fighting in only one of several places of tension that may need the commitment of military resources. In such a situation the stronger country may be unwilling to expend human life and material resources beyond a certain point, whereas its nationalist opponents, fighting for what they regard as the integrity and life of their nations, place no limit on the sacrifices they will make. This was the essential dynamic in both the unsuccessful attempt by Britain to put down the American independence movement and the more recent failure of the French to hold on to Algeria; and a related example of a superpower that could not overwhelm a small power because of the small power's greater will to fight is, of course, seen in the U.S. failure in Vietnam from 1964 to 1973.

It is also true that the military superiority an aggressor counts on can be negated by the entry of additional countries into the war. Hitler's attempts in the late 1930s to pick off his European neighbors one by one provoked the formation of the worldwide military coalition that eventually defeated him. The North Korean invasion of South Korea in 1950 appears to have been based on the mistaken assumption that the United States would not intervene in a Korean war.

Despite the many lessons history provides of aggressors' miscalculations of the pertinent balances of power, however, the existence of an apparently large imbalance of military power between adversary countries tends to stimulate the war hawks in the militarily superior country, and the imbalance can be the most significant factor in pushing decision makers into acts that precipitate war.

Challenges to a Prevailing Balance

Another situation in which armament levels can themselves increase the likelihood of wars between political antagonists occurs when it appears virtually certain that the prevailing balance is about to be significantly altered by new deployments. If the prevailing equilibrium of force is challenged by the arms program of side A, and side B, for reasons of domestic economics or other constraints, finds it highly undesirable to initiate compensatory arms programs of its own, side B may be tempted to consider a preventive war while the balance is not yet unfavorable. Serious discussion of a preventive war against the Soviet Union, for example, resulted from the anticipation in policy circles in the United States and the United Kingdom in the period from 1947 to 1949 that the Soviets would soon attain a nuclear-weapons capability likely to unbalance the post–World War II equilibrium of Russian conventional military superiority in Europe on the one side and America's possession of the atomic bomb on the other.

Sometimes a challenge to a prevailing imbalance also is provocative. The outbreak of hostilities between Israel and the Arabs has on a number of occasions been triggered by new Arab arms buildups (sometimes including arms infusions from the Soviet Union) that portended an elimination of Israeli military superiority. In the 1967 war Israel decided to strike first, in a war it regarded as inevitable, while it was still militarily stronger than its enemies. And Japan's bombing of the American fleet at Pearl Harbor, Hawaii, on December 7, 1941, was motivated at least in part by its desire to hobble American naval capabilities in the Pacific before they could be built up in the two-ocean naval program authorized by the U.S. government in 1939.[18]

Inherently Destabilizing Deployments

Even when they are part of an essentially equalized balance, certain types of military deployments can provide an adversary or both adversaries with high incentives to strike first when war threatens. Enemy weapons or troops concentrations that are major elements of the enemy's military capability may be highly vulnerable if attacked in their present locations or condition of readiness. As a political conflict escalates to the brink of war, the existence of such exposed urgent and valuable targets can present an almost irresistible temptation to strike first. If the enemy is assumed to perceive a similar advantage in striking first at one's own vulnerable deployments, the temptations are multiplied and reinforce each other, particularly if the forces that the enemy would use first are themselves immediately vulnerable.

The fact that America's ships deployed at Pearl Harbor in 1941 were not only the core of the military capability the United States could use against Japan in a war (which the Japanese apparently believed was inevitable anyway) but were also clearly sitting ducks for a surprise air attack undoubtedly provided the clinching arguments when Japanese decision makers weighed the risks of their action.

An earlier classic case of military deployments inducing attack resulted from the mobilization of the Russian army against Austria on the eve of World War I. As Austria prepared to humble Serbia militarily in retaliation for the assassination of Archduke Francis Ferdinand by a Serbian nationalist, the Russians, to deter the impending invasion of their client's country, mobilized their own military forces. Because the Russians feared provoking Germany to join with Austria in fulfillment of the terms of the existing German-Austrian alliance, the czar announced that his mobilization was directed only against the Austrian threat to Serbia. However, the Russian armies were so organized that it was impossible for them to engage in a partial mobilization. That the whole army had to get ready to fight unavoidably threatened Germany as well as Austria. Moreover, given the prevailing techniques of warfare in 1914, the country that first completed the mobilization of its forces might well be able to win the decisive, early battles of the war. The consequence was an immediate mobilization of forces by Germany and its declaration of war against Russia.

The Cold War strategic arms competition between the United States and the Soviet Union contained a destabilizing feature of fearsome dimensions: the efforts on each side to maintain capabilities that could hobble the other side's offensive strategic forces in a war. The mere possession of these counterforce capabilities increased the likelihood that a nonnuclear war or other extreme crisis between the superpowers would escalate to a strategic nuclear war: the more effective such capabilities were, the higher the incentive to get in the first strike in an exchange of strategic blows. The most dangerous situation exists when both sides possess substantial strategic counterforce capabilities vulnerable to the other side's counterforce attack. In an escalating war or crisis, each antagonist therefore may feel that it must use or lose its counterforce weapons. Neither would wait to retaliate until it had absorbed the opponent's first strike. (Disabling counterforce strikes could be aimed at either the weapons themselves or the command and control centers from which they are operated, or both. ABMs, if in the arsenal of the side that strikes first, would blunt retaliation by any of the victim's ICBMs that survive the attack or are launched preemptively.) And since each side would probably program its vulnerable strategic forces to be launched on warning of strategic attack by the enemy, the opportunities for terrible miscalculation would be intense. The nightmare is that in an escalating crisis each side rushes to put its forces on high alert and prelaunch readiness—moves interpreted by the other side's intelligence analysts as preparations to launch a preemptive counterforce blow—leading to irresistible pressures on both sides to strike first to preempt the other side's preemption.

Efforts to reduce such dangerous instabilities, discussed in Chapter 10, reflect the growing awareness that particular configurations of arms races are more prone to war or escalation than others.

Clearly, the notion that only political conflict causes wars and that arms races are only the symptoms of political conflict is a vast and dangerous simplification of the complicated relationships between possessing weapons and resorting to violence.

NOTES

1. For a more formal theoretical analysis of many of the relationships looked at in this chapter, see Bruce Bueno de Mesquita, *The War Trap* (New Haven: Yale University Press, 1981).

2. Leonard S. Spector, *Nuclear Ambitions: The Spread of Nuclear Weapons, 1989–1990* (Boulder: Westview, 1990).

3. Fred Charles Iklé, "Can Deterrence Last Out the Century?" *Foreign Affairs* (January 1973), 51(2):267–285; and Paul Nitze, "Deterring Our Deterrent," *Foreign Policy*, 25 (Winter 1976–1977), 195–210.

4. Harold Brown, *Department of Defense Annual Report, Fiscal Year 1982* (Washington, DC: U.S. Department of Defense, January 16, 1981), pp. 38–44.

5. For the development of strategic force–planning concepts through the 1970s, see Lawrence Freedman, *The Evolution of Nuclear Strategy* (New York: St. Martin's, 1983). A lively account of the debates among the strategists is provided by Fred Kaplan, *The Wizards of Armageddon* (New York: Simon & Schuster, 1983).

6. *Report of the President's Commission on Strategic Forces* (Washington, DC: Office of the President, April 6, 1983), pp. 2–3.

7. *Ibid*. p. 6.

8. *Ibid*. pp. 5–6.

9. Richard Halloran, "Pentagon Draws Up First Strategy for Fighting a Long Nuclear War," *New York Times*, May 30, 1982.

10. Leslie Gelb, "Weinberger Calls His 'Basic Outlook' Unchanged," *New York Times*, June 15, 1982. See also Secretary Weinberger's letter to the *Boston Globe*, June 23, 1982.

11. President Ronald Reagan, Address to the Nation, Washington, DC, March 23, 1983; full text in Department of State, *Current Policy*, no. 472.

12. Office of Technology Assessment, Ballistic Missile Defense Technologies (Washington: U.S. Government Printing Office, 1985), pp. 55–64.

13. *Ibid*.

14. Fred S. Hoffmann, "Ballistic Missile Defenses and U.S. National Security," excerpts from a 1983 report prepared for the Undersecretary of Defense for Policy, in Harold Brown, Fred S. Hoffmann, Paul Nitze, and Ronald Reagan, *Essays on Strategy and Diplomacy: The Strategic Defense Initiative* (Claremont, Calif.: Keck Center for International Strategic Studies, 1985), pp. 5–15.

15. John Lewis Gaddis, *The Long Peace: Inquiries into the History of the Cold War* (New York: Oxford University Press, 1987).

16. John Mueller, *Retreat from Doomsday: The Obsolescence of Major War* (New York: Basic Books, 1989).

17. Statistical studies of the incidence of war have not succeeded in establishing any significant correlation between arms races and the onset of war, other than the obvious fact that countries that fight one another must to some extent have armed against one another. Lewis Richardson in *Arms and Security* (Pittsburgh: Boxwood Press, 1960), p. 740, concludes that "the evidence, as far as it goes, is that only a minority of wars have been preceded by arms races." More recent quantitative studies have not contradicted Richardson's findings. See J. David Singer and Melvin Small, *The Wages of War, 1816–1965: A Statistical Handbook* (New York: Wiley, 1972).

18. See two articles by Samuel P. Huntington: "Arms Races: Prerequisites and Results," *Public Policy* (1958), 41–83; and "To Choose Peace or War," *United States Naval Institute Proceedings, 83* (April 1957), 360–366.

CHAPTER 6

The Culture of War

National inclinations to go to war are shaped significantly by deeply ingrained habits of heart and mind respecting the use of force. As indicated in Chapters 4 and 5, these habits are strongly influenced by the geopolitical situation of the country: its need to struggle against other countries in order to protect or enhance its security and well-being, and its power for effectively prosecuting these struggles through peaceful or violent means. These mostly material circumstances affect and are given subjective meaning by the belief systems of the country's peoples, producing a national culture regarding its conduct in its international struggles. I have coined the term *culture of war* to denote how countries' belief systems affect their use of military force.

The various national cultures of war are all housed within a global culture, featuring a persisting pattern of attitudes and behavior conditioned by the anarchic structure of the world polity. But the persisting global culture of war also exhibits variations across the centuries, as developments in technology, economics, and politics have altered war's characteristics and the relations between force and diplomacy.

THE PERSISTING LARGER PATTERN

Virtually all countries resemble each other insofar as they must all exist in an anarchic international system that places a premium on and legitimizes being able to maintain one's interests with force. Throughout history, therefore, war has been regarded as a normal aspect of international politics.

Countries also resemble each other in regarding large-scale violence among their own citizens as an illegitimate aberration. Within countries

100

recurrent intergroup or antigovernment violence, even the recourse to violence by government to repress dissidence, is generally viewed as an indication that something is drastically wrong, either with those who are behaving violently or with the structure and processes of the political system. Domestically, if individuals are unable to secure their possessions against predators or prevent presumed rights from being violated, the usual expectation is that the official agencies of the whole community—the state—will be available to restrain the aggressive parties, to adjudicate the conflict, and to enforce the results of such adjudication. Pervasive murder and mayhem are held to be inconsistent with the norms of domestic civil society and not simply a continuation of politics by other means.

The global culture of violence, looked at in the large, thus exhibits a double standard: people the world over feel constrained to act nonviolently and with basic civility in handling their conflicts with comembers of their national community but feel relatively unconstrained in using brute force when acting as a nation in prosecuting their conflicts with other nations.[1] I use the qualified term *relatively unconstrained* because within the generally permissive international culture of violence there have been significant variations in attitudes from era to era and from place to place concerning when it is legitimate to go to war and what moral limits should be put on how war is fought. Some of these changes in attitude can be shown to have affected national decisions on war and peace in important ways.

VARIATIONS IN ATTITUDES TOWARD THE USE OF FORCE IN INTERNATIONAL RELATIONS

The contemporary world's corpus of norms and legal conventions on the use of force internationally have been derived in substantial measure from the "just war" concepts that were formulated in the Catholic Church during the first four centuries after Christ and subsequently refined in theological discourse and papal pronouncements during the medieval era.

In contrast to the dominant pre-Christian "might-makes-right" philosophy of statecraft,[2] Catholic just-war theory and its modern secular derivations have provided criteria for governments and publics in determining when it is permissible to begin war (*jus ad bellum*, justice of war) and what kinds of acts are permissible in fighting a war (*jus in bello,* justice in war). This is not to say that these criteria have in fact acted as strong constraints on the use of force. But they do provide standards against which governments can, and sometimes are, held accountable by their constituents and by other governments and peoples.

Just Cause

The central *jus ad bellum* principle is that war is morally wrong unless fought for what is considered a just cause. There will always be debate over the precise definition of this inherently ambiguous concept, but discourse through the ages has rather consistently ruled out or ruled in certain reasons for going to war: Simple plunder—the use of force to rob others of their wealth or deprive them of their land for reasons of one's own greed—is obviously illegitimate (this does not mean it is all that rare; indeed, a totally amoral realism might not condemn it). At the other extreme, self-defense to counter an attack against one's homeland is universally regarded (except by a minority of absolute pacifists) as a legitimate cause for going to war. The universal approval of self-defense, however, makes it likely that those initiating war for morally suspect motives will drape their actions under the self-defense mantle and even go so far as to provoke their adversary into striking the first blow.

Opposing aggression.   In modern times, the legal concept for unjustly initiating war is *aggression;* conversely, a country countering aggression has a presumptively just cause for war. Outlawed in both the Covenant of the League of Nations and the Charter of the United Nations, aggression predictably has become the way every party to a war characterizes the actions of its enemy, making its own behavior, by definition, self-defense. Thus, in the Vietnam War Hanoi's justification for pouring paramilitary and later mainline military forces into South Vietnam in the 1960s was that they were required to defend the country (all of Vietnam) against U.S. intervention in the country's civil war—the latest in a series of imperialist aggressions. Washington's justification for deploying combat units into South Vietnam and subjecting North Vietnam to aerial bombardment was that the actions were part of a collective self-defense effort at the request of Saigon to defend South Vietnam's independence against communist aggression.

In an effort to infuse the legal norm against aggression with some objectifiable meaning that was not so susceptible to cynical manipulation, the United Nations established a special committee to clarify the concept. The recommendations of the committee, adopted by the General Assembly in 1974, define aggression as "the use of armed forces by a State against the sovereignty, territorial integrity, or political independence of another State, or in any other matter inconsistent with the Charter of the United Nations." The resolution specifically singles out the "first use of armed force," with the exception of "cases in which the use of force is lawful"; but the "lawful" uses of force are not enumerated. It does, however, enumerate (while stipulating that the list is not exhaustive) acts that qualify as aggression:

(a) The invasion or attack by the armed forces of a State of the territory of another State, or any military occupation, however temporary, resulting from such invasion or attack, or any annexation by the use of force of the territory of another State or part thereof;

(b) Bombardment by the armed forces of a State against the territory of another State or the use of any weapons by a State against the territory of another State;

(c) The blockade of the ports or coasts of a State by the armed forces of another State;

(d) An attack by the armed forces of a State on the land, sea or air forces, or marine and air fleets of another State;

(e) The use of armed forces of one State which are within the territory of another State with the agreement of the receiving State, in contravention of the condition provided for in the agreement or any extension of their presence in such territory beyond the termination of the agreement;

(f) The action of a State in allowing its territory, which it has placed at the disposal of another State, to be used by that other State for perpetrating an act of aggression against a third State;

(g) The sending by or on behalf of a State of armed bands, groups, irregulars or mercenaries, which carry out acts of armed force against another State of such gravity as to amount to the acts listed above, or its substantial involvement therein.[3]

A problem with this UN exercise in defining aggression is that the larger the range of acts deemed to be aggression, the more justified countries feel in using military force to put down such actions, with or without UN authorization. Ironically, rather than reducing the role of force in world politics, the good intention of forging an international consensus against military aggression runs the risk of producing the opposite: an increase in self-righteous military action by states that have convinced themselves they are upholding the rules of the international community.

Anticipating legalistic or politically unscrupulous attempts to expand the concept of self-defense and other lawful uses of force to cover military moves that are themselves acts of aggression, the resolution stipulates that "no consideration of whatever nature, whether political, economic, military, or otherwise, may serve as justification for aggression."

Yet, in deference to the concerns of Third World governments, the following potentially gaping loophole is provided:

> Nothing in this Definition . . . could in any way prejudice the right
> to self-determination, freedom and independence, as derived
> from the Charter, of peoples forcibly deprived of that right . . . ,
> particularly peoples under colonial and racist regimes or other
> forms of alien domination; nor the right of these peoples to strug-
> gle to that end and to seek and receive support . . . .[4]

The last qualification leaves open the legal status of military intervention by external powers to aid struggles for self-determination and the like, especially when such intervention is requested by liberation movements to counter governments using force against them.

Legitimate and illegitimate intervention. The traditional legal norms of the international system, often referred to as the Westphalian norms (see p. 106), give pride of place to national sovereignty and the noninterference by countries in one another's domestic affairs. The leading provisions in the 1974 UN resolution on aggression are in this sense fully consonant with the larger corpus of international law and with the writings of political philosophers who have bothered to deal with this subject (there are very few). This tradition contains what might appear to be a highly restrictive set of criteria for the legal permissibility of military intervention across national borders. State practice, to be sure, has often departed from the professed norms.

Adapting a formulation of the nineteenth-century philosopher John Stuart Mill to contemporary realities, just-war theorist Michael Walzer, offers a restatement of the requirements that must be met, singly or in combination, for military intervention across state boundaries to be legitimate:

> —when a particular set of boundaries clearly contains two or more political communities one of which is already engaged in a large scale military struggle for independence; that is, when what is at issue is secession or "national liberation";
>
> —when the boundaries have already been crossed by the armies of a foreign power, even if the crossing has been called for by one of the parties in a civil war, that is when what is at issue is counterintervention;
>
> —when the violation of human rights within a set of boundaries is so terrible that it makes talk of community or self-determination or "arduous struggle" seem cynical and irrelevant, that is, in cases of enslavement or massacre.[5]

These criteria, Walzer concedes, may well "open the way for just wars that are not fought in self-defense or against aggression in the strict sense." And this properly is their purpose. But he cautions that "they need to be worked out with great care. Given the readiness of states to invade one another, revisionism is a risky business."[6]

Rules for Fighting War

Over the course of the history of international relations there have been more dramatic changes in the conduct of warfare than in the causes of war. Although the ideas about what constitute justifiable reasons for going to war have remained relatively constant over the centuries, there has been a growing sense that the traditional *jus in bello* norms have become anachronistic.

Medieval Europe.   War in the Middle Ages, like interpersonal dueling, was regarded as an honorable undertaking among feudal princes and was supposed to be fought chivalrously and according to the just-war rules of the Church. Certain weapons were held to be unfair, levels of violence were to be proportionate to the stakes at issue, and non-combatants were to be spared. The rule book could be thrown away, however, if the war was against Muslims (as during the Crusades) or other non-Christians, or even Christians outside of the Roman Catholic faith.

The wars of religion.   With the sixteenth-century breakup of Christendom into its Protestant and Catholic camps—each side regarding the other as doing the work of the devil—war among Christian states became as vicious as wars against the infidel. Defenders of the faith not only felt justified in intervening with force in another state on behalf of their coreligionists, but all chivalrous restraints on fighting were discarded. One of the most brutal periods in world history was that of the horrible Thirty Years' War in central Europe, between Protestants and Catholics, which killed nearly half of the total population in the German and Austrian regions. In many localities the countryside was so devastated of sources of food that survivors resorted to cannibalism.[7]

The period of classical diplomacy.   The Peace of Westphalia, promulgated in 1648, was based on the realization by the princes of Europe that in wars of religion there could be no hope of maintaining rules of proportionality and protections of citizens. Accordingly, they agreed that henceforth the predominantly Protestant states should remain Protestant and the predominantly Catholic states should remain Catholic, with each tolerating the minority religion within its jurisdiction. Moreover, the Westphalian negotiators affirmed two corollary principles of interstate relations, advocated by Hugo Grotius and other leading philosophers of international law as necessary for preventing the kind of carnage Europe had just experienced: (1) the government of each country is unequivocally sovereign within its territorial jurisdiction; and (2) countries must not interfere in each other's domestic affairs.

Remarkably, for nearly a century and a half following the Thirty Years' War, even though wars were plentiful, the behavior of the great powers toward each other did approximate the Westphalian norms. Reinforced by the diplomatic and military requirements of effective performance in the classical balance of power (see Chapter 4, pp. 77–79), the monarchs of the day by and large respected one another's sovereign authority, refrained from sponsoring subversive movements within one another's territorial jurisdictions, and when they went to war, did so for limited goals and with constrained fighting strategies.

The era of nationalism. The successor era of nationalism (which is still with us), however, was not compatible with the culture of moderate statecraft and rule-constrained warfare. Because war was fought for the vital interests of the nation—its way of life and its very survival—or not at all, wars once started were very difficult to terminate before one side or the other had won decisively. Ordinary citizens provided the bulk of the fighting forces for the nation in arms; new technologies of mechanized and mass-destruction warfare blurred distinctions between the home front and the field of military engagement; targeted military industries and supply lines were located in centers of population—circumstances not compatible with the rules of proportional violence and scrupulous regard for the safety of noncombatants. (In the nineteenth century some wars—the Crimean War and the Franco-Prussian War, for example—still conformed to the more limited classical model; the new model of total war was seen most starkly in the wars of Napoleon and the U.S. Civil War).

The twentieth century. The Hague Peace Conferences of 1899 and 1907 were a culmination of efforts by international lawyers and humanitarians in the nineteenth century to shore up the traditional rules of war against the erosive effects of the new military technologies and societal changes. Despite all of their loopholes, the Hague rules still constitute the core of the modern war rules that appear in the military manuals of the armed forces of most countries.

The Hague Convention Respecting the Laws and Customs of War on Land, signed in 1907, prohibits "attack or bombardment, by whatever means, of towns, villages, dwellings, or buildings which are undefended." It also requires signatories to spare, as far as possible, "buildings dedicated to religion, art, science, or charitable purposes, historic monuments, hospitals, and places where the sick and wounded are collected," but adds the elastic qualification: "provided they are not being used at the time for military purposes."[8] The parallel Convention Concerning the Bombardment by Naval Forces prohibits attacks on undefended ports and towns, but then states that "military works, military or naval establishments, depots of arms or war matériel, workshops or plans which could be utilized for the needs of the hostile fleet or arm, and ships of war in the harbor, are not . . . included in this prohibition."[9]

After World War I introduced bombing from airplanes, the Hague rules regarding naval bombardment were extended to cover this new form of warfare. The Hague Rules of Aerial Warfare, adopted in 1932, stipulate that aerial bombardment is "legitimate only when directed at a military objective, that is to say, an object of which the injury or destruction would constitute a distinct military advantage to the belligerent. The rules characterize these legitimate bombing targets as "military forces, military works, military establishments or depots, factories constituting important and well-known centers engaged in the manufacture of arms, ammunition or distinctively military supplies; lines of communication or transportation used for military purposes." The rules prohibit aerial bombardment of civilian populations and structures "not in the immediate neighborhood of the operations of land forces" but explicitly allow for aerial attacks on some civilian centers "provided there exists some reasonable presumption that the military concentration is sufficiently important to justify such bombardment."[10]

Thus, at the start of World War II the rules of war on the books, with their explicit provisions for "military necessity," could be read as a virtual license to kill and destroy everything and anything that was a part of the enemy's war-fighting machine. And this was indeed what happened. Lawyers on both sides found legal justification in the Hague rules for massively bombing anything that was contributing to the war effort, especially factories and lines of communication and transportation, even if they happened to be located within centers of civilian population. By the middle of World War II even the Hague rules' limiting criterion of "military necessity" was dropped as the belligerents engaged in calculated terror bombing of each other's cities. The purpose, explained in various government directives, was to spread destruction over a large area to "destroy morale," and "to secure the heaviest possible moral and shock effect," thereby ensuring that the enemy's "capacity for armed resistance is fatally weakened."[11]

The nuclear age. By the time the first nuclear bombs were ready to be dropped on the industrial cities of Hiroshima and Nagasaki in August 1945, most of the responsible decision makers had no qualms about killing tens of thousands of civilians in an aerial attack on an enemy city. World War II had already produced at least fifty million fatalities, nearly thirty-five million of them civilians, and terror bombing of enemy population centers was nothing new.

Yet the atomic incineration of Hiroshima and Nagasaki produced a vast cultural aftershock: the realization that another world war might spell the extinction of the human species. A new antiwar culture emerged, more amorphous than earlier pacifist movements (see Chapter 8) but more widespread than ever, pervading even the military establishments of the superpowers, where strategies for deterring war through keeping its awesome horrors omnipresent gained ascendancy over strategies for fighting war.

Winston Churchill, never one to shirk from use of force as an instrument of diplomacy, articulated the likely implications of the emergent antiwar culture: "It may well be that we shall, by a process of sublime irony, have reached a stage in the story where safety will be the sturdy child of terror and survival the twin brother of annihilation."[12]

The term *Cold War* itself expressed the conviction in both the United States and the USSR, even among factions most hostile to the rival superpower, that the enmity should not, could not, become a hot war.[13]

These convictions were reinforced as both sides developed "Assured Destruction" strategic nuclear arsenals—each capable of surviving the largest strategic attack the other could launch and retaliating with sufficient lethal power to destroy the other as a functioning society. The Mutual Assured Destruction (MAD) deterrent relationship was codified and institutionalized in a series of strategic arms control agreements, beginning with the SALT accords of 1972 and continuing with the strategic arms reduction (START) negotiations of the late 1980s and early 1990s.

But the MAD culture contained a fundamental moral and strategic paradox. To deter war between the superpowers reliably, the MAD arsenals would have to be accompanied not only by credible threats on both sides to turn any war between them into a strategic nuclear war, but by strategies and deployments that would ensure that any such strategic war would escalate to holocaust levels.

Deeply troubled by these implications, the National Conference of U.S. Catholic Bishops issued a pastoral letter in 1983 alleging that official U.S. strategy was wholly inconsistent with any just-war principles worth the name, and that it would be morally impermissible for anyone to attempt to implement it. "We do not perceive any situation," said the bishops, "in which the deliberate initiation of nuclear warfare, on however restricted a scale, can be morally justified." Nor was it morally permissible, they concluded, even to *retaliate* with nuclear weapons in response to a nuclear attack. But the Catholic bishops stopped short of condemning outright the *threat* to use nuclear weapons for the purpose of preventing the weapons from being actually used. Instead, they relied on the formulation by Pope John II that "in current conditions 'deterrence' based on balance, certainly not as an end in itself but as a step on the way toward a progressive disarmament, may be judged morally acceptable."[14] The pope's position provided a bridge between the strong antinuclearism among the American Catholic bishops and the continued endorsement of nuclear deterrence by the German and French Catholic churches, for as long as the Soviets retained conventional military superiority in Europe.

Stimulated by the international controversy stirred by the Catholic discourse, the United Methodist Council of Bishops issued their own document on what they called the "nuclear crisis." The Methodists went even further than the American Catholic bishops in their nuclear abolitionism, arguing that "the moral case for nuclear deterrence, even as an interim ethic, has been undermined by unrelenting arms escalation. Deterrence no longer serves, if it ever did, as a strategy that facilitates disarmament."[15]

Meanwhile, at official levels, the need to live with mutual-holocaust arsenals produced another kind of anxiety: namely, that the MAD superpower relationship could paralyze the ability of decision makers to relate force to diplomacy in a hostile world, where credible military options were still deemed necessary to protect national interests. The effort to revive confidence on the part of political leaders in Washington and Moscow in the usability of their military prowess, especially on behalf of allies who might be bullied by the rival superpower, prompted military planners on both sides to develop strategies and weapons for fighting controlled nuclear war.

The result was a MAD-*plus* world of deployments and strategies for using strategic nuclear forces flexibly in a wide range of attack scenarios against military targets, while withholding sufficient city-destroying capabilities to deter the enemy from escalating to holocaust levels.[16] Presumably, the belligerents would be induced by their mutual fear of national (if not species) suicide to play by the city-avoidance rules. The ascendancy of this new strategic culture—dubbed by critics as having gone "from MAD to NUTS"[17]—was reflected in the continuing growth of the strategic war-fighting arsenals of the superpowers into the late 1980s, despite the SALT and START accords, to the point where each side was deploying well in excess of 10,000 strategic nuclear warheads.

A parallel effort to escape from the strategic pitfalls and moral implications of the MAD world was President Reagan's Strategic Defense Initiative (SDI), a research and development program announced in

March 1983 that was directed toward the deployment of a defensive shield capable of protecting the country from nuclear attack. Arguing that "to rely on the specter of retaliation" to deter nuclear war was "a sad commentary on the human condition," Reagan asked

> Wouldn't it be better to save lives than to avenge them? . . .
>
> What if free people could live secure in the knowledge that their security did not rest upon the threat of instant U.S. retaliation to deter a Soviet attack, that we could intercept and destroy strategic ballistic missiles before they reached our own soil or that of our allies?

His answer was to

> call upon the scientific community, . . . those who gave us nuclear weapons, to turn their great talents now to the cause of mankind and world peace, to give us the means of rendering these nuclear weapons impotent and obsolete.[18]

The new culture of strategic war in Reagan's vision contemplated a hypothetical duel between offensive nuclear missiles and futuristic defensive weapons deployed largely in outer space, a battle that would spare the populations of the belligerents. Presumably, the defense would dominate the offense, and everyone would know this in advance, so neither side would be tempted to start such a war. But in contrast to the MAD philosophy, if deterrence failed, the nation (and humanity) would survive while the aggressor was being defeated.

The thrust, if not the motive, of both the "discriminate deterrence" and the "Star Wars" schools of strategic thought was to make the world, even in the nuclear age, safe for great-power warfare. If weapons would shoot mainly against weapons and not cities, then war could be waged proportionately and noncombatants could be spared; war, happily, could once again become a normal instrument of great-power diplomacy. And sooner or later, under the assumption that the risks could be controlled, nuclear-armed adversaries would come to blows.

AFTER THE COLD WAR

The demise of the Cold War rivalry between the two nuclear-armed superpowers interrupted the new arms race in strategic war-fighting capabilities and the revival of nuclear war-fighting doctrines. A series of strategic nuclear arms reduction agreements quickly ensued under the premise that such weaponry could be drastically reduced now that war between the superpowers had become politically unthinkable.

But war has not yet become unthinkable between other countries, and some of them, such as Iraq and Israel before and during the 1990–1991 Gulf War, are inclined to use, or threaten to use, the most lethal weapons they possess or can obtain.

No longer able to rely dependably on their superpower protectors, and consequently less controllable by them, the countries in the Middle East, the Persian Gulf, Africa, and South Asia are, if anything, less constrained than during the Cold War to use force to prosecute their standing resource and jurisdictional conflicts and to settle old intercommunal scores. Lebanon remains a tinderbox likely to spark a regional conflagration at any time between her counterintervening neighbors. The region-wide rivalry between fundamentalist and modernizing Muslims threatens to explode into an era of wars of religion reminiscent of the century of Protestant-Catholic conflict in Europe at the end of the Middle Ages.

The post–Cold War breakup of Yugoslavia and the resulting revival of brutal interethnic violence in the Balkans–where occurred the eruptions of 1914 that brought on World War I–hardly presage an era of peace. No less volatile and potentially just as brutal are the ethnic and nationality conflicts loosed in the areas of Eurasia formerly under Soviet control.

Nor have the Americans or the Russians indicated that they have reduced their propensity to use force in conflicts with *weaker* opponents. The habit of unsheathing a terrible swift sword against those who defy one's will was very much in evidence in the Bush administration's 1989 invasion of Panama to depose and capture General Noriega, and in the high-technology Desert Storm operation to oust Saddam Hussein from Kuwait. The Russians, even while heavily preoccupied with internal economic reconstruction, have felt compelled to dispatch their military forces to former republics of the USSR in order to protect Russian ethnic minorities from repression.

In short, the changes in the the structure of international society occasioned by the disintegration of the superpower-run Cold War coalitions were not in themselves sufficient to bring on an era of peace. The inherited culture of violence, in both its international and national dimensions, continues to play a large role in disposing countries to resort to threats or the use of force in prosecuting their international conflicts.

With the culture of war still exercising great weight in world affairs, a crucial determinant of whether a particular conflict will be managed violently or nonviolently is the quality of diplomacy on the part of the governments involved: the subject of Chapter 7.

NOTES

1. Reinhold Niebuhr, *Moral Man and Immoral Society* (New York: Scribners, 1932) explores the sources and implications of these paradoxical attitudes toward domestic violence and international war.

2. The prototype of prevailing pre-Christian theory and practice is provided in Thucydides's account of the justifications the Athenians offered for their brutal treatment of the Melians in the Peloponnesian War. Thucydides, *The Peloponnesian War.* Translated by Rex Warner. London: Cassell, 1954), pp. 358–366.

3. "Definition of Aggression," United Nations General Assembly Resolution 3314 (XXIX 1974), adopted by the General Assembly without a vote on December 14, 1974.

4. *Ibid.*

5. Michael Walzer, *Just and Unjust Wars: A Moral Argument with Historical Illustrations* (New York: Basic Books, 1977), p. 90.

6. *Ibid.*

7. On the conduct of war in Europe during the era leading up to and including the Thirty Years War, see Evan Luard, *War in International Society: A Study of International Society* (New Haven, Conn.: Yale University Press, 1987), pp. 337–345.

8. Convention (IV) Respecting the Laws and Customs of War on Land, signed at the Hague on October 18, 1907, in Josef Goldblat, *Agreements for Arms Control: A Critical Survey* (London: Taylor & Francis, 1982), pp. 122–124.

9. Convention (IX) Concerning Bombardment by Naval Forces in Time of War, signed at the Hague on October 18, 1907, in Goldblat, *Agreements for Arms Control,* pp. 127–129.

10. Hague Rules of Aerial Warfare (1932), quoted by Myers S. McDougal and Florentino P. Feliciano, *Law and Minimum World Public Order: The Legal Regulation of International Coercion* (New Haven, Conn.: Yale University Press, 1961), pp. 643–645.

11. *U.S. Strategic Bombing Survey, Overall Report,* Vol. 2 (Washington, D.C.: U.S. Government Printing Office, 1945), p. 71; and the Bombing Survey's *Report on the Effects of Strategic Bombing on the Japanese War Economy* (Washington, D.C.: U.S. Government Printing Office, 1946), pp. 37–38.

12. Winston Churchill, speech in the House of Commons, *Hansard Parliamentary Debates*, 5th series (March 1, 1955), vol. 537 cols. 1894–1895.

13. John Lewis Gaddis, *The Long Peace: Inquiries into the History of the Cold War* (New York: Oxford University Press, 1987). An alternative hypothesis is advanced by the historian John Mueller in his *Retreat from Doomsday: The Obsolescence of Major War* (New York: Basic Books, 1989). Mueller argues that even if nuclear weapons had never been invented, the superpowers would have been deterred by the prospect of another war on the scale of World War II. He views the ascendancy of an antiwar culture in the industrially developed world as the maturing of an evolutionary process, albeit proceeding with fits and starts, traceable back to the reactions to the Napoleonic Wars and the U.S. Civil War and operating on both rational and subrational levels. On the level of rational calculation of national interests, societies have come to realize that modern war is antithetical to prosperity and economic growth. On the deeper psychological level, Mueller finds war to have become "a thoroughly bad and repulsive idea . . . like dueling and slavery, subrationally unthinkable and therefore obsolescent" (pp. 110–116).

14. National Conference of Catholic Bishops on War and Peace, *The Challenge of Peace: God's Promise and Our Response* (Washington, D.C.: United States Catholic Conference, 1983).

15. United Methodist Council of Bishops, *In Defense of Creation: The Nuclear Crisis and a Just Peace* (Nashville, Tenn.: Graded Press, 1986).

16. A systematically argued case for MAD-plus capabilities was published as a Report of the Commission on Integrated Long-Term Strategy, titled *Discriminate Deterrence* (Washington, D.C.: U.S. Government Printing Office, 1988). Chaired by Fred C. Ikle and Albert Wohlstetter, the members of the commission (all of whom signed the report) included Anne L. Armstrong, Zbigniew Brzezinski, William P. Clark, W. Graham Claytor, Jr., Andrew J. Goodpaster, James L. Holloway III, Samuel P. Huntington, Henry A. Kissinger, Joshua Lederberg, Bernard A. Schriever, and John W. Vessey.

17. Spurgeon M. Keeney, Jr., and Wolfgang K. H. Panofsky, "Mad versus Nuts: Can Doctrine or Weaponry Remedy the Mutual Hostage Relationship of the Superpowers?" *Foreign Affairs* (Winter 1981/82), 60(2) 287–304.

18. Ronald Reagan, Address to the Nation, Washington D.C., March 23, 1983, U.S. Department of State, *Current Policy* No. 472.

CHAPTER 7

The Role of Diplomacy

Lacking a powerful central arbiter of conflicts among them, countries in the nation-state system characteristically prosecute their international conflicts by bargaining, sometimes peacefully, sometimes violently. Bargaining involves offering or withholding positive inducement and threatening or easing threats in order to persuade the other party to accept particular outcomes. Diplomacy, the officially conducted bargaining process among national governments, is normally an admixture of the positive and the coercive. How such diplomatic bargaining is conducted can determine whether adversaries come to blows or find other ways of dealing with the situation that has brought them into conflict.

Scenario A: The structural factors are adverse to peace. The parties to the conflict have been locked in a global power rivalry for fifteen years. Each of their defense establishments has been sized and configured under the assumption that the other is its principal enemy. Now, in a confrontation over an issue of vital geopolitical significance to both of them, their military forces are deployed in menacing formations, ready to engage in lethal combat. And yet, as in the Cuban missile crisis of October 1962, war is avoided.

Scenario B: The protagonists are structurally independent of one another, being located in different regions of the world and lacking pretensions to global hegemony. They have had a long-standing quarrel, however, over their competing claims to sovereignty of a group of sparsely populated oceanic islands that are only of tertiary economic and military value to each of them. And yet, as in the Falkland Island War of 1982, they come to blows.

War is avoided in the Scenario A, where the basic situation is highly conducive to the outbreak of hostilities. In Scenario B, where war is not implied by the basic situation, hostilities erupt. *Why?*

An essential piece of the story in these and other cases of violent and nonviolent management of international conflict is *diplomacy*. War or peace are rarely, if ever, completely foreordained simply by the situation. The decisions of the adversaries to fight or settle are almost always the resultants of an exchange of offers (some seriously discussed, some rejected out of hand) and threats (which may or may not be regarded as credible or worrisome). Not only the substance of the offers and threats, but also the skill with which they are delivered and elaborated—by the antagonists themselves or by intermediaries—will often be a crucial determinant of whether war breaks out.

This chapter focuses on four prototypical cases of diplomacy that played an important role in contributing to the onset of war: British diplomacy in the summer of 1914; the post–World War I "peace diplomacy" of the victors; the interactions between Washington and Tokyo in the summer and fall of 1941; and the U.S.-Iraq relationship preceding Saddam Hussein's 1990 invasion of Kuwait.

The requirements of successful war-avoidance diplomacy will be discussed in Part II.

CASE 1. BRITISH EQUIVOCATION FOLLOWING SARAJEVO

There was much in the structure of international politics in the summer of 1914 that propelled the great powers into the first "world war" since the Napoleonic wars at the beginning of the previous century. Europe was in a loose bipolar configuration—the most dangerous kind of polarization (see Chapter 3)—pitting the Triple Entente of France, Russia, and Britain against the Triple Alliance of Germany, Austria-Hungary, and Italy, and making it likely that a war between any member of one camp against any member of the other camp would plunge the whole continent into war. But the two-way polarization was not sufficiently tight or disciplined to prevent members from getting into wars that were not in the interests of the whole coalition. Rather, the rival coalitions were loose overlays, not really limiting the sovereign autonomy of the states, on top of a complex set of bilateral rivalries of widely varying significance to different members of each camp. One of these rivalries, the competition between Russia and Austria-Hungary for hegemony over the Slavic peoples in southeast Europe, provided the critical mass for the explosive chain reaction following the June 28, 1914, assassination in Sarajevo of the visiting Austrian archduke.

But the scope of the chain reaction of July and August 1914, although highly determined by the international structure and volatile nationalistic animosities of the day, was not irrevocably given by the situation. Skillful diplomacy might have been able to avoid the seemingly inevitable war between Austria and Serbia even after the assassination of the archduke; at the least, it could have localized and quarantined the conflict so as to avoid sucking the great powers into a continentwide and eventually intercontinental war: a horrible paroxysm of violence that left ten million dead and twenty million wounded and, in the end, only exacerbated the systemic instabilities that brought on the war.

British diplomacy in particular bears major responsibility for allowing (and inadvertently encouraging) the Balkan conflict to expand into world war. Kaiser Wilhelm II of Germany, of course, deserves most of the blame heaped on him by historians for encouraging Austria to humiliate Serbia and for his ignorant assumption that Germany's threats to counter a Russian intervention would deter the Tsar rather than provoke him. It fell to London, however, to counter-deter Germany decisively from going to war against Russia (the prospect of the activation of the Franco-Russian alliance did not in itself threaten the Kaiser's alliance with likely military defeat). Instead, during the four weeks between the assassination in Sarajevo and Austria's commencement of military action against Belgrade on July 28—which was followed during the next few days by the irreversible mobilization of the armed forces of Russia, Germany, and France—the British government maintained a posture of neutrality, while desperately trying to organize a peace conference and to mediate the conflict. Ironically, London's well-meaning peace diplomacy was a crucial cause of Berlin's fatal miscalculation that it could win the impending war.

In a careful reassessment of the voluminous diplomatic and historical materials, Jack Levy finds "German perceptions of the strong likelihood of British neutrality" to be "the key to the escalation of the crisis." Levy attributes these German perceptions largely to the "British failure to give a clear and timely commitment in support of its allies."[1]

British Foreign Secretary Sir Edward Grey was evidently banking on the improved Anglo-German relationship of the previous three years to give his statesmanship credibility in Berlin. Grey did warn Berlin informally that in the event of a German attack on France, he could not guarantee that Britain would continue to stand aside. Historians of the period point to concerns in the British cabinet that a deterrent threat would strengthen hard-line elements around the Kaiser and reduce the influence of the peace faction led by Chancellor Bethmann-Hollweg. In fact, British equivocation did just the opposite. Not only did it make Kaiser Wilhelm even more responsive to the hard-liners' argument that Britain would not actually fight on behalf of its traditional rivals, Russia and France, but it also strengthened the hand of General von Moltke and other military leaders committed to the Schlieffen Plan for attacking France through Belgium (see Chapter 4)—the act that precipitated Britain's entry into the war on August 4.[2]

Two days before, upon Germany's invasion of Luxembourg, the British Government did finally warn Berlin that a military invasion of neutral Belgium would be regarded as an act of war against Britain and demanded that Berlin state immediately that it would respect Belgian neutrality. The Kaiser had second thoughts, but General Von Moltke told him it was too late to turn back. German troops poured across the Luxembourg-Belgium border. Britain declared war. In the capitals of all the belligerents the line henceforth was that they had no alternative.

CASE 2. 1919–1939: THE DIPLOMACY OF THE PEACE AS A CAUSE OF WORLD WAR II

The entry of the United States into World War I (provoked by Germany's submarine warfare against U.S. trans-Atlantic shipping) transformed the war aims of the anti-German coalition from the traditional European diplomatic objective of defeating a would-be imperial hegemon into a crusade, in President Woodrow Wilson's words, to "make the world safe for democracy"—a war "to end all wars." The enlarged aims, elaborated in Wilson's Fourteen Points, featured "open covenants of peace, openly arrived at," a diplomacy in which "there shall be no private understandings of any kind" the "removal, so far as possible, of all economic barriers . . . among all the nations," the reduction of national armaments "to the lowest point consistent with domestic safety;" the "freest opportunity for autonomous self-development" for the peoples of Austria-Hungary, and a "general association of nations . . . formed under specific covenants for the purpose of affording mutual guarantees of political independence and territorial integrity to great and small states alike.[3] But by transforming what started as a pure power-political conflict into a righteous crusade for a new world order, the American president—ironically—legitimated the postwar efforts of his European counterparts to impose the victors' harsh peace on their defeated enemies.

Woodrow Wilson came to Paris asking for a peace that would be generous to the defeated countries, a peace of universal justice. It should provide for the self-determination of peoples and for general disarmament. Above all, and of greatest urgency, the postwar arrangements must include a League of Nations to supervise the peace and promote justice through common international action to resolve conflicts and dissuade aggression.[4]

Wilson's counterparts at the Versailles Peace Conference, however, were agents for both the historic power interests of their respective countries and for the popular nationalistic sentiments whipped up by the governments in order to sustain support for the long and bloody conflict (The French lost over 1.5 million lives and the British 917,000, as compared with 127,000 Americans.[5]) They saw the opportunity to reduce Germany's power fundamentally through a punitive peace. Prime Minister Lloyd George of Britain was particularly anxious to take over most of Germany's colonial commerce. French premier Georges Clemenceau, representing a vindictive French nation, was determined to prune its rival down to a minor weight in the new European balance by subjecting Germany to a combination of territorial compensations and financial reparations obligations and by forcing her to disarm her military establishment drastically.

Although the end of the fighting in 1918 was officially defined as an armistice, official representatives of the German government were not allowed full participation in the Versailles Peace Conference. The Germans and their allies were given draft texts of the treaties for their comments and were provided facilities for communicating directly with their home governments, but they were kept from meeting with members of the other delegations or with journalists. The final text of the treaty, handed to the Germans with the threat that war would be resumed if they did not agree to it within seven days, contained the clause that

> Germany accepts the responsibility of Germany and her allies for causing all the loss and damage to which the Allies and Associated Governments and their nationals have been subjected as a consequence of the war imposed upon them by the aggression of Germany and her allies.[6]

The actual negotiations, often bitter, were between the victor powers themselves for dividing up the spoils of war and, most importantly, in the American president's view, for constructing a new world order. The result was the "grand bargain" signed at Versailles in 1919, in which Wilson got his League of Nations (somewhat watered down compared with his preferences) in exchange for acquiescing to a harsher peace toward Germany and her allies than he believed was just. In the bitterest of ironies, however, Wilson's own countrymen prevented him from collecting on his side of the bargain, when Congress refused to approve the Treaty of Versailles.

The specific provisions of the treaties, like the general "war guilt" clause quoted above, clearly implied that the Germans and their allies were to blame for the war and should suffer special penalties for their aggression.

Germany was compelled to renounce all her rights and titles to her overseas possessions—colonial holdings totaling more than a million square miles—and to turn them over to the League of Nations to be administered under the world organization's mandate/trusteeship system. Territorial penalties were also exacted in Europe: France took back the provinces of Alsace and Lorraine, a sweet revenge on its enemy for having taken these provinces from France as a victory prize in the Franco-Prussian War of 1870. In addition, Germany was made to give up the coal mines of the Saar "as compensation for the destruction of the coal mines in the north of France." For fifteen years the Saar would be administered by the League of Nations, after which a plebiscite of its inhabitants would determine its future status. Poland was given sovereignty over the former German provinces of Posen and West Prussia, gaining a wide land corridor to the ethnically German port city of Danzig, which was also taken from Germany and put under League administration as a "free city."

Some of the other territories severed from Germany and Austria-Hungary were also predominantly populated by ethnic Germans, who, if allowed to choose via plebiscite, might have elected to be included within the German state. But the victorious powers had no intention of permitting the principle of self-determination to interfere with their plans for reducing Germany's power and size. Thus, while the borders of the ethnically varied Austro-Hungarian empire were redrawn to provide (insofar as the admixture of peoples permitted) ethnically homogeneous national states, the Germanic provinces were consigned to the pared down state of Austria and prohibited from merging with

Germany proper, and the borders of the new state of Czechoslovakia were extended westward to encompass the two million Germans of the Sudeten region.

The disarmament provisions of Versailles were no less disadvantageous to Germany. German military forces could no longer be deployed in Germany's vast Rhineland region bordering France, Luxembourg, Belgium, and the Netherlands, and the allies were accorded military occupation rights on German territory in the Rhineland west bank area for fifteen years. The German army was permanently limited to 100,000 men, and the navy to 15,000 men and a small number of ships. The country was also prohibited from manufacturing tanks, military aircraft, and other weapons that could be used in offensive operations.

Realizing that their own economic recovery could be negatively affected by the need to take care of a totally bankrupt ward in the center of Europe, the victors' reparations demands on Germany were constrained by their assessments of her capacity to pay and were stated in the form of categories of obligations rather than precise monetary figures. Yet some of the obligations—for example, funds to finance the Allies' war-related pensions to military victims of war and their families—promised to subject the country to long-term external indebtedness. Moreover, the treaty stipulated that Germany could be militarily occupied by the victor powers if she failed to meet her reparations obligations.

With the perspective of hindsight, in light of the experience of a revengeful Germany after World War I as compared with the more responsible Germany after World War II, the Versailles settlement appears to have been imprudently harsh on Germany and a principal cause of the rise of Adolph Hitler and his ability to garner enthusiastic domestic support for the imperialist excesses of the Third Reich. This is not to say that the peace arrangements imposed on Germany were wrong morally. Perhaps the country did need to be punished for its role in encouraging Austria-Hungary to make the moves on Serbia that precipitated World War I. I am speaking of the political *consequences* of Versailles, not its justifiability.

One of the undeniable consequences was to make the Germans more deeply dissatisfied with the status quo than they were before World War I and receptive to a political demagogue who told them that with sufficient strength and discipline they could undo the profound injustice that had been inflicted on them.

The other more idealistic side of the grand diplomatic bargain among the Allies—the institution of Wilson's League of Nations's system—also had some profoundly negative implications for world peace. Wilson's arguments for the League reflected and reinforced the popular view that the world needed a *replacement* for the balance of power system that brought on World War I and the illusion that the new system was embodied in the collective security provisions of the Covenant, particularly Articles 11 through 16:

Article 11 provided that "any war or threat of war, whether immediately affecting any members of the League or not, is . . . a matter of concern to the whole League, and the League shall take any action that may be deemed wise and effective to safeguard the peace of nations."

Articles 12 through 15 established procedures that member nations were obligated to follow "if there should arise between them any disputes likely to lead to a rupture." First, they were to submit such disputes either to the Council of the League, to the Permanent Court of International Justice, or to other certified international tribunals for resolution. Second, they were prohibited from waging war against members who complied with the awards or decisions of these League bodies. Third, the members of the League agreed "in no case to resort to war until three months after the award by the arbiters or the judicial decision or the report of the Council": this was the so-called cooling-off period. But if the appropriate League bodies were unable to render an award or decision, "the members of the League reserve to themselves the right to take such action as they shall consider necessary for the maintenance of right and justice."

The provisions of Article 16, often called the heart of the League's collective security system, included the following:

1. Should any member of the League resort to war in disregard of its covenants under Article 12, 13, or 15, it shall, *ipso facto*, be deemed to have committed an act of war against all other members of the League, which hereby undertake immediately to subject it to the severance of all trade or financial relations, the prohibition of all intercourse between their nationals and the nationals of the Covenant-breaking State, and the prevention of all financial, commercial or personal intercourse between the nationals of the Covenant-breaking State and the nationals of any other State, whether a Member of the League or not.

2. It shall be the duty of the Council in such a case to recommend to the several Governments concerned what effective

military, naval or air force the Members of the League shall severally contribute to the armed forces to be used to protect the covenants of the League.

3. The Members of the League agree, further, that they will mutually support one another in the financial and economic measures which are taken under this article. . . .

4. Any Member of the League which has violated any covenant of the League may be declared to be no longer a Member of the League by a vote of the Council.[7]

The existence of the League, even absent the United States, perpetrated the illusion that war had been outlawed and that there was a mechanism in place to punish aggressors that obviated the need of countries unilaterally, or in alliance with one another, to maintain sufficient military power on their own to counter aggressor states. This would turn out to be an especially dangerous illusion in the 1930s in the Western democracies, because the countries dissatisfied with the post–World War I status quo—especially Germany, Italy, and Japan—had no compunctions about using military force to accomplish their objectives.

The dissatisfied powers knew, and the democracies closed their eyes to the fact, that the essentially conservative structure of the League's organization and decision-making processes would paralyze it from effective collective security responses to swift military power-plays. The League's collective security decisions had to be based on unanimity, excepting the parties to a dispute, but no party to a dispute, if it was a major power, would be without friends on the Council. In any event, the League's collective security enforcement decisions would always be in the form of recommendatory resolutions. There was a strong moral obligation on the part of members to conform to League resolutions, but no country in joining the League gave up a whit of its legal sovereignty.

The Germans, Italians, and Japanese were contemptuous of both the League's collective security system and the grand peace pacts of the day, the Locarno Pact of 1925 and the Kellog-Briand Pact of 1928, that were supposed to substitute for the discredited balance of power system as the means of preventing war. Their contempt was to a large extent warranted. The logic of the League presumed the existence of a common world interest opposing war that would normally override all other national interests: all that was needed was a world institution in place to give expression to the common interest. As it turned out, national desires to avoid fighting other nations' wars overrode the collective obligations of the League, and ironically, the very existence of the League made it easy for countries to pass the buck to the world institution to oppose aggression, providing each nation with a rationale for noninvolvement in the absence of concerted action organized by the League. The spirit of Locarno had also become part of the problem, for the pacts against war, by catering to the popular wishful thinking that coercive statecraft had become obsolete, only strengthened opposition in the Western democracies to the kinds of war-risking confrontations that might have restrained the Machiavellian dictators of 1930s.

The extent of the League's impotence, and the lack of diplomatic resourcefulness in the relevant national governments for taking up the slack, was most starkly exposed in 1935, when Italy, then under the fascist dictatorship of Benito Mussolini, invaded Ethiopia. The League did brand the invasion an illegal aggression, and the Council in this case did invoke the Article 16 sanctions system, asking members to embargo sales of arms and strategic materials to Italy, excepting oil (Italy's most strategically crucial import!). Fifty-two countries made credible attempts to comply with the League's embargo resolutions, but the effects on Mussolini's ability to prosecute his bullying action were negligible.

The only two powers that might have been able to challenge Italy militarily, France and Britain, were preoccupied with domestic problems and were not at all anxious to assume the burden of organizing military sanctions, since none of their vital geopolitical interests were immediately in jeopardy. Within a year, Ethiopia had been totally absorbed by Italy, while the League—true to its legalistic deference to nation-state sovereignty—found itself in the anomalous position of denying a hearing to the erstwhile Ethiopian emperor, Haile Selassie, whom it had been trying to protect from Mussolini's brutal aggression.

The other aggressor nations took note of the League's inhibitory effect on the mobilization of countervailing power. Not only was it unable to provide timely and decisive opposition to Mussolini's power play against hapless Ethiopia, but its presumed role as the world's security agency of first resort provided an excuse for countries to refrain from reacting as they might have otherwise—unilaterally or through alliances to counter acts of aggressive expansion. The Japanese invasion of China in 1937 and Hitler's moves the following year against Austria and Czechoslovakia were, if anything, tempted by the power vacuum surrounding the League's collective security system.

By the time the democracies were ready to reinstitute an alliance to oppose the expansionist powers, it required overt belligerency to give credibility to the intention of its members to resist aggression. And by the time the new alliance could put together enough military power to balance that of the aggressors, the Germans had brutally overrun the European continent and much of North Africa, and the Japanese had conquered almost a third of China and all Southeast Asia.

Even Hitler's bullying and absorption of Austria in 1938 and his demand that Czechoslovakia give up the German-speaking Sudetenland were not enough to make France and Britain respond positively to the Soviet Union's plea for a firm stand by the former allies against further German expansion. Instead, when Prime Minister Neville Chamberlain and Premier Edouard Daladier met with Hitler and Mussolini in Munich, they agreed to let Hitler occupy the Czech Sudeten areas as long as he guaranteed to respect the territorial integrity of the rest of Czechoslovakia. It was not until Hitler violated this promise by seizing Czechoslovakia and Bohemia in March 1939 that the British and French were ready to reinstitute the triangular alliance and explicitly threaten Hitler with war if he attacked Poland. But now the Soviet dictator Stalin was the holdout, insisting on a degree of hegemony for the USSR in Eastern Europe that Britain and France were not ready to grant him. Then, interpreting the Anglo-French rejection of his conditions as evidence that the Western capitalist countries were secretly conniving to allow Germany to destroy the Marxist-socialist state in Russia, Stalin turned the tables and signed his notorious pact with Hitler giving the Soviets control over eastern Poland and adjacent areas in exchange for Stalin's acquiescence to Germany's occupation of western Poland. With the Soviet Union now neutralized and Britain and France in no position to prevent his action physically, Hitler's Wehrmacht thundered across the German-Polish border on September 1, 1939. On September 3, Great Britain and France finally declared war on Germany.

CASE 3. MUTUAL PROVOCATION OF JAPAN AND THE UNITED STATES

A full-scale U.S.-Japanese war in Asia was not part of the grand strategy of either the U.S. government or the Japanese government leading into the summer of 1941, when the diplomatic interaction between Washington and Tokyo became badly botched and put the two countries on a collision course adverse to the vital interests of both. The mutual provocation of the United States and Japan contrasted with the virtually inexorable clash of U.S. and German vital interests maturing during 1940 and 1941. By the fall of 1941, Hitler's military victories had begun to threaten the survival of Britain; it was only a question of time before the United States would become an active belligerent in the European war anyway—probably sometime in 1942, if the Japanese attack on Pearl Harbor on December 7, 1941, hadn't forced Washington's hand.[8] (The U.S. declaration of war against Japan for its attack on Pearl Harbor triggered Hitler's declaration of war against the United States, consistent with the terms of the Tripartite Alliance of Japan, Germany, and Italy).

Anticipating a collusion of Japan and Germany against British interests in Asia, the Roosevelt administration, largely upon the urgings of Prime Minister Churchill, began warning the Japanese in the spring of 1940 that it would not tolerate their attacking the oil-rich British and Dutch East Indies. The administration considered an embargo on U.S. oil shipments to Japan in response to indications that the Japanese were preparing to move into southern Indochina, but this idea was discarded at the time on the premise that denying Japan American oil would give her all that much more of an incentive to grab the East Indies oil fields. Instead, the United States decided to allow the U.S. fleet to remain at Pearl Harbor—a departure from the Navy's usual policy of only temporarily stationing the fleet in Hawaii and permanently basing it on the U.S. West Coast—as a signal that the United States was prepared to intervene militarily in response to a Japanese move south against British or Dutch possessions. The last thing the American government looked forward to, however, was a *two*-theater war, and Roosevelt's top military planners, preparing for the coming war with Germany, were advising against becoming involved against Japan.

More to impress the Japanese than as a part of actual war preparations, the United States entered into military discussions with the British and Dutch in early 1941 on coordinating military operations in the event of U.S. participation in an Asian war. U.S. officials assumed that Japanese intelligence would learn of these planning sessions and would draw the conclusion that Washington was deadly serious about intervening on behalf of the British and Dutch in response to a Japanese attack. Roosevelt also approved a ploy designed by the State Department, despite the objections of the Navy, to dispatch part of the fleet on a visit to Australia and New Zealand. The President liked the idea of having the U.S. ships "popping up here and there" just to "keep the Japs guessing."[9]

These U.S. naval deployments, however, did not send a clear signal to the Japanese about how the United States would respond to their plan to move into southern Indochina. The ambiguity allowed high Japanese officials to convince themselves that their plan to take over southern Indochina would not provoke an American oil embargo; in their view, Washington "knew well enough" that such an embargo would compel Japan to go for the oil in the East Indies. Foreign Minister Yosuke Matsuoka, arguing in favor of taking over the rest of Indochina, advised the Emperor that "a war against Great Britain and the United States is unlikely if we proceed with great caution."[10]

On July 24, 1941, in response to the movement of Japanese troops into southern Indochina, President Roosevelt decided to freeze all Japanese assets in the United States and to give the interdepartmental Foreign Funds Committee authority to release Japanese funds to purchase oil on a case-by-case basis. The Japanese would know that the administration could now directly control the amount of oil going to Japan and would have to reassess whether it wanted to persist in its aggressive moves. The President was not ready to apply a complete embargo, still fearing that this would induce the Japanese to make a grab for the oil of the East Indies. Indeed, the next week he told the Foreign Funds Committee that they could release enough funds for Japan to purchase U.S. oil up to the 1935–1936 level.

But while Roosevelt was out of Washington at the beginning of August for a shipboard meeting with Prime Minister Churchill, the head of the Foreign Funds Committee, Assistant Secretary of State Dean Acheson, refused to release *any* Japanese money, thus instituting a full embargo at least for the time being. Acheson discounted fears that this would provoke war, arguing that "no rational Japanese could believe that an attack on us could result in anything but disaster for his country."[11]

When Roosevelt returned from the Atlantic conference with Churchill, he let the de facto full embargo stand. Perhaps Roosevelt was influenced by the British warrior-statesman's give-them-no-quarter views, or perhaps he realized that to relax the noose after it had been tightened could be misinterpreted by the Japanese as a lack of will in the White House to stand tough, which could tempt them to press even further south toward Malaya and Singapore and eventually down into the oil-rich Indonesian archipelago, in contrast to his earlier view that such an embargo would bring about the very eventuality it was supposed to prevent.

Having invoked maximum economic pressure, the U.S. Government would now have to rely primarily on military deterrence to prevent additional Japanese aggression. In their Atlantic meeting, Churchill had asked Roosevelt to threaten the Japanese that in the event of their further expansion, the United States would have to take measures that "might lead to war." But when Ambassador Nomura visited the White House on August 17, Roosevelt warned only that a Japanese move further south would compel him to take steps "toward insuring the safety and security of the United States."[12] Nor was it clear at the outset just what the Japanese would have to do for the United States to loosen its stranglehold on the Japanese economy.

The Japanese government, knowing that the country would rapidly be reduced to a crippled condition without American, British, and Dutch oil and afraid (despite Roosevelt's mildly worded warning) that war with the United States was inevitable if Japanese armed forces attacked the East Indies, tried to open up negotiations.

On August 28, 1941, Prime Minister Prince Fumimaro Konoe submitted a note to the American president proposing that the two of them meet to work out a settlement. Japan was prepared to agree, in return for the United States resumption of oil shipments, not to advance further south and to withdraw her forces from Indochina "after a just peace has been established in the Far East." U.S. intercepts of Japanese coded messages revealed that a just peace as Japan defined it would include U.S. and British acquiescence in the replacement of the Chiang Kai-shek regime in China (which had been receiving U.S. and British support) with a regime acceptable to the Japanese. Secretary of State Cordell Hull, meeting with the Japanese ambassador on the evening of August 28, let him know in no uncertain terms that the U.S. conditions for normalizing relations required the withdrawal of Japanese forces from all of China as well as Indochina and a nullification of Japan's Tripartite pact with Germany and Italy; moreover, the Japanese government would have to accept these conditions before President Roosevelt would agree to meet with Prime Minister Konoe.[13]

The secretary of state's response fed into the worst Japanese fears: that the United States would deliberately prolong negotiations while keeping the oil embargo in force, thus strangulating Japan's economy and ability to sustain its military machine while U.S. forces were being augmented for the impending Pacific war. Prime Minister Konoe, a champion of negotiations, was forced to resign, and the emperor appointed a new government, headed by General Tojo, to assess the

alternatives freshly. There was intense disagreement on what kind of negotiating concessions to make, if any, but before the end of October there was
a basic consensus among the highest-ranking military officers about the
stark implications of a continuing diplomatic stalemate with Washington:
it would mean war sooner or later, and if a war had to be fought against
the United States, it would have to come early in December if there were
to be even the slightest chance of victory for Japan.[14]

Pessimistically, if not with resigned fatalism, the Japanese military
put their minds to designing a grand strategy for fighting the war. The
strategy that gained approval in the cabinet was not a plan for complete
military victory. Rather, it contemplated winning a series of quick early
victories and then setting up a defensive barrier behind an enlarged perime-
ter of holdings and bases. This would compel the United States to engage
in a costly and long war of attrition to reverse the Japanese gains, an effort
that would wear thin in the American democracy, especially as it would
demand sacrifices over and above what the Americans would be having to
bear in the war against Germany. The objective would be to break the will
of the Americans to fight. A propaganda campaign would be targeted especially on sectors of American society believed to be opposed to continuing the war. Meanwhile, international third parties, such as the Vatican,
would be enlisted to encourage peace negotiations.[15] If Japan could make
the war sufficiently painful for the United States, Washington would lose
heart for persisting in the quest for victory and would be inclined to concede better terms than Japan could have obtained in negotiations under
the asymmetrical conditions of the prewar period.

A war on this design would still be a terrible gamble and enormously
costly to fight, but a consensus was rapidly jelling at the highest levels of
the Japanese government in the fall of 1941 that there was no alternative.

Still, there were some in Japan (the emperor was among them) who
felt that war could be averted by *some* reasonable accommodations to
Washington's demands. Japanese diplomats put out feeler proposals during November that included concessions such as a pledge by Tokyo not
to adhere to the Tripartite Pact if the United States entered the European
war, a promise to withdraw a substantial part of the Japanese forces from
China, and a willingness to moderate the demand that Chiang Kai-shek's
government be deposed prior to their military withdrawal.

In Washington, too, some officials, including Secretary of War
Stimson and President Roosevelt himself, wanted to slow down what
appeared to be a headlong momentum toward a U.S.-Japanese war. Even
as late as the last week in November, and despite the feelings of other

officials that Tokyo might be dissembling, they favored exploring the more moderate Japanese negotiating feelers. And if war were to come, the military preferred it to be later rather than sooner so that U.S. forces in the Pacific theater could be significantly strengthened.

But Secretary of State Hull, sensitive to British concerns that the United States might appear to be weakening its deterrent stance and concerned about public reactions to a Japanese-American deal at the expense of China, opposed any watering down of the U.S. position. Preempting this possibility, Hull on November 25 gave the Japanese ambassador a restatement of U.S. "principles," and he appeared to be vindicated in his tough stance the next day as U.S. intelligence agencies reported that a Japanese naval squadron was moving into the South China Sea.

For the Japanese, Hull's uncompromising reiteration of the standing U.S. demands on November 25 was apparently the point of no return. Prime Minister Tojo regarded Hull's statement as tantamount to an ultimatum and suspected that it meant the United States was planning to attack Japan. On December 1, the Tojo government, with the emperor's endorsement, gave the orders to implement the war plan.

CASE 4. INEPT REALPOLITIK IN THE PERSIAN GULF

If President Saddam Hussein of Iraq had been warned in no uncertain terms by the Bush administration that an Iraqi invasion of Kuwait would compel the United States to oppose him with military force, would he have ordered his troops across the Iraq-Kuwait border on August 2, 1990?

Perhaps Iraq would have moved on Kuwait anyway. Perhaps not. What was going on in the mind of Saddam Hussein at the time is not sufficiently known, if it ever can be. But the record of what did and did not happen in the diplomatic arena in the weeks and days leading up to the August 2 invasion is substantial enough to conclude that Washington gave Baghdad no meaningful incentives to hold back.[16]

The incentives would have needed to be large to dissuade Saddam from using military force. He had compelling economic motives for pouncing on Kuwait: Iraq was struggling under the $80 billion foreign debt incurred during its recent war with Iran, $10 billion of which was owed to Kuwait alone. Kuwait had broken ranks with the regional oil cartel's production controls, driving down the market price of Persian

Gulf oil and costing Iraq billions in lost revenue. Kuwait was allegedly slant-drilling to capture more than its fair share of oil in a major field traversing the Iraq-Kuwait border. In a decisive victory over Kuwait, Saddam could annex unto Iraq as minimum war booty the Ramalia oil field plus the disputed island of Bubiyan, which controls the approach to Iraq's port of Umm Qasr, and he could force Kuwait to wipe off Iraq's debt and to pay Baghdad reparations for past oil profits forgone as well as the direct costs of war. A maximum victory prize might be the permanent incorporation of the entire oil-rich kingdom into the state of Iraq, consistent with Baghdad's long-standing claim that Kuwait was artificially severed from Iraq by the British in their period of imperial rule over the region.

Would Saddam have been deterred by a timely threat of American military counteraction? He might have discounted a U.S. threat to intervene as a bluff: the Cold War was over, and Washington no longer regarded Iraq as a proxy of the rival superpower. If anything, the United States was building up Iraq as a counterweight to the fanatically anti-American Islamic fundamentalists in control of Iran. Saddam knew that the Saudis and Egyptians were advising the Bush administration to avoid a U.S. military intervention and to leave the resolution of the conflict to Arab diplomacy. Moreover, he had reason to suspect that the Americans, remembering Vietnam, would not have much stomach for sacrificing their lives and treasure in another Third World quagmire, especially on behalf of a monarchical regime alienated from indigenous reformist movements.

Looking back on the summer of 1990, it seems that Saddam, if he had discounted a pre-invasion threat by Bush of counterintervention, probably would have been terribly wrong. We have to say probably because we will never know whether the United States would have in fact gone to war had Iraq contented itself with occupying only a portion of Kuwait across the border and used that as a bargaining counter to obtain further concessions. Prime Minister Margaret Thatcher, in urging the American president to use force in the days immediately following Iraq's invasion of Kuwait, indicated that she was afraid of Bush's going "wobbly." As it turned out, it was Saddam's swift military occupation of the entire country and his promise never to give it up that allowed the Bush administration to obtain a mandate from the United Nations to drive Iraq out of Kuwait by whatever means it took. Under this mantle of international legitimacy, the United States assembled a coalition fighting force of 740,000 (540,000 U.S. troops plus 200,000 from allies) to give Saddam Hussein the "mother of battles" he boasted of craving. The United States–led Desert Storm operation to force Iraq out of Kuwait dropped 142,000 tons of bombs on the Iraqis in Kuwait and Iraq itself. The combined air and ground war killed and wounded as many as 100,000 or more Iraqi soldiers (the numbers are still in dispute), destroyed the bulk of Saddam's tanks, artillery, and air force, and finally compelled him, in a set of humiliating cease-fire terms, to agree to dismantle his missiles and capabilities for manufacturing weapons of mass destruction under international inspection.[17]

Clearly the Iraqi dictator had made an enormous miscalculation of the consequences of his invasion of Kuwait. But, just as clearly, there had been a failure on the part of U.S. diplomacy in neglecting to give the Iraqis cause to calculate such consequences *prior* to their fateful move into Kuwait. Indeed, Washington gave Saddam every reason to assume he could pull off the invasion swiftly as a low-risk fait accompli. At the same time, the Bush administration was giving the Kuwaitis to believe that it would protect them against Saddam's bullying, thus reducing their incentives to make a compromise deal with Iraq to avoid war.

As Saddam escalated his verbal threats and deployed his forces menacingly on the Kuwaiti border in late July, President Bush and other U.S. officials communicated their concerns in bland language couched in reassurances that the geopolitical interests the United States shared with Iraq in the region constituted the controlling reality for Washington.

This sense of geopolitical commonality between the two countries had grown throughout the 1980s. It had been Iraq's September 1980 reopening of its on-again, off-again war with Iran that more than anything else induced Teheran to settle its embassy-hostage conflict with the United States. In 1982 the Department of State removed Iraq from its list of terrorist countries so that it could qualify for U.S. aid and credits. In 1984 full diplomatic relations, disbanded in the 1950s when Iraq became a Soviet client state, were reestablished between Washington and Baghdad. A dramatic indication of how determined the Reagan administration was to secure Iraq as a counterweight to Iran was the mild reaction by the White House to the mistaken launching of a missile from an Iraqi jet aircraft against the U.S.S. Stark, which killed thirty-seven U.S. sailors and nearly sunk the ship.

By the time of George Bush's inauguration in 1989, trade between the United States and Iraq had grown to $3.6 billion a year. Despite allegations that Iraqi forces had used chemical warfare against the secessionist Kurds, reports of the worsening human rights situation in Iraq, and growing suspicions during 1989 that Iraq was attempting to develop nuclear weapons, President Bush resisted congressional efforts to get tough with Saddam Hussein. In January 1990 Bush signed an executive order certifying that it would be against the national interest of the United States to halt Export-Import Bank loans to Iraq.[18]

The developing cordiality in U.S. relations with Iraq was temporarily interrupted in April 1990, when Saddam threatened that in a renewed war with Israel he would use chemical weapons that would "eat up" half of Israel. When high U.S. officials expressed dismay and the State Department's spokesperson called Saddam's remarks irresponsible and outrageous, the Iraqis were deeply offended. But relations were put back on track by a delegation to Baghdad of farm state congressmen and senators, headed by Robert Dole, who fawningly assured Saddam of their admiration for him and their support of President Bush's desire for friendly relations between the two countries.

When Iraq began to threaten military action against Kuwait openly in the middle of July 1990, the reaction of the Bush administration was ambiguous at best. Secretary of Defense Richard Cheney told reporters on July 19 that American commitments made during the Iran-Iraq war to come to Kuwait's defense were still valid, and on July 23 the administration ordered U.S. naval vessels in the region to engage in joint exercises with the United Arab Emirates. But on July 24 Department of State spokesperson Margaret Tutwiler told inquiring reporters that "we do not have any defense treaties with Kuwait, and there are no special defense or security commitments to Kuwait." In Baghdad Saddam summoned U.S. Ambassador April Glaspie for an interview, in which the Iraqi president outlined his grievances with Kuwait, and the U.S. Ambassador, following instructions from Secretary of State James Baker, assured Saddam that "we have no opinion on the Arab-Arab conflicts, like your border disagreement with Kuwait."[19] The Baker instruction to Glaspie reportedly asked her to remind the Iraqis that the United States would regard the use of force as "contrary to the U.N. Charter principles," but there is no evidence that she said this to Saddam during her interview.[20]

Two days later, with intelligence agencies reporting a a huge buildup of Iraqi troops just across the border from Kuwait, President Bush sent a mildly worded cable to Saddam emphasizing his desire for improved relations and advising that Iraq's disputes with Kuwait be resolved peaceably. High Defense Department officials tried to toughen up the tepid presidential message, but to no avail. Only three paragraphs long, the cable averred

> I was pleased to learn of the agreement between Iraq and Kuwait to begin negotiations in Jedda to find a peaceful solution to the current tensions between you. The United States and Iraq both have a strong interest in preserving the peace and stability of the Middle East. For this reason, we believe that differences are best resolved by peaceful means and not by threats involving military force or conflict.
>
> I also welcome your statement that Iraq desires friendship, rather than confrontation with the United States. Let me reassure you, as my Ambassador, Senator Dole and others have done, that my administration continues to desire better relations with Iraq. We will also continue to support our other friends in the region with whom we have had longstanding ties. We see no necessary inconsistency between these two objectives.
>
> As you know, we still have fundamental concerns about certain Iraqi policies and activities, and we will continue to raise these concerns with you in a spirit of friendship and candor, as we have in the past both to gain a better understanding of your interests and intentions and to ensure that you understand our concerns. I completely agree that both our Governments must maintain open channels of communication to avoid misunderstanding and in order to build a more durable foundation for improving our relations.[21]

On July 31, just hours before Saddam's troops slashed into Kuwait, Assistant Secretary of State for Near Eastern Affairs John Kelly, testifying before the Middle East Subcommittee of the House Foreign Affairs Committee, was asked about Secretary of Defense Cheney's July 19 statement to reporters about U.S. commitments to Kuwait. Secretary Kelly's answer must have reassured Saddam: "I'm not familiar with the quotation that you just referred to, but I am confident in the administration's policy on the issue: We have no defense relationship with any Gulf country. This is clear . . . ." Kelly was pressed by the committee chairman to clarify what the U.S. policy would be in the event that "Iraq, for example, charged across the border into Kuwait . . . . In that circumstance . . . is [it] correct to say . . . that we do not have a treaty commitment which would obligate us to engage U.S. forces there?" The secretary confirmed that the United States did not have a treaty commitment to cover that circumstance.[22]

The diplomatic failure is captured in *New York Times* columnist Leslie Gelb's finding that "never once in the week prior to attack—as Iraqi troops on the border massed to over 100,000—did Mr. Bush ever say, or even hint, that the U.S. would respond to Iraqi aggression with force." This "diplomatic passivity" evidently gave Saddam to believe that he had "a tacit go-ahead" from Washington.[23]

NOTES

1. Jack S. Levy, "The Role of Crisis Mismanagement in the Outbreak of World War I," in Alexander L. George, ed., *Avoiding War: Problems of Crisis Management* (Boulder, Col. Westview, 1991), pp. 62–102.

2. On British considerations, see Zara S. Steiner, *Britain and the Origins of the First World War* (New York: St. Martin's, 1977), chaps. 7–10.

3. Text of Wilson's Fourteen Points of January 8, 1918, in Frank P. Chambers, Christina Phelps Harris, and Charles C. Bayley, *This Age of Conflict: A Contemporary World History, 1914 to the Present* (New York: Harcourt, Brace, 1950), app. C.

4. Arthur S. Link, *Woodrow Wilson, Revolution, War, and Peace* (Arlington Heights, Ill.: Harland Davidon, 1979).

5. Statistics on lives lost in World War I are from Francis A. Beer, *Peace Against War: An Ecology of International Violence* (San Francisco: W.H. Freeman, 1981), p. 37.

6. Chambers et al., *This Age of Conflict*, pp. 120–124.

7. *Covenant of the League of Nations,* signed at Versailles on June 28, 1919 (Geneva: League of Nations, 1920).

8. My rendering of the U.S.-Japanese relationship leading up to the attack on Pearl Harbor relies heavily on analyses by Scott D. Sagan, "The Origins of the Pacific War," in Rotberg and Rabb, *The Origin and Prevention of Major Wars,* pp. 323–352; and by Robert Devine, *The Reluctant Belligerent: American Entry into World War II* (New York: Wiley, 1965).

9. Sagan, "The Origins of the Pacific War," p. 333.

10. *Ibid.*, p. 334.

11. Dean Acheson, *Present at the Creation* (New York: Norton) pp. 43–52.

12. Divine, *The Reluctant Belligerent,* pp. 132–133.

13. *Ibid.*, pp. 140–141.

14. Sagan, "The Origins of the Pacific War," pp. 340–341.

15. Nobutka Ike, ed., *Japan's Decision for War: Records of the 1941 Policy Conferences* (Stanford: Stanford University Press, 1967), pp. 248–249; cited by Sagan, "The Origins of the Pacific War," pp. 344–345.

16. My account of the interaction between the United States and Iraq prior to the Gulf War relies heavily on the historical reconstruction of the events by Jean Edward Smith, *George Bush's War* (New York: Henry Holt, 1992).

17. The story of how the the Gulf War was fought is told with careful attention to detail in the *U.S. News and World Report* book, *Triumph without Victory: The Unreported History of the Persian Gulf War* (New York: Times Books, 1992).

18. Smith, *George Bush's War,* pp. 44–45.

19. *Ibid.,* pp. 52–57.

20. Leslie Gelb, "Mr. Bush's Fateful Blunder," *New York Times,* July 17, 1991.

21. Michael R. Gordon, "Pentagon Objected to a Message Bush Sent Iraq before Its Invasion," *New York Times,* October 25, 1992.

22. Quoted by Smith, *George Bush's War,* pp. 59–60.

23. Leslie H. Gelb, "A Bush Green Light to Iraq?" *New York Times,* October 22, 1992.

PART II

The Prevention and Control of War

The political psychiatrist . . .
approaches the problem of war and revolution
as one detail of the whole task
of mastering the sources and mitigating the consequences
of human insecurity in an unstable world.

— Harold Lasswell

It may well be that we shall, by a process of sublime irony,
have reached a stage in the story
where safety will be the sturdy child of terror
and survival the twin brother of annihilation.

— Winston Churchill

Mankind has to go out of violence
only through nonviolence.
Hatred can be overcome
only through love.
Counter hatred only increases
the surface as well as the depth of hatred.

— Mohandas K. Gandhi

CHAPTER 8

Efforts to Purge War
from the World

The recognition that a world war fought with today's weapons could threaten the survival of the human species has convinced many government officials, social scientists, theologians, political activists, and other concerned citizens that there is no more urgent or important task than the banishment of the institution of war itself. Partial measures, from this perspective, not only are inadequate but are likely to be counterproductive. Especially dangerous are the notions of "limited war" and "firebreaks" between different levels of warfare, for these can encourage the delusion that modern war and its effects are manageable, with risks that can be controlled—and that therefore crossing the threshold from peace to war need not be regarded as the awesome step it is.

The condemnation of war as a social institution and the search for alternative means to deal with intense international conflicts, though never before so widespread a popular concern, antedate the nuclear age. There is a long history of prominent thinkers and political leaders who have come to the conclusion that war is never, or hardly ever, sane or morally justified and who have attempted to translate their convictions into workable proposals for eliminating war as an instrument of statecraft.

These efforts have been of two kinds: (1) the political-constitutional restructuring of world society, usually based on the assumption that the primary cause of war is the anarchic nation-state system itself; and (2) the reeducation and moral-psychological reform of human beings, based on the assumption that wars are started by people who have distorted values, perhaps not adequately sensitized to the horrors of violence or aware of viable alternatives to war. Sometimes the two approaches have been fused, but most proposals have given primacy to one or the other as the essential precondition for eliminating war.

RADICAL TRANSFORMATION OF THE WORLD'S POLITICAL STRUCTURE

If a single government could be established over all of the world society, exercising a sufficient monopoly over the tools of violence to overwhelm attempts by subordinate groups to use violence, then war could be eliminated or, failing that, rapidly suppressed by the central world government. The logic of this idea has appealed less to practicing statesmen than to philosophers, some of whom have attempted to give political flesh and bones to their visions. Attention need not be given here to proposals for merging or federating states under the aegis of an imperial power—for example, the poet Dante Alighieri's plan in *De Monarchia* and the "Grand Design" of King Henry IV of France. Rather, the focus of this section is on the voluntary restructuring of the world polity for the express purpose of eliminating interstate war.

Crucé's Proposal

In 1623 a French monk, Emeric Crucé, formulated an early proposal, called *Le Nouveau Cynée,* to give the fragmented world society a central governing structure. Membership in the proposed community of states would be universal, encompassing not only the European states but also Turkey, Persia, India, China, and kingdoms in Africa, as well as the pope and representatives of the Jews. All of the important entities would send delegates to a permanent Council of Ambassadors, whose decisions, arrived at by majority vote and enforced, if need be, by the pooled armed might of the majority, would be binding on all members. Crucé's *Cynée* also provided for an elaborate structure of voluntary negotiation and arbitration and for a world court to resolve disputes, prior to action by the Council of Ambassadors; the plan was that the world body's military enforcement would be an ultimate sanction that rarely would have to be used.[1] Predictably, because no monarch of the time was willing to subordinate his sovereign realm to a higher authority, the ideal scheme remained only a paper exercise for want of a powerful sponsor.

Penn's Plan

Seventy years later, in 1693, the prominent colonizer and Quaker missionary William Penn published a similar plan in his *Essay Toward the Present and Future Peace of Europe*. As the title suggests, Penn confined his call for political union to the monarchs of Europe, and like Crucé he insisted that they subordinate their sovereignties to the rules and decisions of a general parliament representing all of them. Decisions would require a three-fourths vote, with the wealthier states having more votes than others in the parliament. And also like Crucé, Penn, compromising his Quaker pacifism, provided that member states would combine their military strength when necessary to compel reluctant states to submit to the procedures and decisions of the all-European government:

> If any of the sovereignties that constitute the imperial State shall refuse to submit their claims or pretentions to them, or abide and perform the judgement thereof, and seek their remedy by arms, or delay their compliance beyond the time prefixed in their resolutions, all other sovereignties, united as one strength, shall compel the submission and performance of the sentence.[2]

Bellers's Plan

A plan resembling Penn's was published by John Bellers in 1710 in his essay *Some Reasons for a European State*. Bellers advanced the dialogue on the potential merger of states by dealing with the problem of unequal power of states expected to become constituent parts of the new Federation. He proposed that all Europe be divided into one hundred equal provinces, each of which would have one representative in the Central Senate and contribute equal military units to a common force. The military contingents, Bellers believed, would "prevent the rash from such dismal adventures as are the consequences of war, while they know that every man in the Senate hath one or two or three thousand men to back what he concludes there."[3]

Saint-Pierre's Project

A more elaborate scheme for a powerful supranational state to prevent war was submitted to the French monarchy in 1712 by the Abbé de Saint-Pierre in his *Project of Perpetual Peace*. Saint-Pierre conceived of an all-European Union whose central authority would be a Senate of Peace. Composed of two representatives from each of the twenty-four states of Europe, the Senate would sit permanently at the Dutch city of Utrecht, presided over by a president called the "Prince of Peace" and chosen weekly by rotation among the members. The only treaties and territorial changes permitted among the member states would be those approved by a three-fourths vote of the Senate. If disputes arose among members, the Senate would first appoint mediating commissioners to try to achieve a compromise; if the mediations failed, the Senate would arbitrate the dispute, with the understanding that its awards would be binding on the members.

States entering into treaties on their own, refusing to abide by decisions of the Senate, or making preparations for war would be brought to submission by the combined forces of the Union. And the defeated offending states would be made to pay the financial costs of the war, with their principal ministers subject to punishment by death or life imprisonment as disturbers of the peace.

The enforcement process provided for in the *Project* would depend on the Union's command of a military force superior to the forces of its members. Each member state was to provide an equal number of troops; smaller states unable to finance their recruitment would be subsidized from funds contributed to the Union treasury by the wealthier states. The Generalissimo of the Union Forces, appointed by and responsible to the Senate of Peace, would have supreme command over the generals of the member states.[4]

The French minister André Fleury did not reject the desirability in the abstract of such a radical transformation of the world polity but exhibited the sophisticated statesman's typical reaction to such schemes: "You have forgotten an essential article," he told the abbé, "that of dispatching missionaries to touch the hearts of princes and to persuade them to enter into your views."[5]

Rousseau's Criticism of Saint-Pierre's Project

The philosopher Jean-Jacques Rousseau admired Saint-Pierre's work, but in embracing it gave it the kiss of death. In his 1761 publication explaining the abbé's logic, *Extrait du projet du paix perpetuelle de Monsieur l'Abbé de Saint-Pierre* and in his 1762 publication assessing its feasibility, *Jugement sur la paix perpetuelle,* Rousseau convincingly demonstrated the utopian nature of the contemplated centralization of power.

Saint-Pierre was correct, wrote Rousseau, that the only way to bring peace to Europe would be to set up a commonwealth

> with powers to pass laws and ordinances binding upon all its members; it must have a coercive force capable of compelling every state to obey its common resolves . . . ; finally, it must be strong and firm enough to make it impossible for any member to withdraw at his own pleasure the moment he conceives his private interest to clash with that of the whole body.

But despite the necessity of such a union to achieve peace, it could never be brought into existence: it was "an absurd dream" requiring sovereigns to perceive that the common interest in peace outweighed their particular interests. This could not be, since peace was not an end in itself for most statesmen but, like war, a condition or means for the realization of other interests. Moreover, Rousseau argued, the separate sovereigns would oppose giving whatever commonwealth could be formed the powers it would require to enforce laws throughout the realm: "Is there a single sovereign in the world who . . . would bear without indignation the mere idea of seeing himself forced to be just, not only to foreigners, but even to his own subjects?"[6]

In these and related essays, especially his *L'Etat de guerre,* Rousseau advanced the elemental idea that sovereign national governments are mankind's historic response to the anarchic "state of war" within domestic society and that their merger in a federation requiring substantial diminution of the power of the separate governments would be feared, by those states that had achieved substantial security within the existing order, as a retrogression toward either a state of war or a forced subjugation by an imperial sovereign. Such a federation could be brought into being, he concluded, only by violence on such a scale as would stagger humanity.[7] In other words, international anarchy, the correlate to national sovereignty, is paradoxically the necessary condition for domestic peace.

Thinking about World Order in the Nineteenth and Early Twentieth Centuries

Rousseau's criticisms of the feasibility of establishing a world government to eliminate war provided philosophical support for the dominant view among political and legal thinkers and statesmen for the next century and a half: the society of states would have to rely principally on diplomacy and the balance of power to prevent war. If there were to be any institutionalized arrangement among nations to moderate their conflicts and encourage cooperation, it could be no more than a confederal organization of still-sovereign states to facilitate mediation and other voluntary conflict-resolution procedures and—most ambitiously— to mobilize concerted action against states that were overaggressive, or immoderately expansionist, or otherwise contemptuous of the norms of the moderate state system. (Efforts to seek peace without a fundamental transformation of the system of sovereign states, such as Immanuel Kant's in the realm of philosophy and those of the League of Nations and the United Nations in the realm of practice, will be treated in the next chapter.)

A revival of interest in truly supranational government was sparked by organizations such as the United World Federalists following the failure of the League of Nations to keep the peace after World War I. Chapter VII of the United Nations Charter, containing the basic international security provisions of the UN, in some respects reflects the efforts to give the new organization enforcement teeth that the League of Nations had lacked; but, as will be shown in Chapter 9, the charter provides only a framework on which supranational enforcement machinery can be constructed if the major member states choose to construct it, which they have not chosen to do—for essentially the same basic reasons Rousseau pointed to earlier.

Clark and Sohn's Proposal for World Law

A detailed proposal for transforming the United Nations into a peace-enforcing world state was developed in the late 1950s by two distinguished international legal experts, Grenville Clark and Louis B. Sohn of the Harvard Law School, who published it in their volume *World Peace through World Law*.[8] To accomplish the goal of the title, say the authors, "nothing less will suffice than a comprehensive plan whereby there would be established on a world scale institutions corresponding to those which have been found essential for the maintenance of law and order in local communities and nations."[9] Since police forces are necessary to maintain law and order even within a mature community or nation, "similar forces will be required to guarantee the carrying out and maintenance of complete disarmament by each and every nation and to deter or suppress *any* attempted international violence."[10]

Accordingly, Clark and Sohn propose a "World Peace Force" composed of 200,000 to 600,000 full-time professional volunteers to act as an enforcement arm of the controlling bodies of a revised United Nations organization. The force would be provisioned with "the most modern weapons and equipment," initially to come from the transfer of weapons and equipment discarded by national military forces during the disarmament process. Subsequently, the arsenal of the World Peace Force would be produced by a United Nations Supply and Research Agency. The World Peace Force would not have nuclear weapons as part of its normal operating equipment, but it could obtain them from a reserve held by a UN Nuclear Energy Authority, should they be needed to deter the use of nuclear weapons by a country that had clandestinely retained some in violation of the disarmament agreement.

Overall direction of the World Peace Force would be completely and continuously the responsibility of the deliberative political organs of the revised United Nations. Its military commanders, appointed by the Executive Council of the UN, could be removed at any time by the council, and the commanders would have no discretionary authority in advance of any contingency.

Clark and Sohn's revised United Nations would make the Executive Council responsible to the General Assembly, much as the British cabinet is responsible to the House of Commons. The General Assembly would have a weighted system of voting based primarily on the populations of member nations. Decisions of the assembly and council would have the status of world law, enforceable directly upon individuals and member nations through a strengthened UN court system serviced by a 10,000-person civil police force in addition to the World Peace Force.

In essence, Clark and Sohn have proposed a representative world federal government with enforcement powers superior to the powers of any of its constituent units. If sufficient consensus existed among the powerful constituent units to found such a system by disarming themselves and transferring their weapons to the world government, the prospect of such a world government able to make enforceable decisions might have some plausibility. But the authors do not attempt to outline the political and economic conditions required to bring about the required consensus. *World Peace through World Law,* therefore, remains an exercise in abstract constitution-building, leaving it to political scientists and statesmen to stipulate and construct the political conditions that might make the scheme a realistic proposal.

Falk's Strategies for Radical Change

Another prominent American professor of international law, Richard Falk, has attempted to construct a set of "transitional strategies" to provide a realistic base for just such radical transformation of the world's political system.

Falk's own preferred world polity, as he calls it, is designed to serve four basic values: the minimization of large-scale collective violence; the maximization of social and economic well-being; the realization of fundamental human rights and conditions of social justice; and the maintenance and rehabilitation of ecological quality. A World Polity Association would be built on a "central guidance system" having all the attributes of a world supranational state (although Falk shies away from the terms *world government* and *world state*). Its central deliberative body would be a three-chamber General Assembly, with different bases of representation in each chamber and checks-and-balances voting arrangements among the chambers to ensure that world laws are based as much as possible on the consent of the governed.[11]

Like Clark and Sohn, Falk envisions a World Security System with armed forces of its own "to maintain international peace under all possible circumstances," ensuring that the legislative and judicial decisions of the World Polity Association are adhered to, and enforcing the disarmament agreement that must precede establishment of the new system. Falk hopes that most of the enforcement will be by nonviolent techniques but does not rule out the use by the World Security Forces of violent weapons, and even nuclear forces, to counter groups that retain or build weapons of mass destruction in violation of the disarmament agreement.[12]

Falk is a realist, however, in recognizing that "no world order solution which presupposes the substantial modification of the state system can be achieved unless the advocates of the new system are aligned with important social and political forces within the existing structures."

Accordingly, he outlines a transition process with associated strategies and tactics to create and enlarge constituencies for his preferred polity that, by virtue of their size and political power, would compel officials with formal authority in the state system to negotiate the required institutional transformations. The transition process comprises three stages:

1. An era devoted to raising the consciousness of the general population and of specific interest groups to realize that they cannot adequately maintain their security and other values in the existing world order and that a drastic change along the lines of the preferred world polity is therefore necessary

2. An era of political mobilization converting the new consciousness into active interest-group lobbying and electoral politics to bring pressure on existing elites and put forward new political elites in countries throughout the world, resulting in committing national governments to the required institution building at the global level

3. An era of transformation during which disarmament of the nation-states and the simultaneous buildup of world institutions and power are undertaken and completed

Falk and contemporaries of similar outlook recognize that their current efforts to raise consciousness must contend against the multitude of tangible incentives, sanctions, and doctrines reinforcing continued majority acceptance of the status quo. In their pessimistic moments they grant that it may take a catastrophe—that is, a worldwide economic collapse, an immediately looming breakdown of life-sustaining ecologies, or World War III—to shake loose the prevailing attachments to the nation-state system. They are also aware that a consensus against perpetuating the existing world system is hardly the same as a consensus on the structure of its successor, for the latter will require a worldwide convergence of values to implement institutional designs that is nowhere in evidence now. Undaunted by these difficulties, they continue their writing and speaking to persuade as many as they can that, because the existing system is sufficiently irrational and bound ultimately to destroy itself, a new system is necessary and can be made feasible.

Whether or not such schemes for the wholesale restructuring of the world polity will one day be feasible, they provide contemporary statespersons with no practical means for dealing with immediate threats of war. This is a principal reason that the schemes are largely ignored by government officials.

UNIVERSAL ADOPTION
OF A PACIFIST MORALITY

In contrast with champions of global structural reform, pacifists locate both the cause of war and the ability to prevent war within individuals. To have peace depend on eventual changes in the structure of the world polity not only is insufficient, they say, but provides justification for resorting to war until the restructuring is finished. The pacifist regards war as unjustified whatever the structure of the polity—even anarchy or brutal empire. These and all other political structures, as well as the role of violence within them, result from the ways humans behave toward each other. To change the political structure without changing the individual moralities of most human beings will only deflect immoral behavior (violence being the grossest immorality) and rearrange its manifestations in society. A world society that establishes a world government without first universally educating humans on the immorality of all violence will still experience war: it will simply be called civil war.

Pacifists believe that the only way finally to purge war from the world is to convince people that all violence is wrong, whether it is committed by states against individuals, by individuals against states, by states against states, or by private individuals against each other. Though they acknowledge other injustices in world society, pacifists insist that war must be regarded as the greatest injustice; otherwise any war will be rationalized as a just war. The concept of just war allows each side to convince itself of the legitimacy of using violence to defend the nation's sovereign independence or its way of life, as well as to protect allies from more powerful enemies.

Pre-Christian and Early Christian Pacifism

Contemporary pacifists trace the roots of their moral philosophy to the pre-Christian period, citing both the wisdom of Asian sages such as Lao-tzu and Buddha and portions of the Hebrew scriptures, especially Isaiah, whose prophet would have nations "beat their swords into plowshares, and their spears into pruning hooks." But the principal early source of their inspiration is the moral imperatives enunciated by Jesus in the Sermon on the Mount, as recounted in the New Testament:

You have heard that they were told, "An eye for an eye and
a tooth for a tooth." But I tell you not to resist injury, but if
anyone strikes you on your right cheek, turn the other to him too;
and if anyone wants to sue you for your shirt, let him have your
coat too. And if anyone forces you to go one mile, go two miles
with him. . . .

You have heard that they were told, "You must love your neighbor
and hate your enemy." But I tell you, love your enemies and pray
for your persecutors, so that you may show yourselves true sons
of your Father in heaven, for he makes the sun rise on the bad
and good alike, and makes the rain fall on the upright and the
wrongdoers. (Matthew 5:38–46)[13]

Until the fourth century many Christian church fathers invoked these
passages to protest any use of war by the state. But after the conversion
of the emperor Constantine, establishing the union of church and state
in Rome, Christian theology retreated to the more pragmatic doctrine
advanced by Augustine of dividing wars into two categories, the just
and unjust, with the just wars those waged on behalf of the empire of
Christendom against the barbarians. In later centuries, pacifism was advocated by small and politically ineffectual sects of Christians, while
the dominant churches gave their blessings first to the Crusades to regain the Holy Lands from the Muslim infidels, and then to the wars of
religion between Protestant and Catholic states that devastated Europe
for a hundred years before the Peace of Westphalia in 1648.

The Reassertion of Pacifism by Erasmus

In the early sixteenth century Erasmus of Rotterdam took exception
to the Church's departures from Jesus' teachings on nonviolence. Claiming that violence was contrary to the essential nature of man, in 1514 he
published an eloquent but futile plea to the "Christian" statesmen and
politicized churchmen of his time to renounce war:

Ye say ye make war for the safeguard of the commonwealth; yea,
but noway sooner nor more unthriftily may the commonwealth
perish than by war. . . . Ye waste the citizens' goods, ye fill the
houses with lamentations, ye fill all the country with thieves,

robbers and ravishers. For these are the relics of war. . . . If ye love your own subjects truly, why resolve you not in mind these words: Why shall I put so many, in their lusty flourishing youth, in all mischiefs and perils? Why shall I depart so many honest wives and their husbands and make so many fatherless children?[14]

Contributions of Thoreau and Tolstoy

Most Renaissance and modern social and political philosophers, even while deploring the killing and disruption of civic life caused by war, have regarded war as they have the state's use of violence against its domestic enemies: as a necessary evil, a means often justified by the ends of state security, order, and justice. It was not until the nineteenth century, in the wake of the devastating nationalistic wars of the Napoleonic period, that an influential counterculture of pacifism emerged again. The most prominent of the new pacifists were literary intellectuals: the American poet and essayist Henry David Thoreau[15] and the Russian nobleman and novelist Leo Tolstoy[16] blended a back-to-the-simple-life philosophical anarchism with the basic Christian ethic of nonviolence, and both urged individuals to refuse to cooperate with governments that would make them go to war against the dictates of reason and conscience.

The Nonviolent Resistance of Gandhi and His Followers

The pacifist leader from whom contemporary devotees of nonviolence draw most inspiration, Mohandas K. Gandhi, was himself a close student of the pacifist philosophers Thoreau, Tolstoy, the Quakers, and Jesus. Fusing this Western pacifist tradition with the Buddhist, Jain, and Vedic Hindu philosophies of nonviolence and inventing new techniques of exerting political pressure, Gandhi developed nonviolent resistance into a political force that, he argued, could make war obsolete.

Gandhi championed the philosophy and practice of nonviolence not only as a way of life for individuals but also as an instrument of politics for groups and nations. The central and animating concept was *ahimsa,* the brotherhood, common dignity, and moral interdependence of all human beings, which when deeply felt would render a man or woman incapable of deliberately inflicting harm on others. Its essential method was *satyagraha,* or "soul force," the active resistance to evil and cultivation of the good, first in oneself and then in others—good being the truth and nonviolence of ahimsa, and evil being falsehood and violence. British colonial rule over India violated the dignity of Indians and falsified the truth that they were brothers of the English, not their subjects; Indian independence, therefore, was a necessary condition of ahimsa. But independence had first to be achieved through nonviolent resistance to British overlordship, and by peaceful techniques of noncooperation: work stoppages, boycotts of British goods, sit-ins and lie-ins against attempts by British officials to use their power—never with hate against the individual British official and always with a reasoned and communicated explanation for the resistance to the evil act. Gandhi persuaded millions of Indians to join him in the satyagraha method of agitating for national independence, in contrast with millions recruited by rival Indian nationalist movements that relied on violent subversion of British rule. For a complex of reasons, the British finally granted full independence to India after World War II; undoubtedly one reason was the sympathy and respect for the Indian cause that Gandhi had evoked in many Britons.

When asked whether an independent India would adopt satyagraha as an instrument of state policy, internally and externally, Gandhi was candidly pessimistic; his belief that the independent government set up by Jawaharlal Nehru in 1947 would rely on armed police to enforce domestic order and on a well-equipped military establishment to protect India's borders was a principal reason Gandhi declined to join the government. However, he remained distressed to the end of his life— he was, ironically, killed by an assassin's bullet—that an independent India would not try the noble experiment satyagraha. The following dialogue, which took place with an American questioner in 1940, reveals his feeling about extending nonviolence to the nation-state system:

Questioner: Suppose a free India adopts Satyagraha as an instrument of state policy, how would she defend herself against probable aggression by another sovereign state?
Gandhi: I fear that the chances of nonviolence being accepted as a principle of state policy are very slight. . . .

But I may state my own individual view of the potency of nonviolence. I believe that a state can be administered on a nonviolent basis if the vast majority of the people are nonviolent . . . Supposing, therefore, that India attained independence through pure nonviolence, India could retain it too by the same means. A nonviolent man or society does not anticipate or provide for attacks from without. . . . If the worst happens, there are two ways open to nonviolence. To yield possession but non-cooperate with the aggressor. Thus, supposing that a modern edition of Nero descended upon India, the representatives of the state will let him in but tell him he will get no assistance from the people. They will prefer death to submission. The second way would be nonviolent resistance by the people who have been trained in the nonviolent way. They would offer themselves unarmed as fodder for the aggressor's cannon. The underlying belief in either case is that even a Nero is not devoid of a heart. The unexpected spectacle of endless rows upon rows of men and women simply dying rather than surrender to the will of an aggressor must ultimately melt him and his soldiery. Practically speaking there will be probably no greater loss in men than if forcible resistance was offered. There will be no expenditure in armaments and fortifications.[17]

By so explaining the essential characteristics of a country's nonviolent defense against an aggressor, Gandhi stipulates conditions that, according even to his own speculations, make it very unlikely that it could become the dominant regime of international relations. Most of the people in a state practicing nonviolence must themselves be dedicated to the philosophy and trained in nonviolent action. They must be willing to yield physical possession of their country to an aggressor rather than engage in violence to prevent its being taken over. They must not submit to the aggressor's regime, however, even if he takes over the country, and they must be willing to be killed rather than submit. Ultimate success, or the eventual relinquishing of control of the country by the aggressor, follows from the assumption that the moral superiority, or soul force, of such absolutely dedicated and pervasive resistance changes the aggressor's desire to subdue the country.

Since almost all the people of the world would have to be devotees of nonviolence for war to be purged from world society, and since the required moral conversion of humankind would take a long time (decades? centuries?), during the process of conversion those who did not believe in the philosophy still would run most of the world. The few countries with war machines dismantled or paralyzed by the activities of domestic believers in nonviolence would be open to military occupation or domination by adversaries with war machines still operating.

Gandhi and his disciples might be willing to accept this as a temporary result, in the belief that matters indeed might have to get worse before they got better. Gandhian absolutists, in any event, would define success as being morally right rather than merely physically preserving themselves.

Statesmen, however, normally put political objectives ahead of morality—even when constrained by moral considerations—and would act on the assumption that their highest political objective, as mandated by the constituents of the polity for which they are responsible, is to maintain the physical survival of the people of the country. To be sure, this objective may sometimes require surrender to a militarily more powerful opponent (as Japan was forced to surrender in August 1945, but only as a last resort) when it becomes clear beyond doubt that the alternative to surrender is ultimate defeat with an even greater loss of life.

The renewed appeal of Gandhi's ideas in the contemporary period is a product of the growing fear that going to war with the massive lethal power now available to belligerents will unavoidably negate the objective of national survival. The Gandhian prescription of choosing instead to live under conditions imposed by the opponent, while working to subvert his regime, may be the more practical, let alone moral, alternative even for nations that have not yet been militarily defeated in war. Indeed, there is a growing body of historical research on Danish and Norwegian nonviolent subversion of the regimes Hitler imposed on those countries during World War II that supports the argument that the techniques developed by Gandhi may be more effective means of preserving the dignity and eventual liberation of a militarily occupied country than violent resistance, which is likely to provoke greater retaliatory violence with more destructive weapons.[18]

Some of Gandhi's disciples have attempted to elaborate and apply his concepts and techniques of nonviolent resistance to the contemporary problems of deterrence and defense under the threat of nuclear holocaust. In the 1980s, Gene Sharp, the director of the Program on Nonviolent Sanctions in Conflict and Defense at Harvard University's Center for International Affairs, even took on the task of showing that countries could better protect themselves against potential Soviet aggression if they were to organize themselves for determined nonmilitary resistance instead of continuing to rely on the increasingly incredible threat of nuclear escalation. In his cogently reasoned treatise *Making Europe Unconquerable: The Potential of Civilian-based Deterrence and*

Defence, Sharp argued that NATO countries had mindlessly reacted to their predicament by digging themselves into a deeper hole where "the capacity to defend in order to deter has been replaced by the capability to destroy massively without the ability to defend."[19] Under Sharp's proposed alternative grand strategy,

> deterrence and defense are to be accomplished by civilian forms of struggle—social, economic, political and psychological. Many kinds of political noncooperation, strikes, economic boycotts, symbolic protests, civil disobedience, social boycotts, and more extreme methods of disruption and intervention are among the weapons of this policy. . . . The aims are to deny the attackers their objectives and to make [the] society politically indigestible and ungovernable by the attackers. Consolidation of foreign rule, a puppet government, or a government of usurpers becomes impossible. In addition, the civilian defenders aim to subvert the loyalty of the aggressor's troops and functionaries, to make them unreliable in carrying out orders and repression, and even to induce them to mutiny.
>
> . . . Potential attackers are deterred when they see that their objectives will be denied them, political consolidation prevented, and that as a consequence of these struggles unacceptable costs will be imposed on them politically, economically, and internationally.[20]

Sharp builds the case for the policy of nonviolent resistance on strategic rather than moral grounds, distinguishing his approach from the traditional pacifism that rejects all violence a priori and puts peace ahead of all other social objectives. He insists that nonviolent resistance, like the strategies it proposes to supplant, be evaluated on grounds of cost-effectiveness for assuring the survival of a community and its values. On these grounds, he concludes, it is much superior to the strategies for securing the integrity of the community through the threat of nuclear retaliation in response to intolerable provocations. For if nuclear deterrence fails, the consequence is likely to be holocaust and national annihilation; but "the failure of civilian-based defense preparations to deter invasion . . . does not bring likelihood of annihilation, but instead application for the first time of the real [nonviolent] defense capacity."[21]

THE GALTUNGIAN SYNTHESIS

Like many pacifists, Johan Galtung, the influential contemporary Norwegian social scientist, sees the solution to the problem of large-scale violence in the reform of basic interpersonal and intergroup relationships. But Galtung regards violence as a much broader phenomenon than physical attack and destruction. In his definition it includes "anything avoidable that impedes personal growth."[22]

Like the advocates of world government, Galtung maintains that a wholesale transformation of the structure of the existing world political/institutional system is a necessary condition for the ascendancy of nonviolent human relationships, but he differs from many world federalists in his insistence that the structural reforms need to reach down into the basic organization of social, economic, and political relationships within and between local communities. Galtung's nonviolent world would consist of

> many small societies, more of them and smaller than the countries
> in today's world. . . . I strongly hold that only in smaller societies
> can the distance between the ruler and ruled be small enough
> to permit self-expression to everybody, and only with smaller
> societies can large-scale hegemonial tendencies be avoided
> [in Galtung's lexicon "hegemonial" relationships are closely
> associated with violence].[23]

These small, territorially based societies would be crisscrossed and tied together by a "strong web of nonterritorial organizations . . . putting everybody in community with local neighbors as well as with distant neighbors."

Cheap means of mobility would be available to everyone, and there would be no visa or passport restrictions. Citizenship would become "more like membership in an association, to be discarded when there is no longer any commitment" to a particular society. But,

> could there also be multiple citizenship or no citizenship at all?
> Why not? Some persons might opt for multiple membership at
> both the community and the social levels, and they might refuse
> citizenship in anything corresponding to today's nation-states.
> The world would not go under for that reason.[24]

Galtung is not content to leave all regulation of interpersonal and intergroup relations entirely to voluntary cooperative processes, however. He recognizes that

> there must somewhere be some central authority that can make and enact plans for such matters as world food distribution, world employment, world ecological balance, world water and oxygen budgets and that can administer the riches that belong to all, such as the seabed and oceans, the bio-atmosphere, the cosmos, subterranean deposits.[25]

Though he admits that "the reconciliation of this need with the need for decentralization would continue to be problematic," Galtung outlines one possible design for a world authority to preserve maximum decentralization consistent with imperatives for world order and justice, a design quite similar to Falk's preferred world polity. It provides for direct election of representatives to a House of States (representing the territorial units), a House of Minorities (representing emerging states), a House of Transnational Associations ("like a parliament or congress"), and a House of Supranational Organizations (representing functional groups). All four houses would articulate the concerns of their constituencies, some of which obviously would overlap, and would pass resolutions. When it comes to making binding decisions, however, Galtung places most authority, initially at least, in the House of States.[26]

Galtung envisions that the basic means of obtaining compliance with the decisions of the world central authority would be the authority's "remunerative power," not coercive force:

> I see a world central authority as having enormous resources for constructive use at its disposal, which means capital, goods and know-how. The authority should be able to disburse all three where they are needed . . . , but there could also be above-normal remuneration to those who comply particularly well with the international norms. In short, I am thinking of a system of positive sanctions much more than negative sanctions, for the simple reasons that the latter do not seem to work as an instrument of compliance and the former are at the same time vehicles of global development.[27]

The Galtungians, like the Gandhians and the advocates of a supranational federal world government, quite consciously are dealing with the long term. When it comes to dealing with immediate threats of war, they must join their contemporaries in choosing among the relatively limited means of controlling conflict available within the still-prevailing nation-state system.

GENERAL AND COMPLETE DISARMAMENT

There is an attractive simplicity to the notion that war can be eliminated as an instrument of international relations if states will give up their military arsenals. Its attraction lies in its apolitical neatness: it requires no precondition that adversaries first solve their political conflicts or agree on a new world constitutional system, and it expresses no need to effect a moral revolution turning all human beings into Christians or Gandhian saints who love their enemies. All it requires is a mutual recognition that the costs and risks of war in the modern world outweigh any gains a state might hope to achieve by going to war, that no statespersons or nations really want war, and that the only reason nations prepare for war is to deter others from resorting to force of arms against them and their allies. Disarmament would be tangible confirmation of the universal recognition that war is no longer a cost-effective means of advancing state interests, and it would remove the self-defense rationale that most states invoke to justify their arsenals and war-fighting strategies. Any government that began to build an arsenal in an otherwise disarmed world would be admitting to the world, including its own people, that it had aggressive designs; other states would isolate it economically and politically, and its own citizens would organize against it.

Periodically, the attractiveness of the idea of general and complete disarmament generates popular support from war-weary or frightened populations, and statespersons have occasionally become its champions. (Most official diplomatic efforts at disarmament have been limited to specific weapons and have attempted to set tolerable ceilings on retained arms. Some of these specific arms-limitation efforts will be looked at in detail in Chapter 10.)

Woodrow Wilson's Fourth Point

President Woodrow Wilson, in the fourth of his Fourteen Points defining the peace that would follow World War I, came close to embracing general and complete disarmament by insisting that "national armaments will be reduced to the lowest point consistent with domestic safety."[28] This formula surely would have been difficult to negotiate among sovereign states of vastly different sizes and domestic systems of law and order, but assuming that some agreement could have been reached on different levels of "domestic" police forces, it would have constituted as much of an approximation as could be expected, short of world government or moral-pacifist revolution, of a blueprint for a disarmed world. When it came to incorporation of Wilson's peace proposal in the Treaty of Versailles, however, other heads of state found Wilson's fourth point too radical; the American delegation was compelled to explain that "domestic safety" implied not only internal policing "but the protection of territory against invasion." Article 8 of the completed treaty finally contained the totally noncontroversial statement that "the maintenance of peace requires the reduction of national armaments to the lowest point consistent with national safety."[29] The rationale for standing armies and awesome national arsenals was once again legitimized.

The Superpower Disarmament Charade

The idea of general and complete disarmament was revived by the Soviets in September of 1959. Addressing the United Nations General Assembly, Premier Nikita Khrushchev said that

> the Soviet Government, after examining from all angles the
> situation which has arisen, has reached the firm conclusion that
> the way out of the impasse must be sought through general and
> complete disarmament. This approach completely eliminates the
> possibility of any state gaining military advantages of any kind.
> General and complete disarmament will remove all the obstacles
> that have arisen during the discussions of the questions involved
> by partial disarmament, and will clear the way for the institution
> of universal and complete control.[30]

Then, anticipating that the United States and its allies would not find this a workable proposal and would brand it mere propaganda, the Soviet leader reiterated some of the Soviet Union's standing proposals for "partial disarmament," on which it was still "prepared to come to terms."[31]

The U.S. government's counterproposals, presented in February 1960, predictably focused on feasible measures "to create a more stable military environment" as the urgent first step—feasible meaning verifiable through reliable national means of inspection. Once such measures could be successfully implemented, reducing the risk of war, the world could move on to a "second stage of general disarmament." As explained by Secretary of State Christian Herter,

> Our objective in this second stage should be two-fold: *First,* to create universally accepted rules of law, which if followed would prevent all nations from attacking other nations. Such rules of law should be backed by a World Court and by effective means of enforcement—that is, by international armed force. *Second,* to reduce national armed forces, under safeguarded and verified agreements to the point where no single nation or group of nations could effectively oppose this enforcement of international law by international machinery.[32]

This U.S.–Soviet dialogue, or rather, debate, over general and complete disarmament was transparently an elaborate stage play, cynically concocted by leaders on each side to pander to the hopes of the presumably unsophisticated general population. The Soviets were proposing that all nations should destroy all their weapons without any reliable procedures to ensure that some parties to the agreement would not retain theirs while the others disarmed: controls would follow disarmament. The Americans were proposing that world government should be set up prior to general disarmament. Neither presented its grandiose proposals with the idea that the other could possibly accept them. Indeed, neither side would have been willing to implement its own proposals.

The superpowers continued this charade during the early 1960s, until the Cuban missile crisis focused the minds of statespersons on the need to get down to serious negotiations. The high point, or perhaps low point, in the general and complete disarmament game was the presentation by both governments of elaborate draft treaties to the Eighteen Nation Disarmament Committee in the spring of 1962. The Soviet draft treaty provided for a four-year disarmament process, to be carried out in three consecutive stages, at the end of which the states would retain "only strictly limited contingents of police (militia) equipped with light firearms, and intended for the maintenance of internal order and for the discharge of their obligations under the United Nations Charter."[33] The Kennedy administration's counterproposal was for general and complete disarmament in a decade-long process, also to be implemented in three stages. At the completion of the process, "states would have at their disposal only those nonnuclear armaments, forces, facilities, and establishments as are agreed to be necessary to maintain internal order and protect the personal security of citizens." In the American plan, a United Nations Peace Force would be built up simultaneously with the phased reductions in national armament to ensure, at each step, that somewhere in the international system there was sufficient military power to deter or suppress aggressive threats or use of arms.[34]

On the surface, the superpowers had converged on the goal of general and complete disarmament to be accomplished by a phased approach, and even on many of the types of substantive reductions within each stage. Most encouraging was the Soviet acceptance, in principle, of an International Disarmament Organization with the function of overseeing the process from the start and the authority to ensure verification of all agreed reductions at each stage. But in their detailed provisions for such a supervisory body, the key to the practicality of even the first stages of limited arms reduction, the superpowers were as far apart as ever. The Soviets insisted that the International Disarmament Organization should be under the direct control of the UN security Council, where they could veto any verification or control measures they disliked.[35] By contrast, the American plan provided that the "International Disarmament Organization and its inspectors would have access without veto to all places necessary for the purpose of verification."[36]

From the late 1960s on, during the period of serious U.S.–Soviet negotiations to limit strategic forces, both Moscow and Washington abandoned their competitive catering to popular hopes for general and complete disarmament. In early 1986, however, the Soviet leader, Mikhail Gorbachev, reopened the propaganda contest by proposing a program for "ridding the earth of nuclear weapons, to be implemented and completed within the next 15 years, before the end of this century."[37] Like the general disarmament schemes of the early 1960s, the Gorbachev proposal also included a phased process, starting with agreements that were not entirely unrealistic. Stage one, for example, would reduce by one-half the nuclear arms that could reach the other superpower's territory. But the Soviet leader made clear that even stage one would be impossible to negotiate unless the Reagan administration first abandoned its Strategic Defense Initiative. The consensus in the U.S. government was that Gorbachev was playing to the public galleries and had not really offered a serious proposal for negotiation. President Reagan's response and the serious arms reductions that did ensue are detailed in Chapter 10.

Thus far even with the end of the Cold War, general and complete disarmament schemes have proven to be the stuff that dreams are made of and not really negotiable; for complete worldwide disarmament would require either the establishment of a powerful supranational authority to enforce it or a degree of trust among previously armed rivals that would allow each to accept on faith claims by the others about the content of their arsenals. In short, the massive political or moral changes that need to be instituted in the world-transforming approaches to peace—world government, universal nonviolence, or the Galtungian synthesis—are also the preconditions for total nuclear disarmament or general disarmament. Any such grand disarmament scheme that fails to provide for political and moral transformation can be no more than an exercise in wishful thinking or propaganda.

NOTES

1. On Crucé's proposal see F. H. Hinsley, *Power and the Pursuit of Peace* (London: Cambridge University Press, 1963), pp. 20–28; also Edith Wynner and Georgia Lloyd, *Searchlight on Peace Plans* (New York: Dutton, 1949), p. 33.

2. William Penn, *An Essay toward the Present and Future Peace of Europe by the Establishment of an European Dyet, Parliament or Estates* (London: Society of Friends, 1936).

3. Quotations from the Bellers plan taken from Hinsley, *Power and the Pursuit of Peace*, pp. 38–39. See also Wynner and Lloyd, *Searchlights on Peace Plans*, pp. 36–37.

4. Abbé de Saint-Pierre's *Project of Perpetual Peace* is outlined by Wynner and Lloyd, *Searchlight on Peace Plans*, pp. 37–38.

5. Minister Fleury's reaction to the abbé's *Project* is quoted by Frederick Schuman, in *International Politics: The Western State System and the World Community* (New York: McGraw-Hill, 1958), p. 205.

6. Hinsley presents Rousseau's reaction to the abbé's *Project* in *Power and the Pursuit of Peace,* pp. 48–49.

7. See Stanley Hoffmann's essay, "Rousseau on War and Peace," in his *The State of War: Essays on the Theory and Practice of International Politics* (New York: Praeger, 1965), pp. 54–87.

8. Grenville Clark and Louis B. Sohn, *World Peace through World Law* (Cambridge, Mass.: Harvard University Press, 1960).

9. *Ibid.*, p. xi.

10. *Ibid.*, p. xxix.

11. Richard A. Falk, *A Study of Future Worlds* (New York: Free Press, 1975), pp. 224–275.

12. *Ibid.*, pp. 242–248.

13. *The New Testament.* An American Translation by Edgar J. Goodspeed (Chicago: University of Chicago Press, 1948).

14. Lewis Einstein, ed., *Erasmus Against War* (Boston: Merrymount Press, 1907).

15. See Henry David Thoreau, *On the Duty of Civil Disobedience* (Boston: Fellowship Press, 1853).

16. See Leo Tolstoy, *The Kingdom of God Is within You* (New York: Crowell, 1899); and *The Law of Love and the Law of Violence* (New York: R. Field, 1948).

17. M. K. Gandhi, *Non-Violent Resistance* (Ahmedabad, India: Navejivan Trust, n.d.), pp. 383–387.

18. See Gene Sharp, *The Politics of Nonviolent Action* (Boston: Porter Sargent, 1973); and Adam Roberts, ed., *The Strategy of Civilian Defense* (Harrisburg, Pa.: Stackpole Books, 1968).

19. Gene Sharp, *Making Europe Unconquerable: The Potential of Civilian-Based Deterrence and Defence* (Cambridge, Mass: Ballinger, 1985), p. 31.

20. *Ibid.*, p. 50.

21. *Ibid.*, pp. 107–108.

22. Johan Galtung, *The True Worlds: A Transnational Perspective* (New York: Free Press, 1980), p. 67.

23. *Ibid.*, p. 92.

24. *Ibid.*, p. 93.

25. *Ibid.*, p. 93.

26. *Ibid.*, p. 348.

27. *Ibid.*, p. 351.

28. Woodrow Wilson, Address to Congress, January 8, 1918. Text in Henry Steele Commager, ed., *Documents of American History since 1898* (Englewood Cliffs, N.J. Prentice Hall, 1973:1, pp. 137–139.

29. U.S. Department of State, *Foreign Relations of the United States, 1918 Supplement* (Washington, D.C.: U.S. Government Printing Office), vol. 1, p. 405.

30. Nikita S. Khrushchev, Address to the U.N. General Assembly, Fourteenth Session, Plenary, *Official Records,* 799th mtg. (United Nations: September 10, 1959), p. 36.

31. *Ibid.*, p. 37.

32. Christian A. Herter, "National Security with Arms Limitations," *Department of State Bulletin,* 42 (March 7, 1960), 355–356.

33. Soviet Draft Treaty of March 15, 1962, United States Arms Control and Disarmament Agency, *Documents on Disarmament 1962*, vol. 1 (Washington, D.C.: U.S. Government Printing Office, 1963), 103–127.

34. United States Treaty Outline of April 18, 1962, *Documents on Disarmament 1962*, vol. 1, pp. 351–382.

35. Soviet Draft Treaty, *ibid.*, pp. 123–126.

36. U.S. Treaty Outline, *ibid.*, p. 352.

37. Excerpts from Mikhail Gorbachev's comprehensive arms control proposal of January 1986, *New York Times*, January 17, 1986.

CHAPTER 9

Efforts to Reduce the Role of War in the International System

The apparent infeasibility of attempts to purge war from the world in the foreseeable future has compelled those determined to improve the odds for human survival to search for ways at least to reduce the role of war in the existing system.

Some of the approaches to reducing the role of war emphasize legal and institutional mechanisms, some diplomatic strategies and tactics, and still others limits on the deployment and use of military force. Having more modest goals than the complete elimination of war, these near-term approaches assume, for the time being, both the continued existence of the nation-state system and the reliance of statesmen, at least in part, on military balances of power and alliances designed to secure the interests of their countries.

This chapter analyzes four principal kinds of war-reduction efforts: international law, diplomatic accommodation and restraint, collective security institutions, and special measures to settle disputes and resolve conflicts. All are attempts to control the most dangerous tendencies in international relations rather than to overhaul the structure of world politics. Arms-control measures are also a part of this approach, but their special requirements and implications warrant treatment in a separate chapter.

INTERNATIONAL LAW

Practitioners and theorists working on peace and security issues in the field of international law tend to share the conviction that statesmen can and must agree to certain limits on the permissible behavior of countries, without which the system of sovereign states would degenerate into brutish anarchy.

This elementary premise was given its classical philosophical statement in 1625 by the great Dutch jurist, Hugo Grotius, in his treatise *On the Law of War and Peace*. Grotius reiterated a secular version of the medieval church doctrine that there is a law above nations—natural law—which follows from the assumption that humankind is at base, and ultimately, one community. The substantive content of natural law can be determined for particular relationships among states by right reason. From the nature of man right reason can deduce the laws that should govern the interaction of individuals in civil society, and similarly it can deduce from the nature of states the laws that should govern the interaction among states in international society.

On the assumption that human nature is characterizied essentially by sociability, the desire for a peaceful life that has led men and women the world over to establish communities of law and order, Grotius reasoned that the highest laws of these communities, or states, are those necessary to maintain a peaceful social life. And because the nature of states, derived from the nature of human beings, is defined primarily by this function of maintaining domestic communities of law and order, the governments of the separate states must be sovereign within their own realms.

Grotius argued, therefore, that the laws governing relations among nations must first and foremost protect the sovereignty of the states themselves, through rules designed to prevent interference in one another's jurisdictions. The other principles of international law, Grotius taught, can be gleaned from the durable arrangements sovereign states have made among themselves, including peace treaties, boundary agreements, and allocations of fishing and navigation privileges in commonly used waters. These customary international laws result for the most part from negotiations undertaken to prevent war or to terminate ongoing wars; peace requires that these customary laws be given presumptive validity. Defending the international legal order may even justify resorting to war to prevent the retrogression of world society into anarchy.[1]

Still operating largely in the Grotian tradition, contemporary jurists in defining international law draw on concepts invoked by the International Court of Justice, on the dominant principles and language of treaties and of the charters of international institutions, and on legalistic rationalizations governments offer to justify their international acts. This dominant tradition of international law is essentially conservative, in the sense of respecting and guarding the basic state-sovereignty structure of world society and the inherited corpus of specific agreements, or customary law, that has proved relatively durable.

The Marginal Influence of International Law on War and Peace

When wars result from acts that violate norms of the state system and widely accepted agreements, invoking international law can provide a framework for appeals by citizens who oppose the warlike actions of their own governments, as well as for appeals by international forums to restore the conditions of peace. But to the extent that wars are themselves the product of unresolved conflicts of sovereignty over territory or population or of new economic or political developments not adequately anticipated in past formal arrangements—in short, most of the determinants of war identified in Part I—international law itself, other than providing some established procedures for settlement of disputes, affords few if any rules for avoiding wars.

The Role of International Law

By codifying the outcomes of disputes resolved through benign bargaining, coercive diplomacy, or war, international law does play a role in discouraging new confrontations that can lead to war. The treaties that define the boundaries of states or their rights of access to particular resources can prevent the kinds of misunderstandings and miscalculations, and tests of strength, that often result from leaving valued areas or assets up for grabs.

A growing area of creative international law is the formulation of agreed-on rules of the road for traffic in nonland areas: rivers, oceans, airspace, and outer space. As these "commons" areas are used more heavily, such rules have become crucial for avoiding accidents, misunderstandings, and confrontations of the sort that can easily engage the prestige of contending states, inflame popular passions, and lead to war.[2]

Environmental policy is another increasingly important field in which international law, by formulating new rules to be negotiated among countries, is crucial to avoiding bitter conflict; guidelines must be developed to deal with environmental pollution that crosses state boundaries or affects commonly used water or air. Without specific environmental impact treaties establishing permissible and impermissible activities, warning and accountability procedures, and liability obligations, countries may become intensely angry at injuries inflicted by other nations on the health and well-being of their peoples. This need was dramatically highlighted in 1986 by the explosion at the Chernobyl nuclear facility in the Soviet Union, which spewed radioactive clouds over many countries.

Particularly in the burgeoning fields of international transportation, communications, and transborder pollution control it has been the modest achievement of international law to remove ambiguities in the rights and mutual obligations of states, thus reducing the need to rely heavily on coercive bargaining with its attendant risks of conflict escalation.

A STATECRAFT OF RATIONAL RESTRAINT

Much international law tends to be an after-the-fact device for reducing the likelihood of war: a clarification of rights and obligations in situations that have already led to intense conflict, under the assumption that future war-threatening situations will be of the same type. But not all situations that can lead to dangerous conflict can be sufficiently anticipated in current legal arrangements. Because circumstances change, the laws codifying the old circumstances can become irrelevant to new clashes of interests and new balances of power.

In international relations, peace more often than not has been the result of prudent statecraft in advance of the legal codification of rights and obligations rather than the result of the implementation of existing law. The succession of the period of relative peace in nineteenth-century Europe, under the Concert of Europe, by the period of general war in the twentieth century shows this dominance of diplomacy over law.

The Concert of Europe

The elaborate set of territorial treaties of consultation that constituted the new law of nations after the defeat of Napoleon Bonaparte in 1815 were designed to prevent a revolutionary imperialist like Napoleon from launching a new rampage of expansion. Unfortunately, the elitist consultative Concert system that developed did not deeply reflect the

underlying social, economic, technological, and political forces transforming the domestic character of states and their relations with one
another. The result was the explosion of the two devastating world wars
of the twentieth century.

Yet a moderate and relatively war-free international system did prevail for most of the post-Napoleonic nineteenth century. However, this
was less due to the constraining force of the new international legal
order than to the diplomatic brilliance of the leading statesmen of that
era — especially Metternich, Castlereagh, and then Bismarck — who ma-
nipulated international relations within a self-imposed set of restraints
against actions that could fundamentally challenge the security of any of
the major states of Europe. It was the dismissal of Bismarck by Kaiser
Wilhelm in 1890, in fact, that signaled the end of the period of restrained statesmanship: international relations quickly degenerated into
the anarchical arms races and power plays that brought on World War I.[3]

Immanuel Kant's Prescription of Restrained Statecraft

Important characteristics of the moderate statecraft of post-Napoleonic Europe were anticipated by the philosopher Immanuel Kant in
his pamphlet *Perpetual Peace,* published in 1795.[4] In our time Henry
Kissinger, a prominent intellectual turned statesman — whose major academic contribution was an admiring history of the diplomacy of Metternich, Castlereagh, and Bismarck — claims to be more a devotee of
the works of Kant than of any other philosopher.[5] (Kissinger's claim is
credible only to the extent that he shares Kant's emphasis on rational
restraint; it lacks credibility if Kant's emphasis on the importance of a
state's domestic constitution is taken into account.)

Kant argued that no war is just and that wars cannot be cleansed of
their inherent evil by the good purposes for which they may be fought.
Rather, war is the greatest evil in human civilization: more than any
other social institution it violates the primary ethical imperative that
humans must treat each other as ends, never mainly as means to other
ends.

For Kant, the key question was how to move the world away from
reliance on war as a normal instrument of statecraft and toward the ideal
of a warless world. He recognized that war is so much a part of international relations that it cannot be simply legislated out of existence; the
goal of perpetual peace therefore must be made a project for statesmen,

with a set of realistic imperatives for, and limitations on, state action that would constitute progress toward the ideal world. The specific international legal instruments Kant proposed as steps in this project were a multistate treaty of permanent mutual nonaggression and a confederation, or permanent congress of sovereign states, through which they could bargain to adjust their differences; but he considered the instruments less important than the commitment of governments to policies of mutual restraint based on respect for each other's domains, national values, and citizenry.

Countries must cultivate a sense of limits beyond which they cannot push each other without provoking war, according to Kant. Like individuals in peaceful domestic communities, nations must learn to treat each other as entities worthy of respect and therefore—most importantly— immune from physical violation. Republican countries, in contrast with monarchical or despotic ones, are likely to adhere to and strengthen such restraint, Kant argued, because of the natural inclination of the ordinary citizenry to tend to their domestic pursuits without the disruptions caused by war.

Kant also urged the abolition of standing armies and eventually of all military force that might be used in external adventures; this would further limit the temptations of states to engage in war-provoking actions.

Between the two world wars of the twentieth century, these Kantian notions found expression in the Locarno Pact of 1925 and the Kellogg-Briand Pact of 1928—both reactions to the failure of the collective security mechanisms of the League of Nations to limit the traditional game of power politics.

The "Spirit of Locarno"

By the end of 1922, the new peace and security system installed after World War I appeared to be on the verge of collapse. When Germany defaulted on the war reparations payments imposed by the victorious Allies, France, in an effort to force the defeated nation to pay, sent troops to occupy the German industrial area of the Ruhr. And because Germany also dragged its heels on implementing the disarmament provisions of the Versailles Treaty, the French in 1925, when the Allies were scheduled to implement the Versailles agreements to end their military occupation of the Rhineland, postponed evacuating their troops.

In an effort to counteract the reforging of an anti-German alliance, Gustav Stresemann, the German foreign minister, fashioned a major peace initiative: he proposed a set of nonaggression and arbitration treaties, principally among France, Britain, Italy, and Germany. These countries, as well as Belgium, Czechoslovakia, and Poland, met in the Swiss town of Locarno in the fall of 1925 in an omnibus negotiation of a pact to remove the scourge of war from Europe. A treaty on the Rhineland provided for that region's full demilitarization, pledging France, Germany, and Belgium to refrain from resorting to war against each other, except for a flagrant breach of the Locarno Pact itself or as a part of a League of Nations action against an aggressor state. France also signed two special treaties of guarantee with Poland and Czechoslovakia providing for mutual assistance against Germany in case that country should violate her new obligations. Finally, Germany signed arbitration treaties with each of the other countries, agreeing to submit her disputes with them to a conciliation commission and then, if necessary, to the World Court and the Council of the League. As the icing on the cake of peace, Germany was admitted to the League of Nations.[6]

The Kellogg-Briand Pact

The official enthrallment with pacts of peace reached its apogee with the General Treaty for the Renunciation of War, signed by fifteen countries in Paris in 1928 and joined by forty-six more over the next two years.

The new peace effort started with a modest proposal by the French foreign minister, Aristide Briand, to the U.S. secretary of state, Frank Kellogg, that the two countries celebrate the tenth anniversary of the American entry into World War I with a statement outlawing war between France and the United States. Briand's initiative was greeted with unexpected enthusiasm in the United States, where the Hoover administration was energized to expand it into a universally binding agreement among all countries to renounce war as an instrument of national policy.

The British and the French governments were not pleased with the American attempt to convert Briand's limited bilateral initiative into a global spectacular, for a universal prohibition against resorting to military force would conflict with such standing alliance commitments as French guarantees to Poland and Czechoslovakia, as well as with British and French colonial responsibilities. France insisted that the prohibition on resorting to force be interpreted as restricting only "wars of aggression," and Britain agreed to join the pact provided that joining did not interfere with its freedom of action in "certain regions of the world, the welfare and integrity of which constitute a special and vital interest for our peace and safety." With these unilateral French and British understandings, the General Treaty, as signed, stipulated that its adherents (1) "condemn recourse to war for the solution of international controversies and renounce it as an instrument of national policy in their relations with one another," and (2) "agree that the settlement or solution of all international disputes or conflicts . . . shall never be sought except by peaceful means."[7]

Kant would have been pleased with these provisions and the simple fact of their being solemnly affirmed on a universal basis, for even though unenforceable, they advanced international standards or imperatives of state behavior needed for lasting peace. He would not have been pleased, however, with the reservations exempting specific wars and collective security obligations, which like the just-war notions of his time allowed a hole wide enough to march an army through any time a signatory country determined the action was in its national interest.

Morgenthau's Rules of Diplomacy

Kantian ideas of rational restraint also underlie the principal recommendations for avoiding a civilization-destroying third world war presented by the twentieth century's most influential realist philosopher of international relations, Hans J. Morgenthau. Morgenthau expressed a limited hope for avoiding cataclysmic war by utilizing and improving diplomacy to control conflicts among countries. He offered nine rules of diplomacy that countries, especially the superpowers, should follow to sustain their interests short of war:

1. Divest diplomacy of the crusading spirit. Universalistic crusades to wipe the forces of evil from the earth or, short of this, efforts of a country to identify its own national interests with a universally valid morality—what Morgenthau called the vice of "nationalistic univeralism"—are incompatible with the accomodation among nations necessary to avoid the total nation-to-nation hostility that results in society-destroying wars. (Henry Kissinger too, as shown in the next section, advocated this kind of restrained realpolitik diplomacy in U.S.–Soviet relations).

2. Restrict the definition of vital national interests—those that cannot be compromised—to national security interests, namely, survival and maintenance of the essential economic well-being of the population. This is the most controversial and difficult to implement of Morgenthau's rules, for it implies abandoning any protection of allies and friends that is not warranted by concern for one's own national security. Before the nuclear age, Morgenthau explained, countries could afford to pursue less restrictively defined national interests, but the prospect of total destruction of the nation in a nuclear war requires the narrower *security* definition of the interests a country should be willing to go to war to defend. (Morgenthau's text renders this rule as: "The objectives of foreign policy must be defined in terms of national interest and must be supported with adequate power." I have rephrased it to reflect his explanation of its meaning better.)

3. Look at the political scene from the point of view of other nations. It is important that a country truly understand its opponents' definitions of their national interests, for otherwise rivals are likely to miscalculate how much they can challenge each other short of intolerable provocation and when the opponent's threat to use force is only a bluff or real.

4. Be willing to compromise on all interests that are not vital. Knowing how to bargain skillfully over secondary interests is an essential part of the diplomatic art. (In fact, Morgenthau's remaining five rules are all facets of this basic diplomacy of compromise.)

5. "Give up the shadow of worthless rights for the substance of real advantage." This is the practical bargaining guidance that follows from distinguishing clearly between vital and secondary interests. It implies that it is unwise for countries to engage their honor, prestige, credibility—machismo, if you will—over anything beyond what is required for national security.

6. "Never put yourself in a position from which you cannot retreat without losing face and from which you cannot advance without grave risks." This means not only having the ability to implement rule 5 but also having good intelligence on the prevailing balance of military power and the scale of values of your opponents, to avoid assuming positions that will be opposed by force of arms. (Khrushchev came perilously close to violating this rule in the 1962 Cuban missile crisis.)

7. "Never allow a weak ally to make decisions for you." This was an important but difficult rule to follow in the post-World War II system of two vast opposing alliances, each led by a superpower. One of the causes of the Sino-Soviet split was the determination of the Soviet Union

to adhere to this rule in the Quemoy-Matsu crisis of the 1950s when the Chinese, for reasons of their own over which the Soviets were not willing to risk nuclear war, engaged in a confrontation with the United States. The rule was violated in the U.S.-South Vietnamese relationship that began in 1954, when the United States took over from France as South Vietnam's protector against North Vietnam, and ended only in 1973, when the United States finally negotiated its withdrawal from Vietnam despite strong objections from South Vietnam.

8. Keep the armed forces an instrument of diplomacy, not its master. The military mind, observed Morgenthau, is trained to think in the absolute—life or death, victory or defeat— and military instruments are designed to destroy an opponent or break his will to resist. The military mind "knows nothing of that patient, intricate, and subtle maneuvering of diplomacy, whose main purpose is to avoid the absolutes of victory and defeat and meet the other side in negotiated compromise."

9. In formulating and conducting foreign policy, the national leaders must not become the slave of public opinion. The often delicate and subtle art of compromise, such as that which produced the mutual recognition by Israel and the PLO in September 1993, requires some degree of freedom from direct democratic control; the necessary bargaining must include conceding some of the other side's objectives and giving up some of one's own, even if the accommodations are unpopular in the short run. The statesperson must "neither surrender to popular passions or disregard them" but "strike a prudent balance between adapting himself to them and marshaling them to support his policies."[8]

Morgenthau recognized that the implementation of these prescriptions for a diplomacy to preserve peace depends on the possession of "extraordinary moral and intellectual qualities" by the world leaders. "A mistake in the evaluation of one of the elements of national power, made by one or the other of the leading statesmen may spell the difference between peace and war. So may an accident spoiling a plan or power calculation." Diplomacy is not enough, but it is essential:

> It is only when nations have surrendered to a higher authority the means of destruction which modern technology has put in their hands—when they have given up their sovereignty—that international peace can be made as secure as domestic peace. . . .
> Yet as there can be no permanent peace without a world state, there can be no world state without the peace-preserving and community-building processes of diplomacy.[9]

Henry Kissinger and Détente

Like Morgenthau, Henry Kissinger subordinated any ultimate vision of a peaceful world polity to here-and-now requirements of preventing a nuclear holocaust. In his academic writings and his statecraft, Kissinger emphasized two essential conditions for a tolerably peaceful international order: (1) an equilibrium of power (primarily military) among the most powerful countries, so that no country can expect to beat any of the others decisively in war or to dictate the conditions under which they must live; and (2) an acceptance by the great powers of the legitimacy of the existing distribution of power and of the territorial and other arrangements of control and influence that are associated with it.

Kissinger's appointment to high office in 1969 came when changes in the world situation and in American domestic politics led him to try his hand at weaving such an equilibrium and legitimacy system. His overriding aim was to reduce the likelihood of nuclear holocaust without reducing American power vis-à-vis that of its principal geopolitical adversary.

Kissinger was able to persuade President Richard Nixon that, because of the Soviet Union's sluggish domestic economic performance, the Kremlin was hungry for trade with the West and so might be willing to assume a "stake in the equilibrium." The United States could make the Soviets pay a current price for expanded commerce in the coin of international moderation, meanwhile luring them into a long-term position of economic dependence. The United States could simultaneously gain additional leverage on the Kremlin by moving to establish cordial relations with the Soviet Union's archrival in Asia. A diplomacy of limited accommodation and mutual restraint, *détente*—or "negotiation rather than confrontation," in Nixon's formulation—might now be able to supplement the military balance of power as the essence of the new statesmanship for avoiding World War III.[10]

Drafted primarily by Henry Kissinger, the Declaration of Principles signed by President Nixon and General Secretary Brezhnev in 1972 gave a remarkably neo-Kantian expression to this strategy:

The United States of America and the Union of Soviet Socialist Republics . . .

HAVE AGREED as follows:

First. They will proceed from the common determination that in the nuclear age there is no alternative to conducting their mutual relations on the basis of peaceful coexistence. Differences in ideology and in the social systems of the U.S.A. and the USSR are not obstacles to the bilateral development of normal relations based on the principles of sovereignty, equality, noninterference in internal affairs and mutual advantage.

Second. The U.S.A. and the USSR attach major importance to preventing the development of situations capable of causing dangerous exacerbation of their relations. Therefore, they will do their utmost to avoid military confrontation and to prevent the outbreak of nuclear war. They will always exercise restraint in their mutual relations, and will be prepared to negotiate and settle differences by peaceful means. Discussions and negotiations of outstanding issues will be conducted in a spirit of reciprocity, and mutual accommodation and mutual benefit.

Both sides recognize that efforts to obtain unilateral advantage at the expense of the other, directly or indirectly, are inconsistent with these objectives.

The prerequisites for maintaining and strengthening peaceful relations between the U.S.A. and the USSR are the recognition of the security interests of the parties based on the principle of equality and the renunciation of the use or threat of force.

[There were twelve principles in all.][11]

At the time of negotiating these accords, Kissinger was not totally convinced that the Soviets really intended to live up to pledges that would involve considerable constriction of their international revolutionary aims.[12] But given the terrible dangers of relying solely on military containment in the nuclear age, he felt it was worth giving the Soviets a chance to become enmeshed in the conservative international order. An adequate balance of military power could be maintained in the background to deter them from revolutionary adventurism, and other coercive pressures—a closer Chinese-American alignment and withdrawal of commercial privileges—could be threatened at any time to remind the Kremlin that peaceful coexistence was conditioned on adherence to the principles signed at the 1972 Moscow summit.

By the time Kissinger left office in 1977, he was disappointed in the results of détente and angry at the Soviets for attempting, especially in Africa, to exploit to their own advantage the unwillingness of the U.S.

Congress, in the isolationist mood following the country's withdrawal from Vietnam, to support coercive countermeasures against Soviet power plays.

Kissinger's grand strategy was also frustrated by congressional refusal to provide him with sufficient tools, in the form of trading and credit opportunities to be offered the Soviets, for conducting the carrot-and-stick diplomacy needed to make détente work. In the Jackson-Vanik and Stevenson amendments to trade and credit legislation, Congress denied the Soviets most favored nation trading privileges (meaning as good as any other nation's) and long-term government credits, both of which Nixon had promised Brezhnev in the 1972 détente package, unless the Kremlin first liberalized its restrictions on Jewish emigration.

Kissinger's experience with détente points up the central limitation of attempts to preserve peace largely through a diplomacy of mutual restraint and accommodation: the top foreign policy officials of the participant countries are required to have at their disposal sufficient resources—carrots and sticks—and negotiating leeway to make the kinds of international adjustments and deals necessary to avoid dangerous confrontations. But unlike conditions in the period of classical European diplomacy from which Kissinger derived many of his insights, contemporary domestic political forces in both the United States and the USSR were not yet ready in the 1970s to provide their diplomats with such resources or negotiating flexibility.

Gorbachev and the End of the Cold War

Defying the predictions of hard-line theorists on both sides of the Cold War divide that neither side would give up the struggle for global hegemony without provoking a world war, the Soviet Union at the end of the 1980s, under the leadership of Mikhail Gorbachev, gave clear indications that it did not want to fight the United States any more, violently or nonviolently. It was hardly inevitable that the Soviet leaders would come to the conclusion at this time that they had more to lose than to gain by persisting with their struggle. The history of the world shows few if any aspirants to global hegemony giving up their ambitions peacefully. Yet this is precisely what Gorbachev was determined should happen.

Gorbachev's calculus of Soviet interests and priorities was entirely rational. When he became General Secretary of the Central Committee of the Communist Party of the Soviet Union in March 1985, he saw that "a major overhaul" was required of the Soviet political economy. As he put it in his 1987 book *Perestroika: New Thinking for Our Country and the World,*

something strange was taking place:

> . . . In the last fifteen years the national income growth rates had declined by more than a half and by the beginning of the eighties had fallen to a level close to economic stagnation. A country that was once quickly closing on the world's advanced nations began to lose one position after another. . . .
>
> An absurd situation was developing. The Soviet Union, the world's biggest producer of steel, raw materials, fuel, and energy, has shortfalls in them due to wasteful or inefficient use. One of the biggest producers of grain for food, it nevertheless has to buy millions of tons of grain a year for fodder. We have the largest number of doctors and hospital beds per thousand of the population and, at the same time, there are glaring shortcomings in our health services. Our rockets can find Haley's comet and fly to Venus with amazing accuracy, but side by side with these scientific and technological triumphs is an obvious lack of efficiency in using scientific achievements for economic needs, and many Soviet household appliances are of poor quality.[13]

A fundamental program of *perestroika* (restructuring) of the Soviet political economy was required, based on "dramatically increased independence of enterprises and associations, their transition to full self-accounting and self-financing, and granting all appropriate rights to work collectives. They will now be fully responsible for efficient management and end results." The reforms, demanding dedicated initiative by people at every level of society, explained Gorbachev, also required "efforts to . . . develop self government and extend *glasnost,* that is openness, in the entire management network."[14]

As it turned out, Gorbachev underestimated the degree of restructuring that would be required. Some of his associates, coached by American advisers, urged a rapid conversion of the economy to full market capitalism—anything less, they argued, would only perpetuate the inefficiencies of the command economy that had brought the country to its present stagnation. And democracy, if Gorbachev was serious about it, demanded that the Communist party relinquish its monopoly of power:

nothing less than a multiparty system offering the people real choices among candidates would suffice. Others went so far as to insist that true democracy must grant the right to the member republics of the USSR to govern their own affairs, even to the point of secession from the Union if that was what their people wanted. Gorbachev at first adamantly opposed these more radical implications of perestroika and glasnost, especially anything smacking of the dismantling of the USSR; but by 1990, both the radical reformers and the Communist party's reactionaries were saying "I told you so" as the fondest hopes of the former and the worst fears of the latter did come to pass. Gorbachev, finally, was unable to sustain his authority as the unraveling of the Soviet system outpaced his prophecies and plans.

Meanwhile, and early in his regime, two fundamental foreign policy implications of perestroika were realistically drawn by Gorbachev and his trusted collaborator and foreign minister Eduard Shevardnadze: There could not be a sufficient reallocation of human energies and material resources toward domestic development tasks as long as the increasingly expensive U.S.–Soviet arms competition continued. And there could be no substantial expansion of commerce with the industrial countries without a new and deeper East-West détente than was originally constructed between Nixon and Brezhnev.

Gorbachev and Shevardnadze correctly perceived that these two international requisites for domestically reforming the USSR could not be realized unless Western Europe and the United States could be convinced that the Soviet Union no longer posed a threat to the West, and they understood that this carried the corollary of a creditable willingness on the part of the Kremlin to reduce Soviet military forces drastically, not only in the strategic nuclear arsenal, but also in the Soviet military presence in East Central Europe.

These foreign policy dimensions of what Gorbachev liked to call new thinking were the centerpiece of his historic address to the United Nations General Assembly on December 7, 1988. "New realities are changing the entire world situation," he said. "The differences and contradictions inherited from the past are diminishing or being displaced." It had become obvious that "the use or threat of force no longer can or must be an instrument of foreign policy."[15]

The era of the Cold War was coming to an end. A return to normal, but not always smooth, state-to-state diplomacy was at hand. Kant would have nodded in recognition that domestic forces were driving the need for world peace.

INTERNATIONAL COLLECTIVE SECURITY

An alternative to enlarging the prospects for peace by prudent and flexible state-to-state diplomacy is a collective security system encompassing and supported by the major powers. A collective security system does not presume ideological consensus among its members, require their agreement on the just international society, or even depend on a commitment to preserve the existing territorial status quo or balance of power. It requires only that member countries renounce the use or threatened use of force as an instrument of foreign policy and make provision to restrain or punish, through cooperative or coordinated action, any country that attacks another with military force for any purpose other than to defend itself against military aggression or to help in a collective security action authorized by the system.

Collective security, so defined, is the basis of the two most significant international experiments of the twentieth century: the League of Nations and the United Nations.

The League of Nations

The widespread idea that World War I was caused by the balance of power/alliance system stimulated a flurry of proposals for a universal alliance against war itself—a league of nations to enforce the peace following the war. President Woodrow Wilson was a true believer in this idea, and it was because of his efforts that the Covenant of the League of Nations was incorporated into the Treaty of Versailles and each of the other major peace treaties of 1919.

The collective security provisions of the League of Nations, outlined in Chapter 7, did not outlaw war itself. War was still legitimate if waged in behalf of the principles of the League—especially if in response to a call by appropriate League agencies for enforcement action, even unilateral military action by members, provided the warring action followed an unsuccessful attempt to utilize the League's conflict-resolution machinery.[16] And, of course, members retained the right of self-defense in cases when military aggression started before League action was possible. In short, the League system did not alter the fundamental ambiguity of the international law against aggression, or basically change the decentralized nature of international law enforcement.

What the League of Nations did was legitimize and provide a framework for collective action against international aggression—to the extent that countries were willing to cooperate in such action. By providing specific mechanisms for determining when illegitimate military attacks had taken place and for facilitating coordinated counteraction against aggressors, the League was a serious attempt to reduce the need of countries to resort to war even in self-defense. Most idealistically, arms races, alliances, and provocative threats of war, such as those that brought on World War I, would no longer be necessary, since deterrence would now be provided by the prospect of concerted international response to any aggressor.

How did the League system of collective security work in practice?

In a number of instances, the League machinery acted as intended by preventing disputes from exploding into war—notably in the border disputes between Albania and Yugoslavia in 1921 and between Greece and Bulgaria in 1925. In these cases, no great power was providing significant assistance to either side, nor had any an important stake in the outcome.

But the League proved to be either irrelevant or impotent when a great power was engaged in aggression. When China brought Japan's 1931 attack on the Asian mainland before the League, charging Japan with blatantly violating the Covenant, the League appointed an investigatory body, the Lytton Commission, and on the basis of its report passed a resolution refusing to recognize the new Japanese-controlled government in Manchuria. Japan thereupon resigned from the League in anger, but remained in physical control of Manchuria without suffering any of the sanctions provided for in Article 16.

In 1923, when Italy, a permanent member of the Council of the League, bombarded the Greek island of Corfu in retaliation for the killing of Italian officers who had been demarcating the Greek-Albanian border, the League proved unable to assume effective jurisdiction of the matter. Under the organization's voting rules, Italy did not have a formal veto, but it was nonetheless in a position to discourage League action.

Twelve years later, in 1935, the League did formally brand Italy's invasion of Ethiopia an illegal aggression, and the Council invoked the Article 16 sanctions system. As recounted in Chapter 7, fifty-two countries cooperated in instituting an embargo on the sale of arms and "strategic materials" to Italy. But the embargo proved to be porous, especially since oil was exempted from it. Moreover, France and Britain, the only two powers who could have challenged Italy militarily, were so preoccupied with domestic problems that neither was willing to assume the burden of organizing military sanctions in response to an action that did not put their own vital geopolitical interests in immediate jeopardy. Italy, like Japan, literally got away with murder, while the powers upon whom the world relied to make the collective security system work stood idly by. Adolf Hitler observed that no country of any weight was prepared to go to war to defend the status quo, let alone to defend a concept of world order; he fashioned his own aggressive plans accordingly.

Following the full-scale Japanese invasion of China in 1937–1938, with the failure of the League to do anything more than declare that members were entitled to apply Article 16 sanctions (which none chose to do), Hitler made his moves: the *Anschluss* with Austria, the ultimatum at Munich, the military occupation of the Sudetenland and then all of Czechoslovakia, and finally his attack on Poland in 1939, which discounted warnings from Paris and London that German military aggression against Poland would activate their alliances with Warsaw. As an indication of how irrelevant the League had become, when England and France finally declared war against Hitler in reaction to his invasion of Poland, they did not even bother with the formalities of attempting to invoke Article 16.

The United Nations

Trying to learn from the failures of the League, the victorious Allies in World War II once again tried to construct a world collective security system. They hoped to do a better job this time on two counts. All the victor powers would belong from the start (the United States had failed to ratify the Covenant and had never joined the League) and would be committed to making the system work. Second, the peace-enforcing machinery of the United Nations would be given teeth in the form of standby military capabilities earmarked for a UN force that could be fleshed out almost immediately to implement Security Council decisions.

The teeth of the UN collective security system are provided for in Chapter VII of the Charter, especially Articles 42 through 47:

- Article 42 stipulates that the "Security Council . . . may take such action by air, sea, or land forces as may be necessary to maintain or restore international peace and security."

- Article 43 obligates all members "to make available to the Security Council, on its call in accordance with a special agreement or agreements, armed forces, assistance, and facilities, including rights of passage, necessary for maintaining international peace and security."
- Article 44 provides that member nations not represented on the Council whose forces are involved in a particular League military operation will participate in the military decision making of the Security Council.
- Article 45 obligates members to "hold immediately available national air-force contingents for combined international enforcement actions."
- Articles 46 and 47 outline the structure and functions of a Military Staff Committee to advise and assist the Security Council on all questions relating to the military requirements of international peace and security. The Military Staff Committee, to consist of the military Chiefs of Staff or their representatives from each of the five permanent members of the Security Council and the military representatives of any member nations whose participation is required, "shall be responsible under the Security Council for the strategic direction of any armed forces placed at the disposal of the Security Council. Questions relating to the command of such forces shall be worked out subsequently."

Because of the impasse between the Soviet Union and the United States, which pervaded most UN agencies from the start, a permanent UN armed force or command, or even a standing framework for rapidly assembling such a force, failed to materialize. An agency for planning UN enforcement operations would be the last place to expect U.S.– Soviet cooperation. The Military Staff Committee, although it has met occasionally since 1947, has assembled no forces to command on behalf of the United Nations. Soviet president Gorbachev proposed that UN-authorized military operations in the Gulf War of 1990–1991 be conducted under the auspices of the Military Staff Committee, but this was rejected by the Bush administration.

The United Nations' police forces that have been formed for limited peacekeeping actions, as distinct from collective security actions, have been organized on an ad hoc basis and have been directly responsible to the Security Council or to the secretary general, bypassing the Military Staff Committee. Their function, conflict control rather than deterrence or punishment of aggression, will be discussed below along with other measures of this type.

Some of the basic UN collective security mechanisms of Articles 42 through 47 were ostensibly used in the United Nations Peace Action to repel the North Korean invasion of South Korea in 1950. In reality a U.S. response draped in the UN flag, the United Nations' role mandated by the Security Council was possible only because of the temporary absence from the Council of the Soviet Union, which otherwise would have vetoed the authorizing resolutions. The Soviet absence allowed the Security Council to designate the United States government and its Joint Chiefs of Staff to direct peace enforcement functions that normally, in the Charter's conception, would have been directed by the UN's Military Staff Committee.

The Security Council resolutions of July 7, 1950, recommended that member states "make . . . forces and other assistance available to a unified command under the United States" and requested "the United States to designate a commander of such forces."[17] The Unified Command established by the Truman administration was essentially identical to the U.S. Far East Command, under which General Douglas MacArthur had been directing battle operations from Tokyo for ten days before the UN vote. General MacArthur was to take his orders from the U.S. government, not from the United Nations, and the shape and pace of the military operations, including the momentous political decision to advance into North Korea, were determined by the Americans in accordance with their views of U.S. national interests. UN endorsements of these unilateral U.S. decisions were sought to give them international legitimacy, and General MacArthur was referred to in all official U.S. statements as "Commander of the UN Forces." But under the cover of universal collective security, the United States was transparently using the United Nations as an instrument for prosecuting its global rivalry with the Soviet Union.

To preserve the definition of the Korean action as a UN collective security operation even after the Soviets returned to the Security Council, the United States formulated a "Uniting for Peace" resolution that the General Assembly adopted in 1950 by a vote of 39 for, 5 against (the Soviet Union and its East European allies), and 11 abstentions. The resolution asserted the General Assembly's authority to act instead of the Security Council "if the Security Council, because of a lack of unanimity of the permanent members, fails to exercise its primary responsibility for the maintenance of international peace and security."[18]

The role of the United Nations in response to Iraq's 1990 invasion of Kuwait, like the UN action in Korea, was an anomaly brought on by circumstances unlikely to recur: The aggressor, Iraq, had no allies among the permanent members of the UN Security Council in 1990 who might oppose the Bush administration's desire to obtain international legitimacy for its plans to oust Iraq from Kuwait by force; the Bush administration had convinced itself and a majority of the American public that allowing Saddam Hussein to keep control of Kuwait would put a Hitler-like aggressor in a position to control the economically and strategically crucial energy resources of the Middle East. Moreover, the ensuing military action against Iraq, like the action in Korea in 1950, was not really a collective security operation; it was, by design of the Bush administration, undertaken by only a handful of countries acting in the mode of a traditional ad hoc military coalition and mobilized and directed by the coalition leader, the United States.

Regional Security Arrangements

Recognizing that situations may arise when it is not possible to forge a worldwide consensus as to which are the aggressor countries and what sanctions should be applied against them, the founders of the United Nations included a series of clauses in Chapter VII of the Charter that allowed particular groupings of countries to organize themselves into regional security communities.

Article 51 allows for "individual or collective self-defense if an armed attack occurs against a Member of the United Nations, until the Security Council has taken the measures necessary to maintain international peace and security." And Articles 52 and 54, under the heading of "Regional Arrangements," encourage members that have formed into regional associations to "make every effort to achieve pacific settlements to local disputes through such regional arrangements . . . before referring them to the Security Council." The Security Council is authorized, where appropriate, to "utilize such regional arrangements or agencies for enforcement action under its authority."

When forming the North Atlantic Treaty Organization in 1949, the United States and its allies cited Articles 51 through 54 to support their claim that NATO is consistent with the letter and spirit of the UN Charter; the Soviet Union and its allies made the same claim in forming the Warsaw Pact in 1955. Other regional groupings, such as the Organization of American States, the Organization of African Unity, the Arab League, and the Association of Southeast Asian Nations, also cite the UN Charter as authority for their existence.

Apart from NATO and the Warsaw Pact, each dominated by a superpower, regional associations have not proved very effective either in organizing collective external defense or in controlling intraregional conflict. One reason is that the recurring conditions that seem to justify violent conflicts between states (discussed in Chapter 3) most often inhere in neighboring countries, resulting in border conflicts, ethnic group rivalries and liberation movements, and in conflicts over commonly used water and other environmental resources (witness the chronic hostility between India and Pakistan, for example, and between Iran and Iraq). Another reason is that jealousies among countries and resentments at would-be hegemons (as, for example, toward Indonesia in Southeast Asia or Brazil in South America) tend to be more intense within regions and to frustrate collaboration, let alone integrative association of a sustained and deeply rooted nature.

The Basic Structural Problem of Collective Security

The weaknesses of both the League of Nations and the United Nations, and even of the smaller limited-membership collective security arrangements, are inherent in the basic structure of the world system of which all these organizations and groupings are subsystems. As long as the primary political units of world society are nation-states, determined to protect their independence above all other values except physical survival and run by leadership groups accountable to domestic interests ahead of world interests, no member nation of an international collective security association will participate in actions likely to put its independence and domestic interests at risk unless such participation is clearly required to protect these interests.

This basic structural inhibition on international collective security action is reinforced by three features of contemporary world society: (1) the deepening and widening economic interdependence among countries; (2) the destructiveness of modern war; and (3) the domestic support required for sustained military operations.

1. Many a country is likely to enjoy a commercial relationship with a country that becomes the target of sanctions imposed by the collective security group to which it belongs. This means that some domestic groups are sure to be opposed to the disruption of normal commerce accompanying the application of sanctions. The more developed a country's economy is and the more it is involved in international commerce, the more this factor is likely to weigh against the country's

participation in collective sanctions not clearly required for its immediate self-interests.

2. If collective security involves participating in military action against an aggressor country, those asked to participate are likely to assess carefully the aggressor's capabilities for military retaliation. Members within the range of highly destructive weapons of the aggressor will show reluctance to become one of the disciplining group. Increasingly, as countries deploy weapons of regional and intercontinental range, this factor is likely to inhibit all collective security actions except those directed against countries without sophisticated weapons.

3. To the extent that a contemplated collective application of sanctions involves going to war against aggressor countries, the economics of contemporary warfare works to inhibit the realization of any internationally organized sanctioning process. Because modern arsenals and armies must be fueled and replenished by many sectors of the domestic economy, countries will weight their anticipated tangible sacrifices heavily against the vaguer world order values supposed to be served by active participation in a proposed international military action. Only when the consequences of nonparticipation are perceived as tangible, immediate, and more disruptive than war are countries likely to participate in a war to secure international peace and security. This means that decision makers, including legislative and popular support groups, would have to be convinced that the contemplated war could be so limited and controlled as to prevent costly disruptions of domestic life.

THE PACIFIC SETTLEMENT OF DISPUTES AND CONFLICT CONTROL

An alternative approach to reducing the role of war in the world is to develop and use nonviolent procedures and instruments to deal with the types of conflicts likely to give rise to military threats and actions, instead of threatening to physically punish the aggressors. This approach, reflected in aspects of the League of Nations system, has carried over into the UN system, where it has been utilized more frequently than have the more dramatic collective security measures.

The standard procedures and instruments of pacific settlement are designed either to prevent conflicts from escalating to the level of violent encounters or to terminate ongoing violences often through the intervention or good offices of an impartial third party.

Mediation and Adjudication

Mediation depends on suggestions of a third party for compromise, which the adversaries are free to accept or reject. *Adjudication* usually involves a formal process, often called *arbitration,* of hearings, findings, and awards administered by a third party; the adversaries agree beforehand that these will be binding on each of them.

In medieval Europe, the Church was the principal institution that offered mediation and arbitration services to warring princes. As the state system matured in the seventeenth, eighteenth, and nineteenth centuries, treaties between sovereigns frequently contained clauses in which the signatories agreed to submit their disputes henceforth to mediation or arbitration by a neutral statesman or international judicial tribunal.

In the contemporary world prominent statesmen are sometimes invited to become mediators, as President Jimmy Carter did in the 1978 Camp David meetings with Israeli Prime Minister Menachem Begin and Egyptian President Anwar as-Sadat, which resulted in the Egypt–Israel Peace Treaty of 1979. (In the secret negotiation of the Israel–PLO accord of 1993, the Norwegian foreign minister served more as host and facilitator of the bilateral bargaining than as mediator.)

When adjudication or arbitration is desired, a dispute usually is submitted to the International Court of Justice (ICJ) or to a special judicial commission to determine the rights and obligations of the parties under international law. Members of the League of Nations were obligated by the Covenant to submit disputes to the ICJ for such adjudication if they could not settle them peacefully by diplomacy or mediation; but the obligation was usually bypassed.

The UN system more realistically leaves to the parties themselves the determination of whether or not to submit disputes to the World Court for adjudication, and some sets of countries have assumed advance obligations, in particular bilateral or multilateral treaties, to submit disputes to the ICJ. Even countries that have undertaken advance obligations with treaty partners to submit various classes of disputes to ICJ adjudication, however, can refuse to accept the Court's jurisdiction in particular cases they fear might go against them as did the Reagan administration in the plea brought before the Court by Nicaragua in 1986.

All in all, the international court system continues to play a meager role in the resolution of disputes, and more often than not is entirely bypassed in conflict among major powers.

Cease-Fires and Cooling-Off Periods

Sometimes what is sought immediately—before the resolution of the issues in dispute—is simply a cease-fire in an existing military conflict or a cooling-off period in a conflict on the brink of war.

Cease-fires are often possible, even though not always instituted at such times, when neither party to a dispute wants to continue bloodshed. All that it takes to terminate the fighting is a push for a cease-fire by a third party or international agency. Third-party initiatives are usually required because of the mistrust warring parties understandably have of each other's real intentions in proposing a cease-fire.[19]

The cease-fire may be in place, meaning that neither side moves from the ground it has occupied in the last round of battle but that both stop shooting at each other. It may be a pullback by one or both sides from the zone of immediate fighting, leaving a no-man's land in between. It may be accompanied by promises not to augment fighting capabilities in the zone of confrontation; it may also involve the interposition of peace-observation or peacekeeping contingents from nonbelligerent countries or international institutions to ensure that the cease-fire or pullback and capability limitations are adhered to. And it may be conditioned on good-faith participation by the adversaries in negotiations to resolve the dispute that precipitated the violence.

A cooling-off period may commence with a cease-fire or, as formerly provided for in Article 16 of the League Covenant, may be instituted to arrest the intensification of a dispute that appears to be heading toward a military confrontation. Typically, the adversaries in a cooling-off sequence agree to negotiate with each other directly or through the good offices of a third party to see if they can resolve their dispute short of war, meanwhile refraining from deploying or augmenting forces that would be used in a resumption of hostilities. The disputants may even withdraw forces already deployed in a threatening mode or remove them from alert status as an indication of their immediately pacific intentions. But as with cease-fires, such cooling-off arrangements usually stand a better chance of being accepted if they are initiated by impartial third parties or international institutions, thus reducing the chance that one of the adversaries will regard the plan as a trick to get it to lower its guard.

Peacekeeping Forces[20]

The most visible interposition of a neutral presence to control inter-state conflict has been the multinational peace-observation groups and peacekeeping forces—the world's "soldiers without enemies."[21] Usually, but not always, organized under UN auspices, these multinational military units have been employed to monitor truces and cease-fires and to occupy space between belligerents to prevent the national armed forces from entering disputed areas or attacking one another.

The first of these UN forces was, strictly speaking, not a force at all, but only a group of military officers assigned to accompany UN mediators in the Middle East to observe and report on compliance of the Arabs and Israelis with various UN-endorsed border arrangements, truces, and armistice agreements. Varying in size from 30 when it was created in 1948 to nearly 600 officers, this United Nations Truce Supervision Organization (UNTSO) has been staffed at different times by military personnel from some 100 countries. Similar UN corps of truce or cease-fire observers have been stationed in Kashmir, West Irian, the Yemen-Saudi Arabia border, and the Golan Heights, between Syria and Israel.

A larger variety of UN military presence, involving thousands of troops deployed between the belligerents to separate them physically and make it necessary for them to crash through the UN glass window, as it were, to violate the truce, was first employed in 1956 on the Israel-Egypt border and at the entrance to the Gulf of Aqaba. This United Nations Emergency Force (UNEF) was mandated first to supervise the withdrawal of British, French, and Israeli troops that had invaded Egyptian territory in the Suez Canal crisis and then to monitor compliance with the armistice. Withdrawal of the force in 1967 at the demand of Egyptian President Gamal Abdel Nasser was one of the precipitating events leading to the 1967 Six-Day War between Israel and her Arab neighbors.

A second UNEF was deployed in the region in 1973 to patrol the new demilitarized zone in the Sinai and to verify the implementation of the Sinai disengagement agreements negotiated at the end of the Yom Kippur War. A parallel United Nations Disengagement Observer Force (UNDOF) was created in 1974 to supervise the small neutral zone created between Syria and Israel in their separately negotiated disengagement agreement.

The most ambitious and controversial of the UN peacekeeping forces prior to the operations in Cambodia and Somalia in the early 1990s was the intervention in the Congo in 1961, known by its French name, Opération des Nations Unies au Congo (ONUC). Directed by Secretary General Dag Hammarskjöld, the ONUC at full strength deployed 20,000 troops from twenty-five countries and a number of fighter aircraft: its authority was a rather loosely worded mandate from the Security Council to help the newly independent Congolese government keep the peace and stabilize control after the withdrawal the previous year of the colonial power, Belgium, and in the face of anticipated secession of the province Katanga. Stretching the Security Council's mandate to allow for limited offensive military action, Hammarskjöld angered the Soviet Union, and after his death in 1961, the Soviets severely constricted the ability of the new secretary general, U Thant, to continue the ONUC. Though the force did not fully stabilize the Congo, the ONUC fulfilled one of its major assigned functions, to provide an external presence in the newly independent, still chaotic Congo to substitute for what otherwise might have been competitive military intervention by the Soviet Union and the United States.

Another major international military presence has been the UN force in Cyprus, created in 1964 and deployed at times in strengths up to 7,000. This force has tried to separate the Greek and Turkish communities to keep them from fighting and has had the task of monitoring zonal and other intercommunal arrangements. But despite the presence of the UN force, a 1974 coup by militant Greeks seeking union with Greece itself ousted the Cypriot nationalist leader Archbishop Makarios; the accompanying intensification of communal strife brought on an invasion by Turkey, at which time the UN force, while keeping aloof from the fighting, helped to protect civilians. With the institution of a truce, the UN force returned to its principal peace-monitoring role.

A rather daring venture into peace*making* through the vehicle of peacekeeping forces is the United Nations Transitional Authority in Cambodia (UNTAC), agreed to in October 1990 by the Government of Cambodia and its domestic opponents as a way to put an end to their civil war. UNTAC was assigned the function not only of monitoring the cease-fire but also of supervising elections and installing a new government in the spring of 1993 and—in an unprecedented assumption of supranational responsibility—staffing and running the key agencies of government in Phnom Penh during the electoral process and installation of a functioning indigenous government. The verdict is still out at this writing as to whether UNTAC has been able to fulfill its mandate adequately.[22]

In Somalia, the UN took another leap into its still uncharted future as a peacemaking institution by assigning itself the mission of restoring civil society in that destitute East African country following a total breakdown of law and order in 1992. Moved to action by the sabotage of UN humanitarian relief efforts by local warlords, the Security Council voted in December 1992 to authorize the Secretary General and member states to "use all necessary means to establish as soon as possible a secure environment for humanitarian relief operations in Somalia."[23] Under this mandate President Bush dispatched 30,000 troops to Somalia with authorization to use force as necessary to allow the relief efforts to proceed. Upon the completion of their pacification mission in the spring of 1993, all but 4,000 of the U.S. forces were withdrawn, making way for a 20,000-person civil-military UN contingent (including the remaining U.S. forces) with a mandate to establish law and order and the rudiments of an indigenous government. But in the summer and fall of 1993, a series of combat skirmishes between UN forces and armed gangs loyal to warlord Mohammed Farah Aidid led to a major reinstitution of U.S. combat power amid growing concerns that the world organization was unprepared to assume such a heavy burden of law enforcement.

The relative success of UN peacekeeping, as well as the obvious logic of the concept, has led from time to time to proposals for creating a permanent UN peacekeeping force with an officer corps under the authority of the UN and permanently assigned troops, some of which the UN might directly recruit. This UN police force would be perpetually ready for dispatch to world trouble spots as needed. United Nations Secretary General Boutros Boutros-Ghali in his widely circulated January 1992 report, *An Agenda for Peace,* held back from reviving this idea. Rather, he asked for a more conscientious implementation of member states of pledges to train and hold in readiness such police contingents to contribute to the UN peacekeeping needs in future conflicts and to broaden the personnel base of such contingents to adapt to the likely expansion of peacemaking operations of the kind dispatched to Cambodia. In the secretary general's words, "increasingly, peacekeeping requires that civilian political officers, human rights monitors, electoral officials, refugee and humanitarian aid specialists and police play as central a role as the military."[24]

To be effective, such an expansion of peacekeeping into peacemaking requires the transmutation of the United Nations into more of a *supra*national organization than it has been up to now. A deficiency, but also a virtue, of the more modest type of UN peacekeeping has been its consistency with the traditional state-sovereignty norms of international society. Under these norms, the deployment of any international peacekeeping forces requires the consent of the government of the country on whose territory it is to be stationed; and the national units (all voluntarily contributed) are subject to direction by a multinational UN command that, through the Secretary General, is responsible to the group of sovereign states belonging to the Security Council—in particular, its five permanent members. The peacekeeping operation has no authority beyond the mandate it is given by this intergovernmental body, and only as long as the member states are able to sustain a consensus on what they want the peacekeeping operation to accomplish.

Although Secretary General Boutros-Ghali, like his predecessors, affirms that "respect for . . . [the state's] fundamental sovereignty and integrity are crucial" to the peace and security functions of the United Nations, he also recognizes that "the time of absolute and exclusive sovereignty . . . has passed; its theory was never matched by reality." The imperative of world order and justice today, he insists, is "to find a balance between good internal governance and the requirements of an ever-more interdependent world."[25]

The more intrusive interjection of the United Nations operatives into situations of domestic strife (as in Cambodia and Somalia) is an effort to find the new balance called for by the Secretary General. But as pointed out in a sympathetic 1992 study, this recent trend "is a potential political minefield" for the world organization:

> The resolution of internal conflicts involves the apportionment
> of power among the hostile parties with sometimes long histories
> of bloodshed and violence. Referenda have losers as well as
> winners. . . . Indeed, even dominant factions may come to perceive
> UN peacekeepers as having lost their impartiality if they remain
> involved in conflicts for protracted periods.[26]

When a local crisis is too politically controversial for the United Nations to handle, countries willing to participate in a peacekeeping operation can go outside the world organization to form a multinational force. A successful example of such a non-UN operation was the special Sinai peacekeeping force deployed at the Egyptian-Israeli border in 1982 after completion of the Israeli withdrawal provided for in the

Egypt–Israel peace treaty. An unsuccessful effort was the multinational force deployed in Lebanon in 1982–1983, which had to withdraw under fire in 1984 as some of the warring elements in that conflict-torn country came to see the multinational force as a tool of a Lebanese government they regarded as illegitimate.

Crisis Management

Another avenue for attempting to prevent international conflicts from turning violent or preventing small wars from escalating in intensity and scope frequently goes under the term *crisis management.* It refers particularly to efforts to avoid the kinds of misperceptions of adversary intentions and capabilities and miscalculations of adversary responses to one's moves that can bring on inadvertent or accidental conflict escalation.

The experience of statespersons and the insights of scholars in this field are collected and synthesized in Alexander George's *Avoiding War: Problems of Crisis Management,* published in 1991. In crisis management, the "devil (or angel) lies in the details," and the George project is properly designed to prod scholars and policymakers to focus on the specifics of the case at hand. Nonetheless, Professor George has been able to distill the historical experience and careful scholarly analysis of particular crises into a set of general guidelines for public officials. He recommends the following:

- "When conflicts are simmering and threatening to erupt into a dangerous crisis," countries should not jump immediately to protect their interests by unilateral actions that are likely to provoke countermoves and crisis escalation, but "should rely in the first instance on timely diplomatic communication and negotiation."
- Especially when embroiled in a crisis with one another, countries should "avoid sudden or secret military deployments" that significantly affect the military balance between them, and should refrain from other attempts to make major gains at each other's expenses.
- When a war-threatening crisis erupts, countries (in taking measures to reduce the vulnerability of their forces and enhance their readiness to defend themselves must "take the greatest care to avoid alerts and deployments that are likely to be perceived by the other side as preparations for significant and imminent *offense* operations." Accordingly,

They should . . . avoid (or at least greatly minimize) the practice of using military alerts and deployments to signal resolution or to exert coercive pressure on the adversary for crisis bargaining purposes. In brief, there should be more use of diplomatic communication and less reliance on military signaling per se.

The sides should seek opportunities to slow down the tempo and momentum of crisis developments . . . to deliberately create pauses in crisis activity . . . in order to provide enough time . . . to exchange diplomatic communications and to give the leadership on both sides adequate time to assess the situation, make well-considered decisions, and respond to each other's proposals.

- The adversaries must limit the objectives of their confrontation and "resist the temptation to inflict a damaging, humiliating defeat on the opponent." While protecting its own fundamental interests, "each side must recognize the other side's legitimate interests and strive for a mutually acceptable formula for terminating the crisis."[27]

The experience of the Cuban missile crisis of 1962, when the super-powers drew each other to the brink of nuclear war and then stepped back, did much to stimulate such studies in this field. It continues to be mined for examples of both what to do and what not to do in intense crises.

Mistake 1: The Kremlin precipitated the crisis by a sudden deployment of offensive missiles to Cuba that appeared to alter significantly the global balance of power at the expense of the United States.

Mistake 2: U.S. strategic forces were put on an unprecedented level of alert, and U.S. regional forces were deployed in attack formation. These moves could have stimulated the Soviets and the Cubans to pre-empt what they began to believe was an inevitable U.S. attack.

Mistake 3: The Soviets maintained loose command and control over relevant forces in Cuba, such as the air-defense battery that shot down a U.S. reconnaissance plane at the height of the crisis, that if used could have triggered a full-scale war.

Fortunately, however, exemplary crisis-management behavior was exhibited at the highest level of both governments:

1. The Soviet strategic forces were not put on a comparable high state of alert to match the United States.

2. President Kennedy rejected pressure from his advisers to use military force at the outset to remove the Soviet missiles, selecting instead the nonviolent blockade (officially called a quarantine) of Soviet arms-carrying ships headed for Cuba as a signal of resolve, while making precisely clear to Khrushchev what the Soviets would have to do to settle the crisis so as to assure that the United States would not use force.
3. President Kennedy also deliberately slowed down the pace of crisis activity—including the apprehension of Soviet ships approaching the quarantine line—so as to give his adversary sufficient time to recalculate his risks.
4. Both presidents in their communications with each other concentrated principally on finding a formula to resolve the crisis without humiliation of either side, which resulted in the crisis-ending quid pro quo of the Soviet removal of their offensive strategic weapons from Cuba in return for a U.S. pledge not to invade the island and a secret assurance that the United States would remove its anti-Soviet missiles based in Turkey.

Professor George points out that crisis management in future conflicts will be more likely to succeed if potential adversaries, before becoming involved in particular intense disputes, develop habits over the long run of communicating with each other "to discuss together problems of crisis stability, to identify types of behaviors that may threaten loss of control and trigger escalation pressures, and to consider and make provision for preventive and remedial measures." This should include the installation of appropriate machinery for rapid precrisis and midcrisis communication at both specialized civilian and military levels and the highest levels of government.[28] Some of the technical means of enhancing crisis-avoidance communications and interaction between the military of potential adversaries are discussed in Chapter 10 under "Confidence-Building Measures."

Creative Conflict Resolution

In recent decades the catastrophic consequences of failing to resolve international conflict without war have drawn scholars from diverse disciplines, as well as experienced practitioners of negotiation from the private and public sectors, into the search for ways of inducing countries in conflict to back away from brink-of-war situations. Clinical psychologists and family counselors, labor-management negotiators, social psychology theorists, attorneys skilled in getting out-of-court settlements, and game theorists—all have experience and wisdom that can be adapted to international conflict resolution.[29]

Diplomats are beginning to pay more attention to this field of inquiry. Some have attended seminars at the Nuclear Negotiation Project of the Harvard Law School and at similar projects to expand their repertoires of options that could be useful for avoiding or terminating dangerous international encounters. On occasion ideas for creative conflict resolution have found their way into high-level country-to-country negotiations with positive effects.

A simple, well-publicized, but probably underutilized idea is the technique of unilaterally making a concession, not with the intent of appeasement, but rather to pressure the adversary to make a reciprocal concession. This negotiating strategy has been elaborated by the social psychologist Charles E. Osgood in his papers on graduated reciprocation in tension reduction (GRIT). The key to the GRIT concept is the invitation explicit in a unilateral de-escalation for the adversary to follow suit, under the promise of further de-escalation if reciprocation materializes. The first unilateral move must not put the initiator at a disadvantage, and the promised further de-escalation should be even more attractive than the first but clearly indicated not to be forthcoming if the adversary fails to reciprocate.[30] Reportedly, President Kennedy deliberately applied Osgood's ideas in 1963 when he announced the unilateral ban on the atmospheric testing of nuclear weapons that preceded the successful Soviet-American negotiation of a partial test ban.[31]

One suggestive line of theoretical and experimental investigation in the field of conflict resolution deals with the vexing problem—typically present in efforts to achieve a cease-fire in wartime and also in many arms-control negotiations—of how to induce cooperation between parties where each side would benefit if both pursued cooperative strategies, as opposed to continuing hostile acts or deployments that would lead both to suffer great harm, but where opportunities are available to each to cheat and thereby gain a substantial advantage over the opponent as long as the opponent does not simultaneously cheat. Researchers have devised experimental simulations that show some strategies are better than others for building cooperative, nonexploitative relationships even among rivals who are highly suspicious of each other's motives and propensities to cheat.[32]

Another creative approach to conflict resolution has been championed by Harvard Law School negotiating expert Roger Fisher, who calls it "fractionating conflict." Again the idea, simple to the point of being self-evident, is often ignored when countries are working themselves toward a major confrontation. The fractionating approach slices country-to-country disputes into small but discrete issues, making it possible to deal with each independently on its merits. Less resolvable disputes are not allowed to stand in the way of ones that can be resolved.[33] Surprisingly, Henry Kissinger, a champion of the opposed theory—issue linkage—showed himself a deft fractionator in orchestrating step-by-step cease-fire and disengagement agreements between Israel and Egypt and between Israel and Syria at the end of the Yom Kippur War. President Carter used the fractionating approach to good effect in the Camp David negotiations, though he used some linkage stratagems to compel agreement as well. It was quintessentially a fractionating approach by the Carter administration, advised by Roger Fisher, that finally secured the release of the American hostages from Iran in January 1981. And in the September 1993 rapprochment between Israel and the PLO, conflict fractionating was at work in the postponement of the resolution of the Jerusalem and "statehood" issues.

In recent years, some of the lessons learned from the Fisher project have been incorporated into programs in nonviolent conflict resolution for inner-city youth, emphasizing *sensitivity training* (open dialogue in order to understand one another's needs, feelings, and points of view), negotiation, bargaining, mediation, and joint problem solving. A pioneering effort, the Resolving Conflict Creativity Program, has been instituted in the New York City school system. Students and teachers in some of the most violent-ridden areas participate in conflict/cooperation simulations and other challenging and entertaining interactions that develop skills in nonviolent interpersonal conflict management in which they can take pride.[34]

A hallmark of creative conflict-resolution approaches is that they are *non*-zero-sum (to use the game theory term for outcomes of benefit to both sides). As opposed to those of coercive strategies, their objectives and their means are predominantly nonviolent; they attempt to divert parties to a conflict from seeking victory (defeat for the opponent) to looking for mutual rewards and satisfaction. They do not presume that either side's values are illegitimate, but rather that most intense conflict among large groups, which is what war is, involves deep convictions on each side that its goals or grievances are just. Creative international conflict resolution does not presume to arbitrate at the level of determining which party is on the side of God or justice and which is not. It tries to find a way around such cosmic issues, putting priority instead on minimizing direct violence.

NOTES

1. The basic concepts of Grotius are well expounded in Walter Schiffer, *The Legal Community of Mankind* (New York: Columbia University Press, 1954), pp. 30–48.

2. For detailed analysis of conflict in and rules of use of nonland areas, see Seyom Brown, Nina Cornell, Larry Fabian, and Edith Brown Weiss, *Regimes for the Ocean, Outer Space, and Weather* (Washington, D.C.: Brookings Institution, 1977).

3. See Henry A. Kissinger, *A World Restored: The Politics of Conservatism in a Revolutionary Age* (New York: Grosset & Dunlop, 1964); see also his essay "The White Revolutionary: Reflections on Bismarck," *Daedalus* (Summer 1968), 97(3):888–924.

4. Immanuel Kant, *Perpetual Peace* (New York: Macmillan, 1917).

5. Kissinger's intellectual debt to Kant is analyzed in Peter Dickson, *Kissinger and the Meaning of History* (New York: Cambridge University Press, 1978).

6. Frank P. Chambers, Christina Phelps Harris, and Charles C. Bayley, *This Age of Conflict: 1914 to the Present* (New York: Harcourt, Brace, 1950), pp. 138–141.

7. *Ibid.,* pp. 141–142.

8. Hans J. Morgenthau, *Politics among Nations: The Struggle for Power and Peace,* 5th ed. (New York: Knopf, 1978), pp. 550–560.

9. *Ibid.*, p. 560.

10. See Henry Kissinger, *The White House Years* (Boston: Little, Brown, 1979); and Seyom Brown, *The Crises of Power: An Interpretation of United States Foreign Policy During the Kissinger Years* (New York: Columbia University Press, 1979), pp. 19–48.

11. "Basic Principles of Relations between the United States of America and the Union of Soviet Socialist Republics," *Department of State Bulletin* (June 29, 1972), 66 (1722):898–899.

12. In *A World Restored*, Kissinger warned against attempts to constrain the revolutionary power by agreements:

Adjustments are possible, but they will be conceived as tactical maneuvers to consolidate positions for the inevitable showdown, or as tools to undermine the morale of the antagonist. To be sure, the motivation of the revolutionary power may well be defensive; it may well be sincere in its protestations of feeling threatened. But the distinguishing feature of a revolutionary power is not that it feels threatened—such feeling is inherent in the nature of international relations based on sovereign states—*but that nothing can reassure it*. Only absolute security—the neutralization of the opponent—is considered a sufficient guarantee, and thus the desire of one power for absolute security means absolute insecurity for all the others. (p. 2)

13. Mikhail Gorbachev, *Perestroika: New Thinking for Our Country and the World* (New York: Harper & Row, 1987), pp. 19.

14. *Ibid.,* p. 33.

15. Mikhail Gorbachev, Address at the Plenary Session of the United Nations General Assembly, December 7, 1988 (translation and text from the Soviet Mission to the United Nations, 1988).

16. *Covenant of the League of Nations,* signed at Versailles June 28, 1919 (Geneva: League of Nations, 1920).

17. United Nations Document S/1587.

18. United Nations Document A/1481.

19. See Paul R. Pillar, *Negotiating Peace: War Termination as a Bargaining Process* (Princeton, N.J.: Princeton University Press, 1983).

20. For an analysis of the peacekeeping undertaken by the United Nations and the prospects for a larger UN peacekeeping role in the post–Cold War era, see William J. Durch and Barry M. Blechman, *Keeping the Peace: The United Nations in the Emerging World Order* (Washington, DC: Henry L. Stimpson Center, 1992).

21. Larry L. Fabian, *Soldiers Without Enemies* (Washington, D.C.: Brookings Institution, 1971).

22. *United Nations Peace-Keeping Operations* (New York: United Nations Department of Public Information, January 17, 1992)

23. United Nations Security Council Resolution 794, December 3, 1992, document S/PV 3145.

24. Boutros Boutros-Ghali, *Agenda for Peace* (New York: United Nations, 1992).

25. *Ibid.,* p. 9.

26. Durch and Blechman, *Keeping the Peace,* p. 16.

27. Alexander L. George, "Findings and Recommendations," in the volume edited by him, *Avoiding War: Problems of Crisis Management* (Boulder: Westview, 1991), pp. 545–567, quotes from pp. 564–565.

28. *Ibid.,* p. 565.

29. For an inventory of diverse conflict-resolution ideas with an applicability to international relations, see Richard Wendell Fogg, "Dealing with Conflict: A Repertoire of Creative, Peaceful Approaches," *Journal of Conflict Resolution* (June 1985), 29(2):330–358.

30. Charles E. Osgood, "Graduated Unilateral Initiatives for Peace," in Clagett G. Smith, ed., *Conflicting Resolution: Contributions of the Behavioral Sciences* (Notre Dame, Ind.: University of Notre Dame Press, 1971), pp. 515–525.

31. Fogg, "Dealing with Conflict," p. 334.

32. See Robert Axelrod, *The Evolution of Cooperation* (New York: Basic Books, 1984), for a creative experimental approach to a version of this problem called "Prisoner's Dilemma" by some game theorists since it seems to fit a hypothetical situation in which two prisoners who have conspired with each other in a major crime are presented by the prosecutor with simultaneous but separate and secret offers to turn state's evidence on the other one: If both prisoners refuse to tell on each other, they will both have to stand trial and run the risk of being convicted or found not guilty; if one cheats on the other by confessing and giving the prosecutor information, the one that helped the prosecutor will ultimately receive a substantially more lenient sentence, and the other will receive maximum punishment for the crime; finally, if each confesses, both will be convicted and neither will get a break at time of sentencing. Clearly, the most tempting strategy to each is to confess and also tell on the other so as to get a substantially reduced punishment for oneself—but if each does this, both lose more than if each kept quiet. If the prisoners could communicate, it would do them well to agree that they should both keep quiet, but even if they did so agree, there would be great temptation to cheat. Game theory itself contains no solution to the problem for either of the prisoners. However, in some computer-assisted simulations devised by Robert Axelrod and his colleagues, it was discovered that if the prisoners were provided with opportunities to play repeated rounds of such a game, they could learn the mutual advantages of cooperating with each other, and that there were certain strategies of retaliation in kind ("tit for tat") that reinforced such learning.

33. Roger Fisher and William Langer Ury, *Getting to Yes* (Boston: Houghton Mifflin, 1981).

34. Myriam Miedzion, *Boys Will Be Boys: Breaking the Link between Masculinity and Violence* (New York: Doubleday, 1991), p. 62.

CHAPTER 10

Arms Control

Arms control is a pragmatic adaptation to the difficulties encountered in each of the approaches to preventing and controlling war that are analyzed above. It starts from the assumption that distributions of military power, for the time being at least, will continue to be weighty determinants of whether, where, and when wars break out and of how they are fought and terminated.

Arms-control efforts are directed primarily toward making the distribution of military power less likely to provoke war. Some efforts also have the objective of ensuring that if wars break out, their destructiveness will be kept to a minimum and they will be ended as quickly as possible. A third objective, making the arms race less expensive, also animates many arms-control efforts.

EFFORTS TO MAKE MILITARY "BALANCES" LESS WAR-PRONE

As shown in the discussion of military balances (Chapter 5), countries tempted to use force against their adversaries will be more, or less, inhibited from doing so by their changing assessments of which side would prevail in the ensuing battle, as well as of the costs, risks, or advantages of waiting to fight at another time. Not only the existing "balance" of military capabilities (the quotation marks are put around *balance* to indicate that the term is applied to unequal, or tipped, balances as well as to essentially equal, or level, ones) but also the changes a balance is undergoing may need to be stabilized or controlled to avert a war.

An arms-control measure designed to effect a military balance need not always be negotiated or mutually instituted. It can be unilaterally adopted. What makes it arms control, as distinguished from normal defense or deterrence policy, is its purpose of relieving the other side of fears of being attacked.

The Naval Limitations of the 1920s and 1930s

Antecedents of contemporary efforts to stabilize aspects of the East-West balance of military power were the naval agreements negotiated among the great powers between World War I and World War II, when naval capability was still the prime indicator of strategic clout.

The Washington Treaty of 1922 established a ceiling on capital ships (large battleships), and a ratio of capital ship tonnage among the naval powers of the day at 5:5:3:1.75:1.75, with Britain and the United States in the first rank, Japan in the second rank, and France and Italy in the third rank. The negotiated ratio reflected the shared desire of Britain and the United States, as friendly naval rivals, to avoid a costly arms race with each other and to keep the upstart Pacific power, Japan, in an inferior position. Japan reluctantly agreed under pressure from Britain, at that time its only great-power ally.

In the London Naval Conference of 1930, the United States, Britain, and Japan extended their tonnage-ratio agreement to encompass most of the main types of warships in their inventories, but with a new proviso, the so-called Escalator Clause, permitting construction above the limits if any signatory considered itself threatened by a nonsignatory power. When Japan withdrew from these obligations in 1933 in reaction to the British and American condemnation of its invasion of China, the other principals were no longer inclined to accept international limits on their naval buildups in the Pacific.

The Anglo-German Naval Agreement of 1935 was a bilateral agreement between England and a remilitarizing Germany to keep their naval armaments programs somewhat restrained. Its principal effect was to legitimize the German buildup—which otherwise might have been in violation of the Treaty of Versailles—but under limits that would allow the British to maintain their traditional naval superiority without having to launch an expensive rearmament program. However, with the approach of war in the spring of 1939, Germany formally renounced the treaty's restraints. The ironic effect of the 1935 agreement, therefore, was to provide Germany with the wherewithal for a crash expansion of its navy while Britain drifted with its normal program.

The Strategic Arms Limitations of the 1970s

The Strategic Arms Limitation Talks (SALT) of the 1970s and the agreements they produced were designed to assure both the United States and the Soviet Union that neither would attempt to gain superiority over the other and to reassure both sides that the strategic forces each deployed were entirely for purposes of deterring war—that is, that they were not for aggression or for victory in a war. These arms-control efforts were also based on the assumption that reinforcing and enlarging the constituencies for East-West cooperation provided the best hope over the long run for avoiding war. The negotiations and resulting agreements, in their tangible evidence of pacific intent, would at least reduce the hostile rhetoric and posturing on each side.

The SALT I negotiation, starting in November 1969 and producing the 1972 Treaty on the Limitation of Anti-Ballistic Missile (ABM) Systems and the 1972 Interim Agreement on the Limitation of Strategic Offensive Arms, was clearly an effort at arms control rather than at disarmament. It reinforced the mutual assured destruction (MAD) basis of the deterrent balance of terror between the United States and the Soviet Union by virtually eliminating (in the ABM Treaty) the deployment on either side of defensive weapons that could substantially reduce the massive destruction likely in a strategic nuclear war and by allowing (in the Interim Agreement) sufficient offensive power on both sides to guarantee that each would retain a capacity to inflict massive damage on the other in a retaliatory blow, no matter how large or well executed the first strike might be. Each side, in effect, was to hold the other's population hostage against any attempt to start a strategic nuclear war, and SALT I was a mutual suicide pact for deterring such a war.

The 1972 ABM Treaty, supposed to be of unlimited duration, permitted each side to have just two ABM deployment sites, with no more than 100 ABM missiles at each. The ABMs at one site were to be oriented to protect the country's capital; those at the other site were to guard an ICBM launching field. In 1974 the superpowers signed a protocol limiting each side to only one ABM site, giving each side freedom to choose to defend either its capital city or an ICBM complex.

Both sides also agreed to limit improvements in their ABM technology, to forgo developing and testing multiple-missile ABM launchers and any sea-based, air-based, space-based, or mobile land-based ABM systems.

The 1972 Interim Agreement on the Limitation of Strategic Offensive Arms froze for five years the number of strategic ballistic missiles, land- and sea-based, deployed or under construction. It provided that the United States could deploy no more than 1054 ICBMs on land and 656 submarine-launched ballistic missiles (SLBMs) on 44 submarines, while the Soviet Union was allowed to deploy up to 1618 ICBMs and 740 SLBMs—though additional SLBMs could be deployed if they were substituted for older ICBMs. The agreement committed the United States and the Soviet Union to continue negotiating to produce an offensive arms treaty by 1977.[1]

The SALT II process, starting in 1972, was an attempt to tie up some of the loose ends left out of the SALT I accords—such as bombers, intermediate-range ballistic missiles, and cruise missiles— and to assure that "essential equivalence" was sustained into the 1980s as new weapons technologies changed the destructive capabilities of the weapons allowed under SALT I.

Two developments in particular threatened to undermine the basic deterrent balance agreed to in SALT I. One was the maturing of technologies for multiplying the number of nuclear warheads each ICBM could carry, resulting in multiple independently targeted reentry vehicles, or MIRVs; if one side installed MIRVs earlier than the other or if its ICBMs were equipped to carry more MIRVs than the other's the numerical ratios in SALT I could become unbalanced. The other complicating development was the improvement in the accuracy of missiles, reducing the ratio of the attacking warheads needed to destroy one missile in a ground silo to almost 1:1 (one attacking warhead to each missile silo to be destroyed). Married to MIRVs, the new accuracy would allow the attacker who struck first to use up only a fraction of his own force in destroying the bulk of his opponent's ICBMs. MIRVs and accuracy together revived the advantage of the strategic first strike, thereby negating a fundamental purpose of SALT: to reinforce the confidence on both sides that neither could contemplate winning a strategic nuclear war.

SALT II attempted to control the destabilizing effects of MIRVs and improved accuracy by establishing limits not only on the number of strategic delivery vehicles each side could deploy but also on the number of such weapons that could carry multiple warheads and on roughly the number of warheads each side could maintain in its strategic arsenal.

The SALT II Treaty—the complicated and detailed set of agreements signed in Vienna on June 18, 1979, by presidents Carter and Brezhnev—was never approved by the U.S. Senate. The unratified treaty limited each side to 2,250 strategic nuclear delivery vehicles, of which no more than 1,320 could be carriers of more than one weapon. Of the 1,320 multiple-weapon delivery vehicles, no more than 1,200 could be MIRVed ballistic missiles: the rest would be bombers carrying long-range cruise missles; and of the 1,200 MIRVed ballistic missiles, no more than 820 could be ICBMs, with the rest SLBMs.

The SALT II Treaty also included special prohibitions on heavy-missile launchers; permission for each side to flight-test or deploy only one new type of light ICBM, not to carry more than ten warheads; a ban on increasing the number of warheads on existing types of ICBMs; a limit of fourteen warheads for each SLBM; and ceilings on the launch-weight and throw-weight of ballistic missiles, with a ban on converting light to heavy missiles.

Verification of adherence to the treaty provisions was to be accomplished, as in SALT I, by "national technical means"—meaning each side's reconnaissance satellites—and the sides agreed not to impede such verification. Since remote reconnaissance could not verify the number of warheads carried by each missile, however, SALT II stipulated a counting rule that once a missile of a particular type had been tested with MIRVs, all missiles of that type would be considered to be carrying the largest number of MIRVs observed in any flight-test of the type; similar counting rules were agreed to for cruise missiles and heavy bombers.[2]

The principal opponents of the SALT II treaty in the United States charged that the numerical limits gave a false sense of equivalence since the Soviets would be allowed to maintain more heavier missiles in their arsenal: the heavier Soviet weapons could carry on the average more MIRVs than the U.S. missiles and could deliver greater megatonnage against their targets. Some members of Congress, basically supportive of the treaty, worried that the verification procedures left too much uncertainty about Soviet compliance with its terms.

These and other issues were still being debated in the Congress at the end of 1979 when Soviet troops invaded Afghanistan, whereupon President Carter asked the Senate to defer its action on SALT II. The deferment became indefinite, and neither the U.S. government nor the Soviet government formally ratified the SALT II treaty. Yet both super-powers found it to their advantage to act as if the pact were binding on them. The Reagan administration, which had been expected to repudiate it, announced six weeks after taking office that "while we are reviewing our SALT policy, we will take no action that would undercut existing agreements so long as the Soviet Union exercises the same restraint."

The statement reflected the judgment of the Joint Chiefs of Staff that for the time being the provisions of SALT II would require no elimination or retardation of ongoing U.S. weapons programs but that without the treaty's limits the Soviets could increase their nuclear warheads at a faster rate than the United States.[3]

ARMS REDUCTION EFFORTS

The START Negotiations

Early in 1981, the newly installed Reagan administration announced that it was thoroughly reviewing the past SALT approach. Most of Reagan's top arms-policy advisers had publicly condemned the SALT II treaty before the administration took office, and Reagan himself had called it "fatally flawed." The president said that the United States would not return to the negotiating table until the new American military buildup was sufficiently under way to allow the United States to "negotiate from strength."

When the U.S.–Soviet strategic arms negotiations, renamed START for Strategic Arms Reduction Talks, resumed in 1982, the American side insisted that the objective of the negotiations should be to achieve real strategic equality through substantial reductions in heavy ICBMs, with specified ceilings for missile throw-weight and numbers of warheads. The Soviets saw in the U.S. proposals a design to reduce ICBMs asymmetrically in categories where the Soviets had greatest strength while allowing the United States to continue its own new strategic buildup and modernization programs. Accordingly, their opening position for the new round of negotiations was that SALT II had provided for essential parity in forces and that the current negotiations should re-endorse the SALT accords, using them as a base for whatever additional adjustments were needed to maintain parity. But when it appeared that the Americans with their emphasis on major reductions might be winning the propaganda battle, the Soviets apparently decided to compete for world approval by publicly announcing their own deeply cutting proposals. Not surprisingly, the Soviet proposals, by emphasizing equality in launchers (as distinct from warheads), avoiding missile throw-weight limits, and insisting on stringent limits on air-launched cruise missiles, were full of asymmetries unfavorable to the United States.

By the time the Soviets walked out of the strategic arms negotiations at the end of 1983 in response to the American deployment of new intermediate-range missiles in Europe (see the discussion of the INF negotiations on p. 211), START was becoming little more than a public relations arena. Indeed, what was supposed to be the central premise of strategic arms control—namely, that weapons with the purpose of destroying the other side's strategic deterrent force were destabilizing—was drastically undermined by President Reagan's endorsement of a major ABM program in his March 1983 Strategic Defense Initiative.

When the superpowers resumed their strategic arms control negotiations in 1985, they were more fundamentally at odds over the basic purposes of the negotiations than at any time since the start of the SALT era. The Soviets argued that the essential condition for further limits on strategic offensive forces, let alone deep cuts, was reaffirmation of the ban on ABMs and an explicit avowal to forgo the kind of space-based, multilayered ABM defense of the country's population that the Reagan administration hoped to attain with its Strategic Defense Initiative. President Reagan, however, insisted that the United States would not bargain away SDI, for it was the best hope of rendering strategic nuclear war obsolete. The Soviets, he said, ought to want to cooperate in turning the world away from a security system dependent on maintaining capabilities for mutual annihilation. If there were to be negotiations on strategic defenses, they should be over how to phase them in, rather than how to preclude them. And to show that the SDI was not an attempt to gain strategic superiority, Reagan said that the United States, as it approached being able to deploy a comprehensive system for shielding its population from nuclear attack, would be willing to discuss ways of sharing the technology with the Soviets.[4]

The announced determination by the Reagan administration to develop a nationwide population defense was antithetical to the preexisting arms-control regime centered on the 1972 ABM Treaty. Not only did the SDI contemplate eventual deployment of the very weapons explicitly restricted by that treaty, but even the announced active pursuit of such a defensive capability, by either side or both, would generate major new compensatory buildups in each adversary's offensive strategic arsenal, which in turn—if the objective of population defense still animated policy—would require ever larger deployments of the defensive system, plus new offensive deployments just to maintain parity in offensive capabilities.

Balanced Force Reductions in Nonstrategic Arms

The different geopolitical situations of the Cold War superpowers and their European alliances were reflected in the 1970s and 1980s in East-West negotiations to reduce the nonstrategic, primarily nonnuclear, weapons and troops of NATO and the Warsaw Pact. Although in formal structure these negotiations were multilateral, involving most members of the rival alliance systems, in practice the East-West bargaining was conducted almost entirely by the two superpowers.

At the outset of the European force-reduction talks in 1973, the Soviet Union established its basic position that the prevailing overall force balance in Europe was essentially equal and that therefore conventional-force reductions in the theater should be symmetrical. The United States represented the Western view that the existing conventional-force balance decidedly favored the Warsaw Pact and that therefore asymmetrical reductions down to common ceilings were required to achieve balance. Another difference at the start of the talks was the Soviet premise that reductions would be distributed across each of the alliances—the Soviets were particularly anxious to limit West German forces—as opposed to the U.S. emphasis on starting with Soviet and U.S. reductions.

Not only these divergent notions of acceptable force-balance outcomes but also the political functions the conventional arms talks had for each of the superpowers did not augur well for success. On the American side, the Nixon administration used the negotiations as a ploy to take the steam from mounting congressional pressures for substantial reductions in the approximately 300,000 American troops stationed in Germany. Henry Kissinger made it clear to the Soviets that their willingness to come to the conventional force negotiating table was a condition for U.S. participation in the Conference on Security and Cooperation in Europe that the Kremlin wanted to use to legitimize the territorial status quo on the Continent. For a long time the unspoken premise at the highest levels of both governments was that the force reduction talks were a charade.

Yet if they could have agreed on a mutually acceptable formula, genuine conventional force reductions in central Europe might have been of considerable geopolitical benefit to both superpowers. A more equal balance of conventional forces would have enabled NATO to reduce its dangerous and anachronistic reliance on the threat of nuclear escalation. And if an overall lower level could have been established for the European force balance, the Soviets would have been less strained in having to allocate forces both to their western front against NATO and their eastern front against China.

Problems with Balance-Stabilization Agreements

There is a compelling logic in efforts to reduce the likelihood of war by preventing both sides in an adversarial relationship from gaining sufficient advantage in military capability to contemplate victory. Balance-stabilization efforts start from the assumption that because neither side will voluntarily place itself in a militarily disadvantageous position, negotiations between adversaries that do not really want to push their conflicts into tests of military strength should produce agreement on mutually acceptable balances and on ways to stabilize them. But it is one thing to state generally the criterion of a stable balance and quite another to agree on its precise characteristics.

The first problem is that of defining and calculating the elements of a military balance of power between any two adversaries with different geographic situations, varied industrial, economic, and technological capabilities, and sets of adversary and alliance relationships differently related to the two-way rivalry to which the military balance is supposed to apply. A country surrounded by land does not have strategic and tactical defense requirements like those of an island country. A country that must import oil and other strategic materials across thousands of miles of ocean has vulnerabilities and needs not at all symmetrical with those of a more strategically self-sufficient adversary. A country with an economic system capable of rapid mobilization of manpower and industrial output for military tasks gives up less security by accepting most arms-limitation agreements than a country with a peacetime economy that would require substantial restructuring to get ready for war. Finally, a country with more than one important military adversary finds it difficult to settle for military equality with an adversary that does not have to worry about others, just as a country with numerous smaller allies (to defend or rely on) has military requirements not really comparable with those of a country with few allies. Given the likelihood that between any pair of adversaries some of these essential differences are always present, arriving at the configuration of a mutually acceptable military balance of power is more an art than a science.

The second problem is that of locking an agreed-on balance into a configuration that will not change so rapidly or clandestinely as to render the initial agreement meaningless almost before the ink is dry. The problem is not so much systematic cheating on an agreement as the inherent volatility of technologies that can change, literally overnight, the capabilities and vulnerabilities of weapons already deployed, to say nothing of weapons that may be deployed if and when an existing control agreement breaks down. Countries are not willing to shut down their research and development laboratories, yet it is in these laboratories, more than on the battlefields, that a given balance of power may be totally overturned. Accordingly, hedging against an adversary's technological breakthroughs has become an imperative of national security, and research and development programs maintained for this purpose often involve more significant components of a military balance—such as accuracy and other factors of the effectiveness of weapons—than those controlled in the negotiated agreements.

ARMS REDUCTION AS A PART OF POLITICAL SETTLEMENT

In their October 1986 summit meeting at Reykjavik, Iceland, President Reagan and General Secretary Gorbachev attempted to transcend the deadlock over SDI by moving onto a higher plane of negotiation. In Gorbachev's words, it was time to "wrench arms control out of the hands of the bureaucrats." And Reagan hoped for a "historic breakthrough." Historic it was, but not in the way Reagan had hoped. As put by John Newhouse, "there can have been no stranger meeting between leaders of big powers . . . in history. . . . Two high rollers were matching idealistic visions and raising each other. They reached a higher and more rarefied place than anyone had been, and then fell off the cliff."[5]

Gorbachev came to the Reykjavik summit with a proposal for the superpowers to reduce their strategic forces by 50 percent each across all categories of weaponry. Not to be upstaged, Reagan countered with a proposal for the elimination of all ballistic missiles over a ten-year period. Gorbachev then upped the ante even further by proposing the elimination of all nuclear weapons. Reagan (to the dismay of some of his aides) accepted, believing a great historical moment had arrived. But at this point Gorbachev returned to the issue of SDI, linking the ban on nuclear weapons to Reagan's agreeing to stop all work on the SDI program except for laboratory research. "He threw us a curve," Reagan recalls in his memoirs. "I couldn't believe it and blew my top."[6] The summit ended without an agreement.

But across a wide spectrum of national security policy analysts in the United States and other NATO countries there were alarms at how close Reagan had come to giving away the store. Former Secretary of Defense James Schlesinger inveighed against the "casual utopianism" that marked the President's performance at Reykjavik and that turned the summit into a "near disaster from which we were fortunate to escape."[7] Most of the criticism was based on the premise that the global balance of power restraining Soviet international aggressiveness depended crucially on the credibility of the NATO (primarily U.S.) threat to respond with overwhelming power, including nuclear weapons as needed, to any Soviet military move against a country outside its sphere of control. To eliminate nuclear weapons from the equation prior to rectifying the conventional force imbalance favoring the Soviets and their Warsaw Pact allies would grant the Soviet side overall superiority in the global balance of power. Moreover, without having to face the likelihood of military conflict escalating to nuclear war, the Soviets would presumably be tempted to engage in aggression, under the assumption of being able to control the risks.

Looking back at Reykjavik, however, from the perspective of the post–Cold War era, the bargain Reagan was willing to strike with Gorbachev (provided he could keep SDI) does not seem such a dangerous grand illusion. Gorbachev was anxious to get out of the arms race and devote Soviet resources to perestroika, and it soon became evident that this also included a dismantling of the Warsaw Pact and the bulk of the nonnuclear capability that heretofore was thought to give the Soviets an advantage if nuclear weapons were removed from the balance.

Indeed, despite the stalemate at Reykjavik, breakthrough after breakthrough did occur in the superpower arms-control arenas, reflecting Gorbachev's determination to put an end to the Cold War and the U.S. government's delight in being able not only to claim victory but also to achieve major budgetary savings from reduced arms expenditures.

First came the successful negotiation in 1987 of the Treaty Eliminating Intermediate-range and Shorter-range Nuclear Missiles (the INF treaty), requiring both sides to dismantle all of their nuclear missiles with ranges of between 500 and 3000 miles. When it was first proposed by the Reagan administration in 1980, the Soviets rejected it as a political ploy, since it would remove their strategic forces specially oriented against Western Europe and China while leaving intact the British, French, and Chinese nuclear capabilities targeted against the USSR. Yet this was precisely what the Kremlin had now accepted. Moreover, the Soviets accepted a degree of inspection on their territory and that of their allies to verify the destruction of their weapons that in the past they would have opposed as incompatible with national sovereignty—"the most stringent verification regime in history," Reagan bragged at the December 1987 signing ceremony in Washington.[8]

Next came the substantial pullout of Soviet general-purpose forces from Germany and Eastern Europe starting in 1989, much of it unilateral and announced before the United States committed itself to reciprocal reductions in the Conventional Forces Europe (CFE) negotiations. These Soviet reductions would remove a crucial weight from the Soviet side of the overall military balance. More than any of the Kremlin's concessions, this surprising development convinced the Bush administration that the Soviets were in fact calling a halt to the Cold War. It also made the United States and NATO security planners more open to agreements, such as those contemplated by Reagan and Gorbachev at Reykjavik, on major reductions in intercontinental strategic nuclear forces.

The resumed strategic force negotiations resulted in the START treaty, signed in July 1991, which required each side to reduce its strategic nuclear warheads by 30 percent, leaving the United States with 9,000 and the Soviet Union with 7,000. President Bush followed this with a proposal, announced in his January 28, 1992, State of the Union address, for further reductions that would leave both sides with 4,700 warheads each, insisting that in the interest of stability the Soviets should eliminate all of their land-based multiple-warhead ICBMs, which were the most powerful and accurate but also the most vulnerable forces in the Soviet strategic arsenal. Responding to this offer in the summer of 1992, the Russian President, Boris Yeltsin—having inherited most of the Soviet strategic forces and counseled by his military advisers that the Bush proposal would leave the United States with most of its strong suit, submarine launchable ballistic missiles (SLBMs), still intact—counterproposed that both sides cut their nuclear arsenals down to 2500 strategic warheads. On January 3, 1993, proclaiming "the Cold War is over," the two Presidents signed a new Strategic Arms Reduction Treaty committing their countries to reduce their nuclear warheads to less than 3500 on each side by the year 2003.[9]

UNILATERAL MEASURES TO MAKE MILITARY BALANCES LESS DANGEROUS

Some arms-control measures need not await negotiated agreements between adversaries. They can be instituted unilaterally without a loss in security to the side taking the initiative, sometimes even with a gain in military effectiveness.

Unilateral arms control can serve various objectives: reduction of an adversary's temptations to attack or to escalate an ongoing military campaign, elimination of menacing forces or deployments that leave an adversary with no real choice other than attack or escalation, assurance of firm and continuing control by top political authorities over military operations.

Reducing the Adversary's Temptations

Unprotected military forces or those deployed in ways that make them seem vulnerable can tempt an adversary with the prospect of easy gain achievable through attacking them. An arms-control orientation to military force planning includes recognizing such problems in a country's force posture and correcting them; this in some cases may require force modernization and augmentation. That arms control is not always antithetical to deterrence or even to effective military performance was recognized in the now-classic primer by Thomas Schelling and Morton Halperin, *Strategy and Arms Control,* first published in 1961:

> Whether the most promising areas of arms control involve reductions in certain kinds of military force, increases in certain kinds of military force, qualitative changes in weaponry, different modes of deployment, or arrangements superimposed on existing military systems, we prefer to treat as an open question.[10]

During the Cold War, concern that the inferiority of NATO conventional force might tempt the Soviet-led Warsaw Pact to initiate military hostilities in a crisis—say, over Berlin—prompted some analysts and policymakers who considered themselves arms controllers to recommend a conventional force *buildup* by NATO.[11] The counter-argument of strategists opposed to a buildup of conventional force was that augmenting conventional forces might reduce deterrence of a Soviet attack by conveying the impression that the West had a tolerable alternative to nuclear escalation and would therefore be completely inhibited from escalating a conflict to the nuclear level.

Measures to reduce temptations for nuclear-armed adversaries to escalate a conventional war rapidly to nuclear levels include pulling back nuclear land mines and battlefield nuclear weapons storage areas from border regions and hardening shelters for attack aircraft and missiles.

Other measures to reduce escalatory temptations involve retiring weapons from deployment if they seem to be so vulnerable to destruction that they are sitting ducks, leading an enemy to feel confident of an advantage in striking first. In 1961, for example, the United States decided to remove its medium-range Thor and Jupiter ballistic missiles from Italy and Turkey precisely because of their vulnerability to surprise attack. The American decision was a unilateral move that did not require reciprocation; and it was only a delay in implementing it that left the Jupiters still in place in Turkey at the time of the Cuban missile crisis, allowing their removal to be part of the quid pro quo President Kennedy offered the Soviets for removing their missiles from Cuba.

In the late 1970s and in the 1980s, as both superpowers deployed highly accurate counterforce strategic weapons, the stationary land-based ICBMs on both sides became relatively easy targets and therefore possible inducements to a first strike in an intense U.S.–Soviet conflict. Accordingly, each superpower, on its own, initiated strategic force modernizations to retire the vulnerable ICBMs and rely more instead on strategic weapons to be fired from relatively invulnerable submarines or aircraft.

Animated by these concerns, some military analysts advocated that Russia and the United States deploy mobile, single-warhead ICBMs to substitute for the vulnerable MIRV-carrying ICBMs in their arsenals— an idea that was later incorporated into the 1993 START provisions.

Eliminating (or Refraining from Deploying) Provocative Military Forces

From an arms-control perspective, certain kinds of military deployments that seem cost-effective to the military planner should be rejected unilaterally as too threatening to potential enemies. When viewed by an adversary, these deployments indicate (incorrectly) that the country plans to start a war or escalate an ongoing war. They are weapons that need not be in the inventory of military forces supposedly maintained only for deterrent or defense purposes.

Some forces are, of course, inherently ambiguous in their functions. Fighter aircraft can be used for air-defense, combat-support, deep-interdiction, and offensive-bombing missions. Army battle tanks can be used to defend a frontier or to launch a blitzkrieg raid across it. And in the age of intercontinental strategic warfare, weapons maintained to deter attack by assuring second-strike retaliation can also be used in a first strike against an adversary's home-based strategic weapons.

Some forces nonetheless carry a strong presumption of aggressive intent, especially if they are not essential for deterrent or purely defensive missions. The intermediate-range missiles the Soviets deployed to Cuba in 1962 were both offensive and unnecessary for defense or deterrence. So, too, were the IRBMs both sides deployed in Europe in the early 1980s, with their high accuracy and short flight-times.

The multiple-megaton MIRVed ICBMs still in arsenals of Russia and the United States are proper candidates for elimination. These monster ICBMs are tempting targets because of their vulnerability and are unnecessary because all their missions can be performed just as effectively by less vulnerable missiles and aircraft—except for the most provocative mission: a first strike to destroy the other side's ICBMs. Consequently, it is this first-strike capability that the military on each side attribute to one another as the motive for deploying huge multiple-warhead ICBMs. Even so—and this is when an arms-control orientation can lead to additional policy options—neither side needs to be able to threaten to destroy the other side's ICBMs in a retaliatory counterforce strike to maintain a credible deterrent against the other side's ever attempting an attack. Many important military targets other than ICBMs could be destroyed in a retaliatory strike; threatening these should be sufficient for deterrence. Moreover, in the remote but plausible possibility that deterrence should not work, the first-striker, in the face of the enemy's having counterforce weapons left to retaliate with, would be sure to fire all his ICBMs in the first strike; but if the opponent had forsworn counterforce retaliation, the first-striker might have the incentive to withhold some destructive missiles. This could leave some chance of terminating the war short of massive nuclear destruction.

Ensuring Political Control of Military Operations

Wars can start and get out of hand independently of decisions by a country's top decision makers, or even in violation of their policies, if military command and control arrangements are weak and not firmly subordinated to the highest national authority. This is an impetus for arms control that is most appropriate to deal with unilaterally, particularly as each country's procedures for ensuring political control must be consistent with its political/constitutional system and therefore in some aspects unique.

Before the days of high-speed global communications, armies and navies had to operate under the most general of directives from their governments. Generals and admirals could make decisions with immense political implications: when to fight, where to engage in battle, when to terminate a war, and so on. But the technological revolution in communications has changed all this, making it feasible to exercise, continuously, detailed control from home headquarters. It is well that it has, for the contemporaneous revolution in weaponry has made it possible to execute enormous changes in the lethal and geographic dimensions of a conflict in a matter of minutes.

The development of nuclear weapons has been the principal stimulus to command and control innovations that ensure military responsiveness to political authority. One of the most important of the arms-control innovations has been the permissive action link (PAL): the weapons in a PAL system remain unarmed—that is, unable to deliver or detonate an explosive charge—until they receive an electronic signal that either arms them directly or allows them to be armed by human operatives. The PAL system permits the national command authority to retain a crucial inhibiting control over the pace of escalation of a conflict, without losing the capacity to decentralize control to local commanders flexibly when this is appropriate. Coupled with direct communications links from top authorities to battlefield commanders, the PAL system even allows a top political leadership that wants to exercise firm tactical direction of a military campaign to do so.

Working against the exercise of centralized, durable political control is the compression in the time that it now takes to inflict massive destruction. ICBMs take a half-hour from launch to impact. Shorter-range missiles take only minutes. Because it can prove impossible to contact and assemble the relevant political decision makers and expect them to make considered decisions in the narrow time frames between detection of an incoming attack and its impact, military planners are inclined to pressure their governments to predelegate authority to subordinates to make the appropriate military responses. Early alerting of forces in crises and devolution of the authority to launch nuclear missiles and even, in certain circumstances, to launch on warning of attack are contemplated as necessary measures for the management of crises.

An arms-control orientation, on the other hand, generally regards early alerting of forces, especially strategic forces, and predelegation of launching authority as dangerous. Accordingly, many arms controllers in recent years have put their minds to the command and control problem, directing their most urgent efforts toward ways of ensuring the survival, under attack, of both retaliatory forces and the highest national command authorities. The more time a country can afford to take to respond militarily to an attack, the more opportunity there will be to retain political control of a war and to terminate it when necessary and appropriate.[12]

CONFIDENCE-BUILDING MEASURES

Another form of arms control allows adversaries to communicate and exchange information in ways that reassure each other they are not about to begin a military attack or escalate an ongoing war to a higher level of conflict.

Such messages of reassurance have always been the province of diplomacy. Some of the recent and currently developing measures, however, are equally forms of arms control, for they require manipulations of military forces or communications describing the whereabouts and disposition of military forces.

The newer forms of confidence-building measures are the products of negotiations primarily in two arenas: the East-West follow-on negotiations after the Conference on Security and Cooperation in Europe, which produced the Helsinki Final Act of 1975, and various U.S.–Soviet and U.S.–Russian forums dating from 1963. Confidence-building measures of this sort have also been instituted between Israel and Egypt to assure each other of adherence to their 1979 peace treaty.

In September 1986 a major confidence-building accord was reached in Stockholm by the thirty-five original signatories of the Helsinki Final Act of 1975 (thirty-two European countries in addition to the Soviet Union, the United States, and Canada). The Stockholm agreement obligated signatories to inform each other of any military exercises involving 13,000 troops or more or 300 battle tanks. If the activities involved more than 17,000 troops, or 5,000 troops in amphibious landing or parachute assaults, all signatories had the right to send observation teams to witness the maneuvers. Troop movements of 75,000 or more required two years advance notification, and those between 40,000 and 75,000 one year advance notification. Exercises engaged in exclusively by air forces or navies were not subject to the notification and observation requirements.

The most innovative provisions of the 1986 confidence-building accord (given the Soviet Union's traditional objections to on-site inspections) were those allowing signatories to carry out inspections on each other's territory if they suspected military activities were being conducted about which they should have been notified in advance. But the countries were hardly leaving themselves wide open to foreign inspection: inspectors were to be accompanied by representatives of the receiving state and could be kept from seeing "areas or sensitive points to which access is normally denied or restricted, military and other defense installations, as well as naval vessels, military vehicles and aircraft." The inspecting state could bring in its own observation equipment and cameras, but aerial inspections would have to be carried out from planes provided and flown by the host country. Moreover, no participating state was obliged to accept more than three inspections on its territory per calendar year or more than one each year from the same state.[13]

Clearly, countries planning to start a war could have found ways — consistent with the letter of the accord — to block on-site observation of their activities. The principal value of the confidence-building measures, however, was that they provided the means for countries to reassure each other against unwarranted suspicion that their military exercises were part of an oncoming attack, and they made it virtually impossible for any signatory to successfully pull off a major surprise invasion of another country, because the aggressor would first have to deny its cosignatories their rights of inspection.

The U.S.–Soviet direct dialogue on confidence-building measures was concerned primarily with avoiding accidents or miscalculations that might result in nuclear war. These discussions produced a series of bilateral agreements:

- The 1963 agreement to establish a direct communications link (the "hot line")
- The 1971 Accidental Measures Agreement requiring each side to notify the other in advance of missile launches beyond its territory in the

direction of the other's territory, as well as immediately to inform one another of any incident, such as the possible accidental or unauthorized detonation of a nuclear weapon, that could cause the outbreak of nuclear war

- The 1971 agreement upgrading the hot line by providing for two satellite communications circuits
- The 1972 Incidents at Sea Agreement enjoining the two sides to adhere strictly to international conventions for preventing collisions at sea and also to provide advance notice of actions on the high seas that might endanger their ships or aircraft
- The 1985 agreement, also including Japan, to safety measures on air routes in the North Pacific

In addition, U.S.–Soviet technical working groups attached to various bilateral arms-limitation forums attempted to formulate agreements on advance notification of missile launches, advance notification of major military exercises, exchanges of military data, and further hot line improvements.

LIMITING THE DESTRUCTIVENESS OF WAR[14]

Throughout history, particular countries or groups of countries have sought to control the ways wars are fought by prohibiting the possession or use of certain kinds of weapons and by prohibiting certain classes of targets. This has commonly been prompted by moral revulsion against inflicting suffering indiscriminately on combatants and noncombatants alike. But just as often the rationale for the limitations, no less than for the arguments against the limitations, has been strategic in that the countries urging limitations would have their relative power enhanced or preserved if they were adopted.

Prohibiting Cruel and Inhuman Weapons

All weapons are, of course, cruel and inhuman insofar as they cause death, suffering, and destruction of highly valued possessions. But acts of war are perceived to be especially cruel and inhuman if they inflict more death, destruction, and suffering than is required to attain a defined political-military objective—in other words, if they are not dictated by military necessity. Often, however, it has been simply technological innovation in weaponry, giving one side an edge over the other, that has been characterized—by those on the inferior side—as morally impermissible.

Early Christian norms. During medieval times the Church, rejecting the notion that all is fair in love and war, tended to oppose all military innovations as they came along, condemning their use in warfare among Christians, though not condemning their use against non-Christians. The Second Lateran Council in 1139, for example, condemned the crossbow (which could penetrate knightly armor) as "deadly and odious to God." Similar denunciations, often reflected in treaties between dynasties or states, were in turn directed at the first firearms, the bayonet, and devices on rifles and artillery that allowed rapid shooting instead of the previous shoot-reload-shoot techniques.

The Hague rules. Before the two world wars of the twentieth century, the largest consensus among governments on the illegitimacy of particular weapons was forged at the Hague Peace Conferences of 1899 and 1907. The first Hague Conference was attended by twenty-six states, mostly European, the second by forty-four, representing nearly all the recognized national governments of the world.

The Hague conferences reaffirmed some traditional prohibitions and promulgated some new ones against "arms, projectiles, or material calculated to cause unnecessary suffering." The use of poisoned arms was prohibited, as was the use of dumdum bullets that flatten and expand on hitting the human body, causing large open wounds. Exploding bullets were not explicitly prohibited in the 1899 and 1907 conferences, though a wide consensus in subsequent interpretations by international lawyers was that the Hague rules implied their prohibition.

World Wars I and II, however, rendered the Hague distinctions between humane and inhumane weapons almost quaint as the belligerents developed and applied new technologies to warfare. Flamethrowers are an example: Early in World War I the French condemned the Germans as barbarian when they introduced the technique of projecting liquid fire against French troops. But by the end of the war the Allies were using flamethrowers against the Germans. Later, in their improved napalm version, flamethrowers became an important element in U.S. battlefield tactics in the Second World War, Korea, and Vietnam. Once such weapons become commonplace, the initial psychological reactions against them tend to fade and they are treated in military command manuals as if the suffering they produce were no less or more humane than suffering produced by the blast, fire, and direct body disintegration from more conventional weapons.

Prohibitions on biological and chemical weapons. The two principal legal instruments that prohibit resorting to biological and chemical weapons are the 1925 Geneva Protocol, prohibiting both the wartime use of asphyxiating, poison, and other gases and bacteriological methods of warfare,[15] and the 1972 Biological Weapons Convention, prohibiting the development or possession of bacteriological and toxic weapons.[16] These standing conventions and current efforts to add to them are in part a reaction to fears of the novel and little-known effects on the human body of biological and chemical substances rather than to evidence that they cause more horrible suffering than other methods of warfare; they also result from assumptions that noncombatants could not be protected from their effects. However, the willingness of governments to forgo their use (while still preserving the right of retaliation for first use by an enemy and, in the case of chemical weapons, of modernizing their arsenals) has been induced mainly by military judgments that they would be of little use on the battlefield and unpredictable in effect.

The special case of nuclear weapons. An important reason for the widespread revulsion against nuclear weapons is the lingering and delayed effects of radiation: as documented in numerous studies of the survivors of Hiroshima and Nagasaki, the suffering is never over, and it sometimes becomes an increasing torture during the remainder of a victim's life. The feeling against nuclear weapons, however, is equally a reaction to the wide circumference of the devastation—instant and lingering—carried in each warhead. Not only is it impossible to protect noncombatants, even those not in the immediate target area, from the effects of a strategic nuclear attack but it has become generally recognized that massive strategic nuclear attacks of the kind contemplated in war plans of the superpowers threaten the survival of the whole human species. Still, the almost universal moral condemnation of nuclear war has not yet led to an agreement among the nuclear-armed powers to outlaw the first use of nuclear weapons.

Protecting Civilian Lives and Property

Efforts to make attacks on noncombatants and their property an offense against basic civic and religious law are as old as the history of warfare itself. These efforts have been a reaction to strategies, which did not have to await the development of modern weapons, of besieging and bombing population centers, holding innocents hostage in order to break the will of the enemy to resist, and attacking civilian sources of military equipment, food, and other provisions to hobble enemy fighting capabilities.

As indicated in Chapter 6, The Hague Convention Respecting the Laws and Customs of War on Land and The Convention Concerning Bombardment by Naval Forces, signed in 1907, plus the Hague Rules of Aerial Warfare adopted in 1932—all technically still the law today—prohibit attacks on all civilian areas "provided they are not being used at the time for military purposes."[17] But what constitutes "military purposes" in the above proviso is left so vague that undefended places presumed to contain military factories and supplies, including fuel and even food and clothing for the military, can be attacked as military targets. Any civilian casualties or destruction to otherwise exempt buildings would, of course, be unintended collateral damage—an unfortunate side effect of the necessary military action.

World War II totally washed away even the rules confining aerial bombardment of civilian targets to those within the immediate zone of land combat. Lawyers on both sides found legal justification in the Hague rules for attacking anything that was contributing to the war effort, including, of course, most factories; and the explicit allowance of attacks on "lines of communications and transportation used for military purposes" could justify bombing practically every modern city.

The nuclear age, initiated by the bombing of Hiroshima in August 1945, appeared to render anachronistic any possibility of fighting a war justly. In a few years, after a brief and abortive—and probably not really sincere—attempt by statesmen to work out an international control and disarmament regime for nuclear weapons (the Baruch Plan and Soviet counterproposals), the United States began to incorporate the notion of a massive nuclear incineration of its new enemy into its deterrence and defense policies. And in 1954 the American secretary of state, John Foster Dulles, publicly declared that in order to deter the Soviet Union from even local aggressions, the United States was maintaining a capacity to retaliate instantly and massively at times and places of its own choosing—meaning especially Soviet cities. By the late 1950s, the Soviets having followed suit, the two superpowers had come to understand, and largely accept, that each was holding the other's population hostage as assurance against being directly attacked: this was aptly called the "balance of terror."

Early in the Kennedy administration, Secretary of Defense Robert McNamara and some military strategists gave serious consideration to adopting a city-avoidance targeting strategy for nuclear war, along with associated damage-limiting measures to protect the American population, such as civil defense shelters and a nationwide antiballistic missile system. But McNamara's own studies led him to abandon the scheme as both strategically unrealistic and enormously expensive, especially in light of indications that the Soviets had no intention of fighting a limited strategic war if they ever came to blows with the United States and, moreover, that the Soviets could field offensive counters to the damage-limiting measures more cheaply than the United States could install them. McNamara also came to the conclusion that the increasingly expensive arms race could be arrested by mutual agreement if the mission of the strategic forces on each side could be limited to holding the adversary's cities hostage against a nuclear first strike—that is, by maintaining a survivable capacity to ensure that the cities would be destroyed in a retaliatory blow. Thus, by the end the 1960s the world was presented with the supreme irony that its most dedicated arms controllers supported the most destructive nuclear strategies—for purposes of deterrence and arms control. The arms controllers were partly vindicated during the 1970s as the morally questionable mutual assured destruction (MAD) relationship between the superpowers proved itself conducive to negotiation of mutual limits on strategic arms.

The prospect of a nuclear holocaust and the reliance on the mutual assured destruction relationship to prevent it cut deeply across the grain of traditional Catholic strictures against killing noncombatants. A committee of American Catholic bishops took up the challenge in the early 1980s with a stringent program of self-education in strategic realities and doctrine. The result was the pastoral letter *The Challenge of Peace: God's Promise and Our Response,* approved by the National Conference of Catholic Bishops in 1983.[18]

The bishops' pastoral letter reaffirms the principle that "lives of innocent persons may never be taken directly, regardless of the purpose alleged for doing so. . . . Just response to aggression must be discriminate;

it must be directed against aggressors, not against innocent people caught up in a war not of their own making" (Section 104). The bishops, convinced by studies showing that once nuclear weapons have been introduced into a conflict the prospects for escalation to a war of total societal destruction are very high, concluded that "the deliberate initiation of nuclear warfare, on however restricted a scale, can never be morally justified" (Section 149). Even nuclear retaliation for a nuclear attack would be morally impermissible if it would kill many innocent people (Section 148).

Needless to say, the Bishop's pastoral letter was not popular among professional strategists or arms controllers. But, as noted in Chapter 6 (p. 111), the questionable morality of prevailing deterrent strategies was part of Ronald Reagan's rationale for his Strategic Defense Initiative.

RESTRICTING THE SPREAD OF WEAPONS

Paradoxically, the end of Cold War, while reducing the likelihood of World War III, may have increased the likelihood of local "hot wars"—a consequence of the disintegration of hegemonically controlled bipolar system into a loose polyarchy of cross-cutting alignments and antagonisms. Because of the unreliability of alliance commitments in such a world, countries have high incentives to provide for their own self-defense, which translates into obtaining up-to-date military arsenals. In the process, the opportunities for paranoia-generating arms races and war-provoking military confrontations and deployments multiply.

Efforts to arrest this system-destabilizing dynamic have a difficult time of it, not only on the demand side, where local arms races feed upon one another and exacerbate the political rivalries that give rise to them, but also on the supply side, where countries with export-oriented arms industries are unwilling to turn away consumers.

The Nuclear Nonproliferation Regime

The most ambitious effort to restrict the spread of sophisticated military capabilities around the world is the nuclear nonproliferation regime. The worldwide revulsion at the instant atomic incineration of Hiroshima and Nagasaki at the end of World War II, its horrible aftereffects, and the dissemination of expert opinion that a nuclear World War III could jeopardize the survival of the human species, put nuclear weapons in a unique arms-control category. Although the power rivalry and intense mutual suspicion between the United States and the Soviet Union prevented them from negotiating a bilateral nuclear disarmament treaty, they did cooperate, even during the height of the Cold War, in trying to prevent the spread of nuclear weapons. Motivated as much by the desire to maintain their hegemony as by revulsion against nuclear war, the two nuclear superpowers jointly drafted and pressured their respective allies to accept the 1968 Nuclear Nonproliferation Treaty (NPT). Some important nuclear suppliers and consumers have never liked the economic and political implications of the NPT. As of 1990, some twenty-five countries (including China, France, India, Israel, South Africa, and Brazil) had neither signed nor ratified the treaty, and quite a few signatories (for example, Iran, Iraq, North Korea, South Korea, and Libya) very likely had been deliberately violating its spirit if not its letter.[19]

Provisions of the NPT.[20]   The Nuclear Nonproliferation Treaty, which has been signed by which more than 140 countries, is the centerpiece of the nuclear nonproliferation regime. The NPT is essentially a "grand bargain" between the nuclear weapon "haves" and the "have-nots." The latter are to forgo acquiring nuclear weapons in return for receiving substantial assistance from the nuclear-capable countries in developing their own peaceful nuclear programs.

- Article I pledges the signatory countries *with nuclear weapons* "not to transfer to any recipient whatsoever nuclear weapons or other explosive devices or control over such weapons or devices directly, or indirectly; and not in any way to assist, encourage, or induce any nonnuclear weapon state to manufacture or otherwise acquire nuclear explosive devices, or control over such weapons or devices."
- Article II pledges the signatory countries *without nuclear weapons* "not to receive . . . nuclear weapons or other nuclear explosive devices or . . . control over such weapons or devices directly, or indirectly; not to manufacture or otherwise acquire nuclear weapons or other nuclear explosive devices; and not to seek or receive any assistance in the manufacture of nuclear weapons or other nuclear explosive devices."
- Article III is a set of restrictions on the transfer, receipt and use of peaceful nuclear materials, technologies, and facilities—safeguards provisions—necessary in fulfilling the bargain to help nonnuclear countries develop peaceful nuclear industries. The article obligates

each nonweapon country signing the treaty to negotiate a specially tailored safeguards agreement with the International Atomic Energy Agency (IAEA) to ensure, primarily through inspection by the IAEA, that there will be no diversion of nuclear energy or materials from peaceful uses to nuclear weapons or other nuclear explosive devices. The nuclear supplier countries also are obligated by Article III to subject their transferred nuclear material and equipment to IAEA safeguards.

• Articles IV and V round off the deal by obligating the signatories to "the fullest possible exchange of equipment, materials and scientific and technological information for the peaceful uses of nuclear energy . . . with due consideration for the needs of the developing areas of the world."

• Article VI reiterates the standing obligation of the nuclear powers to pursue negotiations leading toward the cessation of the nuclear arms race, toward nuclear disarmament, and toward eventual general and complete disarmament. This article was inserted primarily as a concession to the nuclear have-nots, who complained that the NPT consigns them to permanent second-class status and violates the norms of sovereign equality of nations unless the nuclear-armed nations eventually disband their own nuclear arsenals.

A signatory has the right to withdraw from the treaty after three months' notice "if it decides that extraordinary events . . . have jeopardized the supreme interests of its country." The treaty also mandates a reconvening of the signatories in 1995 to decide whether it will continue in force indefinitely or be extended for an additional fixed period.

The Nuclear Club: Official members, suspected members, and aspirants. As of this writing, the standard lists of suspected members of the nuclear weapons club—in addition to the openly-acknowledged membership of the United States, the United Kingdom, France, China, and the post-Soviet area (Russia Ukraine, Kazakhstan, Belarus)—include Israel, India, Pakistan, and South Africa (even though the government in Pretoria in 1991 signed the NPT and announced the termination of its nuclear weapons program). Aspiring members include North Korea, South Korea, Taiwan, and Iran. Iraq, normally on the list of aspirants, is at least temporarily out of the running in the aftermath of the Gulf War. Brazil and Argentina, previously on the aspirant list, agreed in 1991 to adhere to the Treaty of Tlateloco, which designated Latin America as a nuclear-weapon-free zone, but they still both retain the capability to start up nuclear weapons production facilities in a number of months.[21]

The NPT paradox.   As the roster of the Nuclear Club suggests, the NPT approach may be one of those classic cases of an intended solution becoming a part of the problem. The provision of technologies and other support for the peaceful nuclear power projects of countries pledging weapons abstinence has, in practice, allowed many of these countries to acquire and develop nuclear materials, equipment, and know-how that are of dual use (having both military and civilian applications) or are easily utilizable in weapons programs. Moreover, countries and firms well endowed with marketable nuclear materials and technologies have not been anxious to restrict their lucrative exports to countries that have taken the weapons-abstinence vow, especially as they see their competitors cultivating that market; nor has it proven easy to track and monitor imports and exports of the nuclear materials and technologies into and out of even the signatory countries once such items have found their way into the international market. To control the tempting trade, particularly in dual-use items, the United States, Germany, Japan, Russia, Britain, France, Canada, Italy, and a half-dozen or so other important exporters of nuclear technology, calling themselves the Nuclear Suppliers Group, have adopted a uniform code for conducting international nuclear sales. Adherents to the Nuclear Suppliers Group pledge not consummate sales of nuclear materials, equipment, or technology to any customer (whether or not a signatory of the NPT) that does not accept a set of tightened monitoring and safeguard arrangements designed to assure that countries buying nuclear-related items ostensibly for peaceful projects are not in fact using them in weapons programs.[22]

1995: The Year of Truth for the NPT

World Society's need for concerted international efforts to restrict the spread of nuclear weapons is at least as great in the 1990s as it was in the 1960s. The decline of superpower hegemony, the collateral increase in the determination of middle-ranking and smaller powers to provide for their own self-defense, and the increased worldwide availability of the nuclear materials and technological know-how required to make a nuclear bomb have increased the risk that war anywhere in the system will spiral out of control. It is questionable, however, whether the existing nuclear nonproliferation regime is capable of arresting the dangerous trends in the post–Cold War system significantly without a substantial augmentation in the regime's authority and powers.

The standard list of regime-strengthening proposals includes (a) giving the IAEA the right to engage in unannounced or short-notice "challenge" inspections of suspected facilities, (b) expanding the funding and personnel of the IAEA, (c) requiring *all* countries, including the official members of the Nuclear Club, to provide the IAEA with a full accounting of and on-site verification access to their nuclear weapons and non-weapons facilities, stockpiles, and imports and exports of nuclear-related items, (d) tightening government controls over nuclear-related exports, (e) toughening sanctions against governments, firms, and individuals that contribute to the spread of nuclear weapons, and (f) accelerating the reduction of existing nuclear arsenals.

The 1995 NPT review conference thus may turn out to be one of the most significant international meetings ever in the peace and security field. The participating governments will be choosing, implicitly if not explicitly, between three starkly different models for dealing with the prospect of increasing nuclear weapons proliferation: (1) substantially more centralized global regulation of the markets in nuclear materials, technology, and expertise; (2) continuation of the existing NPT system of reliance on restraint by national governments, overlaid with a thin veneer of international monitoring; or (3) nonrenewal of the NPT, which would amount to a basic deregulation of the nuclear market, trusting instead to natural economic disincentives, incentives, and military deterrence considerations to keep weapons proliferation within tolerable limits.

NOTES

1. U.S. Arms Control and Disarmament Agency, *Arms Control and Disarmament Agreements: Texts and History of Negotiations* (Washington, D.C.: ACDA, 1979), pp. 131–152.

2. U.S. Department of State, *Salt II Agreement: Vienna, June 18, 1979.* (Selected Documents, No. 12a).

3. Strobe Talbott, *Deadly Gambits: The Reagan Administration and the Stalemate in Nuclear Arms Control* (New York: Knopf, 1984), pp. 224–226.

4. *Public Papers of the Presidents of the United States: Ronald Reagan 1985* (Washington, DC: 1988), Book 2, pp. 1104–1108, 1130–1135, 1436–1439.

5. John Newhouse, *War and Peace in the Nuclear Age* (New York: Knopf, 1989), pp. 394–395.

6. Ronald Reagan, *An American Life* (New York: Simon and Schuster, 1990), p. 677.

7. James Schlesinger, "Reykjavic and Revelations: A Turn of the Tide," *Foreign Affairs: America and the World 1986*: 434.

8. *Weekly Compilation of Presidential Documents*, Vol. 23, no. 29 (December 8, 1987), p. 1458.

9. Steven Erlanger, "A Last Treaty of the Kind," *New York Times,* January 4, 1993. For detailed analysis of the treaty provisions see *Arms Control Today* (January/February 1993), 23(1).

10. Thomas C. Schelling and Morton H. Halperin, *Strategy and Arms Control* (New York: Twentieth Century Fund, 1961).

11. McGeorge Bundy, George F. Kennan, Robert S. McNamara, and Gerard Smith, "Nuclear Weapons and the Atlantic Alliance," *Foreign Affairs* (Spring 1982), 60(4):753–768, recommend a NATO conventional-force buildup as a necessary correlate to NATO's eliminating its reliance on the first use of nuclear weapons.

12. Much of the work on the command and control problems is done within the Department of Defense or by its technical contractors at a high level of secrecy. The best recent authoritative reflection of this work in the open literature is Bruce G. Blair, *Strategic Command and Control: Redefining the Nuclear Threat* (Washington, D.C.: Brookings Institution, 1985). A journalistic account, but seemingly well informed, is Daniel Ford, *The Button: The Pentagon's Strategic Command and Control System* (New York: Simon and Schuster, 1985). An excellent study published earlier is Paul Bracken, *The Command and Control of Nuclear Forces* (New Haven, Ct.: Yale University Press, 1983). See also Bracken's more recent essay, "Accidental Nuclear War," in Graham T. Allison, Albert Carnesale, and Joseph S. Nye, Jr., *Hawks, Doves, and Owls: An Agenda for Avoiding Nuclear War* (New York: Norton, 1985), pp. 25–53.

13. "Key Sections of Document at Stockholm Meeting on Security," *New York Times,* September 22, 1986.

14. My discussion in this section relies heavily on Myres S. McDougal and Florentino P. Feliciano, *Law and Minimum World Public Order: The Legal Regulation of International Coercion* (New Haven, Conn.: Yale University Press, 1961), pp. 520–731.

15. Protocol for the Prohibition of the Use in War of Asphyxiating, Poisonous, or Other Gases and of Bacteriological Methods of Warfare, *League of Nations Treaty Series,* vol. 49 (Geneva: League of Nations, 1929).

16. Convention on the Prohibition of the Development, Production, and Stockpiling of Bacteriological (Biological) and Toxin Weapons and on Their Destruction. Text in U.S. Department of State, *Treaties and Other International Acts, Series 8062* (Washington, D.C.: U.S. Government Printing Office, 1975).

17. Convention (IV) Respecting the Laws and Customs of War on Land, signed at The Hague on 18 October 1907, in Josef Goldblat, *Agreements for Arms Control: A Critical Survey* (London: Taylor & Francis, 1982), pp. 122–124.

18. For both the text of the 1983 pastoral letter and a detailed account of debates over earlier drafts, see Jim Castelli, *The Bishops and the Bomb: Waging Peace in the Nuclear Age* (Garden City, N.Y.: Doubleday-Image Books, 1983).

19. Leonard S. Spector with Jacqueline R. Smith, *Nuclear Ambitions: The Spread of Nuclear Weapons 1989–1990* (Boulder: Westview, 1990).

20. *Treaty on the Non-Proliferation of Nuclear Weapons* (opened for signature 1 July 1968), in U.S. Arms Control and Disarmament Agency, *Arms Control and Disarmament Agreements* (Washington, D.C.: U.S. Government Printing Office, 1984), pp. 91–95.

21. See Center for Defense Information, "Stopping the Spread of Nuclear Weapons: Still Time to Act," *The Defense Monitor* (1992), 21(3).

22. On the Nuclear Suppliers Group, see Spector and Smith, *Nuclear Ambitions,* pp. 434–436.

The Prevention and Control of War in the Post–Cold War Era: Toward a Comprehensive and Flexible Strategy

CONCLUSION

The Prevention and Control of War in the Post–Cold War Era: Toward a Comprehensive and Flexible Strategy

Just as there are many causes of the persistence and pervasiveness of war, so there are many imperatives in a basic strategy of peace. Single-cause and single-prescription approaches not only are wrong in an analytical sense but they can be counterproductive when it comes to reducing the role of violence in human society, for they create expectations that, when proven to be unrealizable, give rise to a disillusioned, if not cynical, acceptance of war as a normal feature of world politics.

The need for a multifaceted and flexible strategy for preventing and controlling war is especially pressing in the post–Cold War era. No longer can the nuclear balance of terror between the superpowers and the bipolar structure of the international system be counted on to restrain enemies around the world from trying to settle their disputes with lethal force.

The global power of one of the polar centers collapsed with the disintegration of the Soviet empire. Moscow's energies, now almost totally consumed with the imperatives of domestic reconstruction, are unavailable for the imposition of its conception of world order.

The United States, also attempting to redirect its energies to deferred domestic needs after decades of imperial overstretch, has neither the passion of its earlier anticommunism nor the surplus resources to attempt to sustain a Pax Americana. President George Bush's claim that the United States had a vital economic interest in preventing Saddam Hussein from gaining a dominant hold on Persian Gulf oil helped to garner public support for Desert Storm, but Bush's additional talk of a "new world order" and the implication that the United States, now the world's only superpower, would have to take on the role of global policeman, did not sit very well with the American public. Indeed, the impression that Bush was paying too much attention to foreign affairs contributed to Bill Clinton's election victory in 1992. And as the Bosnian crisis escalated in early 1993, the new president was reluctant to commit the United States to anything approaching the military leadership role that Bush had reasserted for the country in the Gulf War.

This systematic change was evident in the September 1993 demarche in the Arab-Israeli peace process (initiated in secret by representatives of Palestine Liberation Organization leader Yasser Arafat and of Israeli Prime Minister Yitzhak Rabin, and brokered by Norway). Russia was merely a bystander. The United States—though its financial and military resources would be called upon to help implement the new arrangements and for inducing some of the more recalcitrant Middle Eastern governments to cooperate—was hardly the global mover and shaker it was when President Carter mediated the Israeli-Egyptian peace process of 1979.

POLYARCHY AS A WAR-PRONE SYSTEM

The prospect for the foreseeable future, therefore, is for some variant of the basic *polyarchic* structure of world politics outlined in Chapter 4 (pp. 71–74): no dominant hierarchy of power and a myriad of overlapping and cross-cutting associations, not all of them congruent with the balance of power and state-sovereignty norms of the traditional international system. In the polyarchic world, the varied loyalties and identities of each country's population—based on nationality, ethnicity, religion, economic role, social class, occupation, or ideology—determine who is on whose side and who is likely to fight or attempt to make peace. Many groups transcend the borders of particular nation-states, and institutions representing the various identities and interests often come into conflict over their respective jurisdictions and over which government has the primary or ultimate authority in particular fields.

With so many cross-cutting loyalties and associations, credible multinational alliances are difficult to sustain. Every country has to be prepared to fend for itself, and war is less deterred than it was in the era of Cold War bipolarity. This radically depolarized structure might seem to have a saving grace: wars that do break out need not engulf the whole system, and—given sensible statecraft—can be quarantined within the locality or region that spawns them. However, not too much comfort can be drawn by the peoples likely to be the victims of attack; not only are they bereft of reliable protectors, but the genocidal weapons available for purchase in the polyarchic world economy increasingly subject peaceable and unarmed communities to blackmail at the hands of unscrupulous adversaries. Compounding the potential for chaos is the fact that even poor nations can employ devastating weapons of terrorism and revenge that the new technologies and open global market allow them to purchase or manufacture on the cheap.

In short, in the polyarchic world, if we continue to accept war (in its increasingly horrendous dimensions) as a normal instrument for prosecuting conflict, we can look forward to a "state of nature"—more brutal than ever imagined by Thomas Hobbes—in which the lives of many of the world's peoples, even the survival of the species itself, are in perpetual jeopardy.

How can this stark prospect be avoided?

THE ELEMENTS OF A POST–COLD WAR STRATEGY OF PEACE

A strategy for reducing the tendency of societal strife to turn violent, particularly in the permissive atmosphere of post–Cold War polyarchy, must be sufficiently resourceful and flexible to be able both to intercept ongoing conflicts at various stages of escalation and to deal with their basic causes. In order to ensure that war is averted, leaders of the involved countries, as well as officials of countries not directly involved, international civil servants, and nongovernmental public interest groups willing to provide good offices and dispute-resolution services, will need to be sensitized to the many ways in which conflicts can get out of hand and to the array of measures and institutions available to avoid, reverse, or terminate dangerous escalatory processes.

In most cases, developments on many levels—structural/systemic, cultural, and individual/psychological—will be interacting with and affecting one another as sources of conflict escalation and will therefore also be appropriate targets for measures of prevention and control.

The need to operate simultaneously in multiple dimensions and at multiple levels is greater than ever in the aftermath of the Cold War, especially where primordial ethnic and nationality rivalries fuse with issues of territorial jurisdiction, sovereignty, human rights, and distributive justice.

Top-Down Conflict Control: Dealing with the Symptoms

Where the causes of war can be traced to the very structure of relationships between the parties to a conflict—such as the system of dominance and subordination within or between communities, the ownership and distribution of property and other economic amenities, the demographic clustering or intermingling of ethnic groups, and the congruence or lack of congruence of governance regimes with the prevailing patterns of material and cultural interaction—ameliorants are appropriately directed toward the rectification of the basic structural contradictions.

But because structural reform is usually a long-term project, the imperative of immediate conflict control often requires the injection of a temporary ameliorant to stabilize or reverse a dangerous course of escalation for the time being while the groundwork for more fundamental structural reform is more gradually put in place. Thus the strategy for preventing and controlling war, even while dealing with conflicts that are clearly structural in origin, must have at its disposal measures for emergency crisis intervention to deal with the most dangerous symptoms as well as basic political and socioeconomic measures designed to rectify systematic deficiencies.

The following discussion summarizes the potential usefulness of internationally available conflict control instruments and strategies for escalating situations in which direct negotiation between the antagonists has been unable to control or reverse the course of escalation sufficiently.[1]

Mediation. Preserving the essential structure of the relationship between parties to a conflict but allowing them to back down from nonnegotiable demands that have contributed to dangerous escalation, mediation is among the least intrusive of conflict control measures and, for that reason, also one of the most useful. Its appeal is that by having suggestions for compromise put forward by the neutral third party, it allows the antagonists to moderate their demands without either appearing to have given in to the other. The utility of mediational processes in moderating war-prone international conflicts has been growing with the spread of representative democracy. Governments that require popular approval in order to act abroad have a tendency to inflate the stakes of international disputes, turning even conflicts over secondary interests into emotional causes deemed to implicate the nation's honor. When the bargaining gets rough and is conducted in the public arena, force may be threatened or used as a bargaining ploy even through it would be irrational for the sides to come to blows. In such situations leaders may be especially fearful of the public condemnation that would accompany their seeming to concede to an enemy's demands in order to avoid a fight, whereas accepting an outcome proposed by a mediator can be sold to the public as the mark of reasonableness and enlightened statecraft.

Peacekeeping units.   An important and increasingly relied-on instrumentality available to antagonists who are unable to resolve an intense dispute but do not want to go to war (or continue fighting) is a *neutral military presence* in the immediate zone of war-prone confrontation. Such "soldiers without enemies," typically (but not necessarily) organized under the auspices of the United Nations, are composed of military contingents contributed by a number of countries not allied with either side in the conflict. Their functions can range from monitoring adherence to the terms of truce agreements to providing military buffers against violation of cease-fire lines or demilitarized zones.

The post–Cold War polyarchy simultaneously enlarges the need for such international peacekeeping and enhances the political feasibility of putting together the needed forces in the form of both a permanent United Nations peacekeeping command and ad hoc improvisations related case by case to specific conflict situations. The need is larger because of the collapse of the capacity of one of the superpowers to perform a conflict control role in Eurasia and among its clients on other continents, the reduced inclination (largely a function of the disappearance of the Soviet threat) of the United States to assume the costs and risks of global policing, and the consequent eruption of conflicts that had been frozen for four decades by the Cold War. The opportunity is greater than at any time since the end of World War II because the depolarization of the international system occurring upon the demise of the Cold War makes it highly likely that for any particular conflict there will be plenty of countries without geopolitical, ideological, or bloc-loyalty commitments to either side who therefore would be appropriate members of peacekeeping contingents.

Peace enforcement. More ambitious than peacekeeping, international peace enforcement usually refers to operations of the military or civilian personnel of the United Nations or a regional security organization to *implement the transition* from war (or a brink of war) to peace. (Sometimes the more comprehensive label peacemaking is applied to such operations, but if so, peace enforcement should be identified as a subcategory to distinguish it from preventive diplomacy, mediation, and other conflict resolution measures.) As with peacekeeping, the role of the peace enforcement units and where they are deployed are supposed to be agreed upon in advance by the belligerent parties, but their functions typically involve considerably more than monitoring a cease-fire or separation-of-forces agreement and may include disarming the belligerents, distributing goods and services, rebuilding infrastructure facilities, running transitional government institutions, conducting elections, and overseeing the installation of a new government. To perform these functions, the peace enforcement units may have to use force, not just in self-defence but to compel elements of the local society to cooperate with the pacification and socioeconomic and political restructuring agreed to. However, if substantial opposition to the international peace-enforcement mandate arises from authoritative representatives of one or another of the indigenous parties to the peace agreement, and they exercise their sovereign right to refuse to cooperate, the other parties will be faced with the choice of disbanding the peace-enforcement operation and withdrawing its units from locales where it is not wanted or transforming it into a full-blown collective security operation.

Collective security. Unlike the peacekeeping or peace-enforcement operations of international organizations, which assume that the adversaries really do not want to fight, collective security institutions and operations are designed to deter or fight against an aggressor bent on using force. Premised on the willingness of members of the collective security regime to sacrifice blood and treasure to preserve the security of any of them against aggression, even from one of the members of the regime, this kind of control on international conflict is unlikely to be applicable to many of the kinds of conflict characteristic of the polyarchic system. Even so, as evidenced by the use of collective security provisions in the United Nations Charter to organize an international response to Iraq's 1990 invasion of Kuwait, the availability of such an international institutional aegis for legitimizing military counteraction against an aggressor can facilitate counteraction that otherwise might be prevented by antiwar factions in the countries militarily capable of standing up to the aggressor.

Thus, the enhancement of the the world's collective security institutions and norms and their application in appropriate cases can help compensate for the disappearance of the local conflict suppression functions of the Cold War coalitions. Although it is difficult to imagine many situations that, on the model of the 1990 Gulf crisis, will find all five permanent members of the UN Security Council in accord on the nature of the threat to the peace and how to counter it, the potential for such a concerted response can be a positive force in discouraging local aggressors from taking advantage of the paucity of credible alliance commitments in the post–Cold War polyarchy.

Systemic Remedies: Dealing with Structural Determinants

Unless applied as components of a more comprehensive set of systemic reforms, mediation, peacekeeping, peace enforcement, and collective security measures for controlling conflict are usually premised on the continuance of the basic political and socioeconomic structures that have caused the conflict or facilitated its escalation to the level of war. Thus, while controlling the conflict at hand, they may not be able to provide much hope against its flaring up again once the immediate ameliorants and escalation suppressants are removed. Realistic strategies for durable peace, whether between two historically antagonistic nations, among a set of countries in a region pervaded by war-prone instabilities, or for the world as a whole, need to address the systemic causes of war and to provide the involved communities with options for fundamental, even radical, restructuring of their relationships.

Achieving congruence between states and peoples.   Where a basic source of violence is the extreme dissatisfaction of ethnic communities at having to live in a state dominated by other ethnic groups, the possible structural reforms include transformation of the unitary state into a federation of confederation, the redrawing of state boundaries and possibly secession, ideally based on a plebiscite that all communities in the region consider legitimate, and enhanced political status or representation for the aggrieved communities in the existing political jurisdiction. The insight we can derive from the world's political history is that a structural adjustment of the incongruence between state and peoples that is achieved by violence tends to engender new cycles of violence by and against communities that feel themselves disadvantaged in the new structure and become determined to subvert it. The commitment to, and development of, nonviolent processes for rectifying state-community incongruencies should therefore be viewed as one of the leading imperatives in a comprehensive strategy for world peace.

Reducing the value of state sovereignty. Another structural approach—now being tried out with the Palestinians in the West Bank and Gaza Strip—is to provide local political authority and international representation to national, subnational, and transnational communities that lack full sovereignty, thereby reducing somewhat the compulsion to attain full sovereignty.

Rectifying glaring maldistributions of material resources. In situations where the source of intense interstate conflict or domestic conflict with international repercussions is a perceived maldistribution of material resources, the avoidance of violence may require either redistribution or the enhancement of decision-making power in institutions having responsibility for the crucial economic allocations. Again, the historical record of nations and empires demonstrates that a regime's failure to rectify relative deprivations perceived to be unjust is one of the recurrent sources of rebellion and that attempts to repress redistributional movements forcibly more often than not increase the likelihood of the repressive regime's being violently deposed. Internationally, imperial systems and even state-to-state relationships are also susceptible to violent opposition by peoples or states perceiving themselves to be unjustly disadvantaged by the political status quo, and although those who benefit from the status quo, possessing superior military capabilities, may be able to sustain their dominance for a time, the determination of the disadvantaged to overthrow the regime will likely express itself eventually in widespread violence, perhaps through terrorist networks, against the privileged. The lesson is that world public order, no less than domestic public order, requires rectification of intensely felt injustices and that the development of regimes and policies for effectuating reasonable redistributions peacefully is an essential aspect of a viable strategy for peace.[2]

Enhancing international accountability.   On a parallel plane is the growing recognition that the contemporary revolutions in communications, transportation, industrial processes, and weaponry have created an unprecedented degree of positive and negative mutual dependence of the peoples of the world that is incongruent with the inherited structure and norms of the sovereign state system.[3] The basically peaceful functioning of the evolving interdependent world society requires structures and norms of accountablity congruent with the realities of international interdependence. Without such accountability, countries will be propelled into otherwise avoidable conflicts, and these conflicts will needlessly escalate out of control.

The basic accountability principle can be stated simply: *Those who can or do substantially affect the security or well-being of others (especially by inflicting harm) are assumed to be accountable to those they can or do affect.*

The needed accountability arrangements can range across a spectrum from ad hoc meetings between those who can affect one another (when information or threats are exchanged or behavioral adjustments are negotiated, after which the parties go home) to permanently sitting decision-making institutions. Accountability arrangements can also vary across another spectrum, intersecting the first one, which ranges from obligations to keep the affected or potentially affected parties informed of what is being (or will be) done to them to agreements not to act without the approval of the affected parties.[4]

Achieving global governance.   Realists and idealists alike locate the most basic cause of war in the overall structure of the nation-state system: its essential anarchy. With no overarching system of rules in the global polity and no authoritative regime powerful enough to enforce order and justice among the states, even pacifically motivated nations are compelled to secure their existence and way of life with their own military force, sometimes supplemented by help from allies. The result is that international conflicts, whatever their structural or immediate causes, are always prone to turn into tests of military power, which in turn stimulate arms races and geostrategic wars to prevent potential enemies from achieving decisive military superiority. Ultimately, even according to Hans Morgenthau, the father of contemporary "realism," the only way for humankind to break out this vicious circle would be to establish a world government. Morgenthau understood, however, that world government was infeasible prior to the evolution of a world community; so the principal task for the statesperson committed to achieving a durable peace, he advised (writing during the Cold War), was to refrain from promoting schemes for world government in the contemporary era and instead to develop the arts of rational and patient diplomacy—the steady pursuit of vital national interests along with a willingness to compromise on secondary and tertiary interests—as the only hope for building world community.

The comprehensive strategy for peace I am recommending for the post–Cold War era would retain Morgenthau's wise counsel against pursuing utopian schemes for full-blown world government. But it emphasizes support here and now for statecraft and and other political action to construct webs of mutual accountability in fields where interdependence is great. These mutual accountablity relationships can serve simultaneously to further a sense of world community and as preliminary scaffolding for more comprehensive and worldwide accountablity relationships, especially in fields such as nuclear arms control and environmental management, where a modicum of global governance is becoming widely recognized as necessary and politically feasible.

Controlling and reducing military deployments.   Most of the basic structural reforms discussed can only be effectuated through long-term projects. In the meantime, in many conflict situations one side or the other will be tempted to resort to violence to get its way. Most countries, therefore, can be expected to continue to deploy military forces designed to defend against or punish would-be aggressors. Some of these deployments, even when meant only to deter war, can appear threatening to the other side; thus, arms-control and arms-reduction arrangements configured to ensure that countries do not come to blows because of mutually provocative military deployments need to be a prominent part of the strategy for preventing and controlling war.

Implementing this imperative in the post–Cold War polyarchy involves new and complex difficulties. The former Cold War rivals and their respective allies, now in the process of reducing their own arsenals to adjust to the reduced need to deter each other, are tempted to earn foreign exchange by peddling their now superfluous weapons—even weapons of mass destruction—in the international bazaar. And there are more customers than ever, as countries large and small, thrown back on their own resources for defense with the disintegration of the superpower coalitions, feel the need to at least match the new weapons obtained by their local rivals. With military technologies having become so volatile (injecting a new electronic guidance component into an old missile makes it an accurate first-strike weapon), bilateral and regional arms races are spiraling out of control and, rather than contributing to local deterrent balances, are resulting in a proliferation of militarily unstable situations where the existence of the weapons themselves can provoke unwanted war.

There are potentially profound structural implications in all of this. The advanced military powers, especially, will have to agree not to respond to the new market temptations, but this means they will also need to devise reliable mutual accountability arrangements to ensure against defections from such compacts. Additionally, increased monitoring powers, more intrusive than the sovereignty norms of the nation-state system have previously allowed, will have to be accorded to supranational institutions such as the International Atomic Energy Agency and parallel agencies that are created to oversee the implementation of chemical, biological, and conventional arms limitation accords.

The Moral Dimension

Contrary to the politically naive realpolitik notion that morality has virtually no role in the relations among nation-states, my reading of history reveals that the willingness of societies to resort to war and the conduct of military operations is strongly affected by prevailing official and public views on when and how it is legitimate to use military force.[5] At a minimum, therefore, an effective statecraft for peace must sensitize officials and the wider public to the moral implications of alternative policies for national and international security and of the military options being considered for particular conflicts.

Recognizing the importance of moral considerations and moral pressures for a strategy of war prevention and control is only the first step. Once we take that step we enter a sea of ethical, philosophical, and theological controversy on the permissibility and impermissibility of various kinds of coercion and violence—a realm of its own with contending schools of though and traditions. Yet the genocidal potential of the military arsenals now in existence justifies the attempt to forge as broad a consensus as possible on the moral imperatives needed to constrain the violent actions of governments and political groups.

Accordingly, I offer here a set of principles, adapted from and building on traditional just war theory, that I believe should be propounded to constrain statecraft in the post–Cold War era.[6] These principles are sufficiently consonant with views that are widespread and growing among officials and laypersons in today's world to constitute the core of a potential consensus that could be translated into international covenants and nationally enforceable law.[7]

1. States and other political authorities and communities should use violence only as a last resort to (a) prevent greater acts of violence or (b) to reverse gains from a recent aggression or comparable illegal action. Often such last-resort justifications are invoked only perfunctorily and passively: We gave the other side every opportunity to make things right (a euphemism for their refusing to capitulate to the terms of our ultimatum). They left us no alternative. A serious adherence to the principle, however, would involve *pro*active efforts to utilize conflict resolution processes and institutions (including third-party mediation) to find mutually tolerable outcomes. Failing satisfactory conflict resolution, the last-resort principle still prohibits sounding the trumpet of war before fully utilizing all available means of nonviolent conflict prosecution—including condemnatory resolutions in the United Nations, expulsions from key international agencies, denial of international credits and commercial licenses, boycotts and embargoes, and the servance of all diplomatic relations—thus giving the adversary sufficient opportunity to comprehend the severity of the anger its actions have provoked and to reconsider whether it wants to risk that such anger escalates to war.

2. Competent authority for determining the legitimacy or illegitimacy of the use of force internationally (including actions by or against communities claiming to be nations) resides in the United Nations Security Council or the International Court of Justice. This does not deny national governments the prerogative to act quickly to defend their countries in advance of such an international finding, but if an emergency prompts a unilateral decision, the government that acts in advance of international authorization is obligated to seek such international legitimation immediately after the start of hostilities. This revision of the traditional competent authority principle (which was a response to the disintegration of the feudal order of medieval Europe and transferred legitimate war-making and conflict-control authority to the precursors of modern national governments) is called for by the post–Cold War flareup of intense ethnic/nationality conflicts over the makeup of political jurisdictions. The contemporary breakdown of congruence between nation and state in many parts of the world argues for the transfer of legitimate war-authorizing decisions to institutions that are accountable to the wider international community.

3. Acts that jeopardize the healthy survival of the human species are impermissible. A product of the era when a nuclear holocaust between the Cold War superpowers was a distinct possibility (and was, in effect, threatened in the deterrent policies of the United States and the Soviet Union), this principle needs fresh reiteration as weapons of mass destruction come into the hands of more political entities and as ecologists learn more about the potential damage to the planet's biosphere that could result from even localized use of these weapons.

4. Deliberate killing of or violence upon unarmed innocent civilians is impermissible. Whatever the military justifications strategists may put forward, the moral imperative of sparing noncombatants from military attack needs to be revived and closely monitored in the event of war. This traditional just war principle requires special reiteration in light of its unconscionable violation in the international and civil wars of the twentieth century—some of which are underway (viz. Bosnia) as I write. The technologically advanced nations have less justification than ever for invoking the rationale of military necessity to escape the clear prohibitions of this principle, for they can inflict all the damage necessary to the war-fighting capabilities of their enemies through the employment of precision-guided weapons with controllable lethal impact. The infliction of collateral damage upon civilian populations as an unintended effect of the presumed need to destroy infrastructure targets (highways, irrigation systems, electric power plants, and the like) should be outlawed. Those responsible for such acts, winners and losers alike, should be subject to criminal proceedings for violating the principle of noncombatant immunity.

5. The number of people killed or maimed as a result of military action (or inaction) generally determines the degree of moral evil of the action (or inaction). A reformulation of the traditional proportionality rule, this principle, like the principle of noncombatant immunity, requires special emphasis because of the easy availability of instruments for inflicting massive violence. Without prejudging what should be done in particular cases, the principle provides a basis for mobilizing political pressures on governments and communities against engaging in war in the first place and at least to limit the destructiveness of wars that are not prevented. It moves less in the direction of absolute pacifism and more in the direction of encouraging active nonviolent resistance to evil.

This principle is not an endorsement of absolute pacifism, since (consistent with principle 1 above) it allows for killing in self-defense when the only way to avoid being (or having one's people or allies) killed or tortured is to kill. To say that self-defensive killing is allowed, however, does not mean that it is devoid of evil, but only that in certain circumstances it may be a necessary evil, less evil than the act it prevents. The underlying premise does accord moral superiority to nonviolent resistance against violence, although it grants that violent resistance may be necessary when other means have failed and the loss of value in allowing the aggressor to get his way is deemed greater than the loss of value incurred by violent resistance. The acts of violence reluctantly chosen must be constrained by the understanding that each act of killing compounds the evil.

The Psychological Characteristics of Decision Makers and Diplomats

Finally, the strategy for peace comes full circle to the starting point of the analysis in Part I on the causes of war: the crucial role of the emotional and cognitive dispositions of the individuals having major responsibility for deciding when to commit their nations to the awful sacrifices that war entails. It is on these individuals—their inclinations to regard the moves of their counterparts in other countries as either hostile or benign, their compulsions to prove how tough and smart they are, their abilities to revise preconceptions on the basis of new information that contradicts their previous assumptions, their preferences for coercive or positive means of influencing people, their basic wisdom or stupidity about the ways of the world, and their moral attitudes toward violence — that the ability to implement the multifaceted strategy outlined here will depend in large part.

There are no reliable tests or selection procedures for prescreening candidates for responsible positions to ensure that they possess the appropriate predispositions. Nevertheless, some traits are better *not* to have in presidents, prime ministers, national security advisers, foreign and defense secretaries, their key aides, and directors of major international agencies operating in the security field and international mediators: ideological rigidity and intolerance of complexity, the psychological need to win every confrontation, the narcissistic compulsion to be loved by everyone, the incapacity to empathize with one's foreign counterparts, the absence of a sense of moral responsibility for the effects of one's actions upon others, and an obsession with holding on to one's high office. These traits are conducive to the misperceptions, miscalculations, and egotistically motivated decisions that bring on otherwise avoidable wars.

In sum, just as it is premature, if indeed it will ever be possible, to formulate a grand theory for predicting just which international conflicts will turn violent, so it is not feasible to devise a grand strategy for preventing and controlling war that can be consistently applied with positive effect in the wide range of war-prone situations that are plausible in the post–Cold War era. Yet, analogous to the practice of applied cardiology in the the absence of an overarching and validated theory of the causes of fatal heart disease, a comprehensive approach to the prevention and control of war, sensitive to the multiplicity of factors that can work against the peaceful management of conflict, can be applied flexibly in evolving situations to discover, intercept, and if possible reverse their most dangerous tendencies.

The prevention and control of war remains, for the time being, more an art than a science: a perpetually evolving and complex art in which effective performance requires intensive training and the continuing assimilation of insights from both analysts and skilled practitioners.

NOTES

1. The post–Cold War requirements and opportunities for enhancing the conflict control capabilities of the United Nations are outlined by Boutros Boutros-Gali, *An Agenda for Peace* (New York: United Nations, 1992).

2. The connection between world public order and global distributive justice is the major theme of a succession of reports on North-South relations by panels of distinguished statespersons. See especially, Independent Commission on International Development, *North-South: A Program for Survival* (Cambridge Mass.: MIT Press, 1980); Brandt Commission, *Common Crisis North-South: Cooperation for World Recovery* (Cambridge: MIT Press, 1983); and World Commission on Environment and Development, *Our Common Future* (New York: Oxford University Press, 1987).

3. See Paul Kennedy, *Preparing for the Twenty-First Century* (New York: Random House, 1993), especially his chapter "The Future of the Nation-State," pp. 122–134; see also Peter F. Drucker, *Post-Capitalist Society* (New York: HarperBusiness, 1993), chaps. 6–9.

4. I have developed the concept of the international accountability and traced various of its institutional and policy implications in Seyom Brown, *International Relations in a Changing Global System: Toward a Theory of the World Polity* (Boulder Col.: Westview, 1992), pp. 160–167. An earlier statement is in Seyom Brown, *New Forces, Old Forces, and the Future of World Politics* (Glenview Ill.: Scott, Foresman, Little, Brown, 1988), pp. 263–281.

5. For how such moral views have affected U.S. policies since World War II see Seyom Brown, *The Faces of Power: Constancy and Change in United States Foreign Policy from Truman to Clinton* (New York: Columbia University Press, forthcoming).

6. For exposition and analysis of the just war tradition see Michael Walzer, *Just and Unjust Wars: A Moral Argument with Historical Illustrations* (New York: Basic Books, 1977); Douglas Lackey, *The Ethics of War and Peace* (Englewood Cliffs, N.J.: Prentice Hall, 1989); and National Conference of Catholic Bishops on War and Peace, *The Challenge of Peace: God's Promise and Our Response* (Washington: United States Catholic Conference, 1983).

7. The discussion of principles for the legitimate use of force is adapted from my presentation "On Deciding to Use Force in the Post Cold War Era: Ethical Considerations," at the Conference on Ethics, Security, and the New World Order, sponsored by the Carnegie Council on Ethics and International Affairs and the National Defense University, Washington, D.C., February 11, 1993.

Index*

*Subentries under all items are listed in the order that they first appear in the text rather then alphabetically. I have selected this form since it more closely parallels the sequence of the exposition.